JOURNAL FOR THE STUDY OF THE NEW TESTAMENT
SUPPLEMENT SERIES
113

Sheffield Academic Press

Discourse Analysis and Other Topics in Biblical Greek

edited by
Stanley E. Porter
& D.A. Carson

Journal for the Study of the New Testament
Supplement Series 113

Published by
Sheffield Academic Press Ltd
Mansion House
19 Kingfield Road
Sheffield, S11 9AS
England

Typeset by Sheffield Academic Press
and
Printed on acid-free paper in Great Britain
by Bookcraft
Midsomer Norton, Somerset

British Library Cataloguing in Publication Data

A catalogue record for this book is available
from the British Library

ISBN 1-85075-545-0

CONTENTS

Part II
OTHER TOPICS

PREFACE

This collection, *Discourse Analysis and Other Topics in Biblical Greek*, brings together into one volume papers first delivered at the Society of Biblical Literature annual meetings in 1992 and 1993. These papers were all presented under the auspices of the Section on Biblical Greek Language and Linguistics. This is the second collection of essays to be produced by the Section. The first was published as *Biblical Greek Language and Linguistics: Open Questions in Current Research* (ed. Stanley E. Porter and D.A. Carson; JSNTSup, 80; Sheffield: JSOT Press, 1993).

In the first four years of its existence, first as a Consultation and now as a Section, we as the co-chairpersons of the Section (and editors of these two volumes) have been greatly encouraged and personally rewarded by the growing profile of those who assemble to discuss matters of Greek language and linguistics. The format of the two sessions of each Society of Biblical Literature annual meeting continues in the same way as it began. One session is devoted to a specific topic, with invited papers and responses, and the other session is open to papers proposed by individual scholars. The response to this idea continues to be positive, and several important topics are to be covered in the designated sessions in the years to come.

The designated session of 1992 in San Francisco, California, considered the degree and kind of Semitic influence upon the Greek of the New Testament. We would like to thank those who participated in that session, and contributed to its informative content. The designated session of 1993 in Washington, DC, considered the topic of discourse analysis. Whereas it was a difficult choice to decide which of these two sets of papers to include in this volume, it was finally thought that the newness and increasing interest in discourse analysis merited its being included here for wider consideration by New Testament scholars.

The open sessions of 1992 and 1993 again included a number of papers on a range of topics in current research. Some were more theoretical in orientation and some attended more to offering various exegetical insights. The editors were faced with the difficult task of deciding which papers to include in this volume. As we stated in the preface to the first volume of essays, there are several important questions to ask when deciding which essays to include in a collection of disparate essays such as this. The question is not simply which papers are the best or worst, since virtually every one of the papers has at least something to commend it. Again, the papers included are those which give an accurate sampling of the kinds of papers presented at the conference, and which possess the greatest significance in the light of issues of interest to those concerned with Greek linguistics. We think that it is fair to say that these essays show that New Testament studies is continuing to show tangible results from attempts to employ sound linguistic method in the study of ancient Greek.

Because this volume divides into two sections, a separate introduction is provided to each part. Part I 'Discourse Analysis' includes an introductory survey of the field of discourse analysis, and the three presentations (edited for publication) and two responses (also edited) first read in Washington, DC, in 1993. This subject area was mentioned in the preface to the first collection of essays as a fundamental topic where there is room for serious discussion and debate, and those attending were not disappointed. Although the topic is a new one, there were many interested and enthusiastic attendees and questioners. This atmosphere was encouraged by the large amount of perceptible difference among the presenters, as well as the respondents. To say the least, the entire session was lively and lived up to most expectations. Part II 'Other Topics' includes a probing introduction and five papers selected from the ten presented in the two open sessions of 1992 and 1993. In the light of the editors' appeal in the preface to the first volume of essays for more papers dealing with the Greek found outside of the New Testament, including the Greek of the Septuagint (LXX), of the papyri and inscriptions, and of non-biblical writers, it is rewarding to find that several of the papers utilize such evidence. The constraints of time prevented the participants from being able to elucidate everything that they considered their subjects warranted, so the full papers are presented here, revised in the light of the informative questioning that followed each.

The editors wish to thank the many participants who made the two years of papers represented here a success, and we look forward to several more years of informative discussion in the Section on Biblical Greek Language and Linguistics.

ABBREVIATIONS

ARAL	*Annual Review of Applied Linguistics*
ARW	*Archiv für Religionswissenschaft*
AV	Authorised Version
BAGD	W. Bauer, W.F. Arndt, F.W. Gingrich and F.W. Danker, *Greek–English Lexicon of the New Testament*
BDF	F. Blass, A. Debrunner and R.W. Funk, *A Greek Grammar of the New Testament*
BETL	Bibliotheca ephemeridum theologicarum lovaniensium
Bib	*Biblica*
BT	*The Bible Translator*
CBQ	*Catholic Biblical Quarterly*
ConBNT	Coniectanea biblica, New Testament
CTL	Cambridge Textbooks in Linguistics
ExpTim	*Expository Times*
FN	*Filología Neotestamentaria*
GTJ	*Grace Theological Journal*
HNT	Handbuch zum Neuen Testament
JBL	*Journal of Biblical Literature*
JETS	*Journal of the Evangelical Theological Society*
JSNT	*Journal for the Study of the New Testament*
JSNTSup	*Journal for the Study of the New Testament*, Supplement Series
Lang	*Language*
LCL	Loeb Classical Library
LLL	Longman Linguistics Library
LSJ	Liddell–Scott–Jones, *Greek–English Lexicon*
NASB	New American Standard Bible
NEB	New English Bible
Neot	*Neotestamentica*
NICNT	New International Commentary on the New Testament
NIGTC	The New International Greek Testament Commentary
NIV	New International Version
NovT	*Novum Testamentum*
NovTSup	*Novum Testamentum*, Supplements
NRSV	New Revised Standard Version
NTS	*New Testament Studies*

NTTS	New Testament Tools and Studies
OPTaT	*Occasional Papers in Translation and Textlinguistics*
PG	J. Migne (ed.), *Patrologia graeca*
ResQ	*Restoration Quarterly*
RevQ	*Revue de Qumran*
RSV	Revised Standard Version
SBG	Studies in Biblical Greek
SBLDS	Society of Biblical Literature Dissertation Series
SBLMS	Society of Biblical Literature Monograph Series
SJT	*Scottish Journal of Theology*
ST	*Studia theologica*
TEV	Today's English Version
TrinJ	*Trinity Journal*
UBSGNT	United Bible Societies' *Greek New Testament*
WBC	Word Biblical Commentary
WTJ	*Westminster Theological Journal*
WUNT	Wissenschaftliche Untersuchungen zum Neuen Testament
ZNW	*Zeitschrift für die neutestamentliche Wissenschaft*

LIST OF CONTRIBUTORS

H. Alan Brehm is Assistant Professor of New Testament at Southwestern Baptist Theological Seminary, Fort Worth, Texas, USA.

D.A. Carson is Research Professor of New Testament at Trinity Evangelical Divinity School, Deerfield, Illinois, USA.

George H. Guthrie is Assistant Professor of Religion at Union University, Jackson, Tennessee, USA.

Andreas J. Köstenberger is Assistant Professor of Biblical Studies and Theology at Briercrest Schools, Caronport, Saskatchewan, Canada.

Eugene N. Lane is Professor of Classical Studies at the University of Missouri, Columbia, Missouri, USA.

Stephen H. Levinsohn is International Linguistic Consultant for the Summer Institute of Linguistics and a Bible translator with the Inga (Quechuan) people in Colombia, South America.

Micheal W. Palmer is Assistant Professor of New Testament, Greek and Philosophy at Bluefield College, Bluefield, Virginia, USA.

Stanley E. Porter is Professor and Head of the Department of Theology and Religious Studies at the Roehampton Institute London, England.

Jeffrey T. Reed teaches Greek and New Testament at Talbot School of Theology, Biola University, La Mirada, California, USA.

Moisés Silva is Professor of New Testament at Westminster Theological Seminary, Philadelphia, Pennsylvania, USA.

Dennis L. Stamps lectures in New Testament at the School of Continuing Education, University of Birmingham, England.

[illegible] of Classics [illegible] the University of [illegible], Wisconsin, USA.

Matthew W. [illegible] of New Testament Greek and [illegible] at [illegible] College, [illegible], USA.

Part I
Discourse Analysis

Discourse Analysis and New Testament Studies: An Introductory Survey

Stanley E. Porter

The study of the New Testament is essentially a language-based discipline. That is, the primary body of data for examination is a text or, better yet, a collection of many texts written in the Hellenistic variety of the Greek language of the first century CE.[1] Whatever else may be involved in the study of the New Testament—and there are many other factors that must be taken into account, such as archaeology, history, literary criticism (of various sorts), sociological criticism, and even theology—to remain a study of the New Testament it must always remain textually based, since the only direct access that we have into the world of the New Testament is through the text of the Greek New Testament.

Having said this, however, I do not mean in any way to imply that this is an easy task, even though it has been represented this way in several quarters. There are those who believe that the use of English or other modern-day translations provides sufficient access, especially if their primary interests are in some of the other areas of related research mentioned above. There are others who believe that their knowledge of the rudiments of Greek is such that they have an unimpeded way into understanding the New Testament. Both views are subject to error. First of all, both of these views fail to realize that there is an appreciable distance between the world of the New Testament and the modern world. In this sense the study of the New Testament is part of a larger hermeneutical endeavour that attempts to mediate this historical distance through various critical means.[2] Whereas there

1. On the question of the nature of the language of the New Testament, see S.E. Porter (ed.), *The Language of the New Testament: Classic Essays* (JSNTSup, 60; Sheffield: JSOT Press, 1990); on language varieties, see R. Hudson, *Sociolinguistics* (CTL; Cambridge: Cambridge University Press, 1980), pp. 21-72.

2. On the importance of realizing and mediating the two horizons of text and

is increasing awareness in many sub-disciplines of New Testament study regarding the importance of understanding the complexities of the original context,[3] many of these studies have not addressed the attendant linguistic issues. Secondly, both of these views fail to appreciate the importance of on-going debate regarding the linguistic structure of Greek, debate informed by critical study using the most informed paradigms and principles of modern linguistic investigation.[4] Whereas there have been some signs of growing interest in matters linguistic in the form of important monographs and collections of essays, the principles of modern linguistics have not been as instrumental in informing New Testament studies as have some other disciplines. After Barr's important ground-clearing work,[5] in recent years there has been important research done in several different areas of Greek study (besides those works specifically treated below), explicitly utilizing the principles of modern linguistics and focusing upon various specific features of the Greek language, including questions of method,[6] syntax,[7] semantics,[8] lexis,[9]

interpreter, see A.C. Thiselton, *The Two Horizons: New Testament Hermeneutics and Philosophical Description* (Grand Rapids: Eerdmans, 1980), esp. pp. 51-84.

3. Context itself is a difficult term to define, but here is meant to include at least the sociological, literary, historical, theological and, certainly, linguistic worlds out of which the text(s) emerged.

4. L. Rydbeck's trenchant comments of 1974 are only now being addressed ('What Happened to New Testament Greek Grammar after A. Debrunner?', *NTS* 21 [1974–75], pp. 424-27, esp. 427).

5. J. Barr, *Semantics of Biblical Language* (Oxford: Oxford University Press, 1961). The controversy caused by this book is well known. What is surprising is how many of the practices he pointed out have continued.

6. E.g. R. Kieffer, *Essais de méthodologie néo-testamentaire* (Lund: Gleerup, 1972); S.E. Porter, 'Studying Ancient Languages from a Modern Linguistic Perspective: Essential Terms and Terminology', *FN* 2 (4; 1989), pp. 147-72.

7. E.g. R. Wonneberger, *Syntax und Exegese: Eine generative Theorie der griechischen Syntax und ihr Beitrag zur Auslegung des Neuen Testaments, dargestellt an 2. Korinther 5.2f und Römer 3.21-26* (Frankfurt: Peter Lang, 1979); D.D. Schmidt, *Hellenistic Greek Grammar and Noam Chomsky: Nominalizing Transformations* (SBLDS, 62; Chico, CA: Scholars Press, 1981).

8. E.g. M. Silva, *Biblical Words and their Meaning: An Introduction to Biblical Semantics* (Grand Rapids: Zondervan, 1983); A.C. Thiselton, 'Semantics and New Testament Interpretation', in I.H. Marshall (ed.), *New Testament Interpretation: Essays on Principles and Methods* (Exeter: Paternoster Press, 1977), pp. 75-104.

9. E.g. J.P. Louw and E.A. Nida (eds.), *Greek–English Lexicon* (2 vols.; New York: United Bible Societies, 1988); S.E. Porter, 'Is *dipsuchos* (James 1:8; 4:8) a

verbal structure,[10] cases,[11] and word order,[12] to name only a few.[13] Much of this work is unknown, even to those who regularly teach Greek and exegesis of the New Testament.[14] The singular disregard for study of the Greek language can only have detrimental consequences for understanding the Greek of the New Testament. The direct evidence of

"Christian" Word?', *Bib* 71 (1990), pp. 469-98; J.P. Louw and E.A. Nida, *Lexical Semantics of the Greek New Testament* (Philadelphia: Fortress Press, 1992).

10. E.g. S.E. Porter, *Verbal Aspect in the Greek of the New Testament, with Reference to Tense and Mood* (SBG, 1; New York: Peter Lang, 1989, 1993); B.M. Fanning, *Verbal Aspect in New Testament Greek* (Oxford Theological Monographs; Oxford: Clarendon Press, 1990); and K.L. McKay, *A New Syntax of the Verb in New Testament Greek* (SBG, 5; New York: Peter Lang, 1993). McKay and Porter have also written a number of articles along these lines. For points of contention see the essays by Porter and Fanning, with introduction by Carson and responses by Schmidt and Silva, in S.E. Porter and D.A. Carson (eds.), *Biblical Greek Language and Linguistics: Open Questions in Current Research* (JSNTSup, 80; Sheffield: JSOT Press, 1993), pp. 18-82.

11. E.g. S. Wong, 'What Case is this Case? An Application of Semantic Case in Biblical Exegesis', *Jian Dao* 1 (1994), pp. 49-73.

12. E.g. J.T. Reed, 'The Infinitive with Two Substantival Accusatives: An Ambiguous Construction?', *NovT* 33 (1991), pp. 1-27; S.E. Porter, 'Word Order and Clause Structure in New Testament Greek: An Unexplored Area of Greek Linguistics Using Philippians as a Test Case', *FN* 6 (12; 1993), pp. 177-205.

13. See also Porter and Carson (eds.), *Biblical Greek Language and Linguistics*, part II, which has four essays on various topics; D.A. Black, *Linguistics for Students of New Testament Greek: A Survey of Basic Concepts and Applications* (Grand Rapids: Baker, 1988); S.H. Levinsohn, *Textual Connections in Acts* (SBLMS, 31; Atlanta: Scholars Press, 1987); P. Cotterell and M. Turner, *Linguistics and Biblical Interpretation* (London: SPCK, 1989); and S.E. Porter, *Idioms of the Greek New Testament* (Biblical Languages: Greek, 2; Sheffield: JSOT Press, 1992). Several commentaries make use of recent work in linguistics, but not many. Worth noting are M. Silva, *Philippians* (Wycliffe; Chicago: Moody, 1988; repr. Grand Rapids: Baker, 1992); D.A. Carson, *The Gospel according to John* (Leicester: Inter-Varsity Press, 1992); and R.H. Gundry, *Mark: A Commentary on his Apology for the Cross* (Grand Rapids: Eerdmans, 1993).

14. It would be unkind (though very revealing) to mention several books that I have in mind which, although they purport at places to be investigations of the grammar of the text, show no knowledge of recent developments in the study of Greek. As a test of linguistic awareness, one needs simply to check the footnotes of books or articles at those places where grammatical comments in the text are supposedly being supported by secondary comment, and where reference is made not even to some of the older grammars (to say nothing of recent work in the area) but to other commentary writers, etc.

this neglect is found not only in the lower numbers of students enrolled in study of the Greek language, but also in the neglect of such issues by scholars and teachers who consider themselves students of the text.

Such neglect of matters linguistic was not always the case in New Testament studies. Last century and into the early years of this century, many of the major critical scholars of the New Testament were also informed scholars of the Greek language.[15] That is much less true today, as the discipline apparently further fragments into various discrete areas of investigation, often drawing their inspiration from other disciplines. If anything, the study of the New Testament is becoming more polyvalent and interdisciplinary, and less synthetic in nature, as various methods from other disciplines come to inform New Testament research. In many respects, however, this is not true of modern linguistics.

Within the discipline of linguistics, one of the most important and most widely discussed and investigated areas of research is discourse analysis or text-linguistics.[16] The emergence of discourse analysis within the last

15. The fact that they utilized the best language models of their day does not mean either that their work has no value for today or that their methods or results should be uncritically exalted as the final word in Greek study. We must use the most informed models of our day.

16. For the purposes of this essay a distinction is not necessary, although many linguists would want to distinguish between text as the written form of communication and discourse as the interpretation of these communication events. Among the basic volumes in discourse analysis worth considering are: W. Dressler, *Einführung in die Textlinguistik* (Tübingen: Niemeyer, 1972); J.E. Grimes, *The Thread of Discourse* (Janua Linguarum s.m., 207; The Hague: Mouton, 1975); T.A. van Dijk, *Text and Context: Explorations in the Semantics and Pragmatics of Discourse* (London: Longman, 1977); E. Gülich and W. Raible, *Linguistische Textmodelle* (Universitätstaschenbücher, 130; Munich: Fink, 1977); R.-A. de Beaugrande and W.U. Dressler, *Introduction to Text Linguistics* (LLL, 26; London: Longman, 1980); T.A. van Dijk, *Studies in the Pragmatics of Discourse* (The Hague: Mouton, 1981); R.E. Longacre, *The Grammar of Discourse* (New York: Plenum, 1983); G. Brown and G. Yule, *Discourse Analysis* (CTL; Cambridge: Cambridge University Press, 1983); M. Hoey, *On the Surface of Discourse* (London: George Allen & Unwin, 1983); M. Coulthard, *An Introduction to Discourse Analysis* (London: Longman, 2nd edn, 1985 [1977]); T.A. van Dijk, *Handbook of Discourse Analysis* (4 vols.; New York: Academic Press, 1985); T.W. Crusius, *Discourse: A Critique and Synthesis of Major Theories* (New York: Modern Language Association, 1989); D. Nunan, *Introducing Discourse Analysis* (Harmondsworth: Penguin, 1993). Recent issues of two journals, *Text* (10 [1990]) and *Annual Review of Applied Linguistics* (11 [1990]), were devoted to discussing discourse analysis.

ten to twenty years in linguistic studies[17] in some ways mirrors what has been happening in the study of the New Testament with regard to the exploration of diverse models, but in other ways moves beyond New Testament studies in arguing for an integrative interpretative paradigm. Discourse analysis as a discipline within linguistics has emerged as a synthetic model, one designed to unite into a coherent and unifying framework various areas of linguistic investigation. It is difficult to define discourse analysis, since it is still emerging (see below on the several emerging schools of thought), but there are certain common features worth noting. Above all, the emphasis of discourse analysis is upon language as it is used. As a result, discourse analysis has attempted to integrate into a coherent model of interpretation the three traditional areas of linguistic analysis: semantics, concerned with the conveyance of meaning through the forms of the language ('what the form means'); syntax, concerned with the organization of these forms into meaningful units; and pragmatics, concerned with the meanings of these forms in specific linguistic contexts ('what speakers mean when they use the forms').[18] Thus the smallest meaningful units in the language (e.g. morphemes) and their composition into increasingly larger units (e.g. words, groups of words, clauses, sentences, paragraphs or pericopes and entire

Of particular interest are: R. de Beaugrande, 'Text Linguistics through the Years', *Text* 10 (1990), pp. 9-17; and idem, 'Text Linguistics and New Applications', *ARAL* 11 (1990), pp. 17-41.

17. To give some idea of its newness, it is still not common to find extended discussion of discourse analysis in textbooks or introductory books on linguistics. Two that do are G. Yule, *The Study of Language: An Introduction* (Cambridge: Cambridge University Press, 1985), pp. 104-14; and V. Fromkin and R. Rodman, *An Introduction to Language* (New York: Holt, Rinehart & Winston, 4th edn, 1988), pp. 224-27. For brief histories, see M. Stubbs, *Discourse Analysis: The Sociolinguistic Analysis of Natural Language* (Language in Society, 4; Oxford: Basil Blackwell, 1983), pp. 1-12; A.H. Snyman, 'A Semantic Discourse Analysis of the Letter to Philemon', in P.J. Hartin and J.H. Petzer (eds.), *Text and Interpretation: New Approaches in the Criticism of the New Testament* (NTTS, 15; Leiden: Brill, 1991), esp. pp. 83-89.

18. N.J.C. Gotteri, 'A Note on Bulgarian Verb Systems', *Journal of the Midland Association for Linguistic Studies* NS 8 (1983), p. 49. See, for example, several standard volumes in these areas for considerable overlap in content as well as overlap with topics discussed in discourse analysis: J. Lyons, *Semantics* (2 vols.; Cambridge: Cambridge University Press, 1977); S.C. Levinson, *Pragmatics* (CTL; Cambridge: Cambridge University Press, 1983); and P.H. Matthews, *Syntax* (CTL; Cambridge: Cambridge University Press, 1981).

discourses) must be seen in terms of both their individual parts and their formation into the whole. This reciprocal movement has been described in terms of micro- and macro-structural analysis (or bottom-up and top-down analysis). The ways in which these units are seen to be united involves analysis of informational structure (e.g. lexical choice), cohesion (e.g. various connective devices), prominence (e.g. the ways in which significant material is highlighted), and linguistic cotext (e.g. the immediate textual environment) and context (the larger environment, including presuppositions and reference). Although discourse itself is a flexible term (with anything from a single word to a much longer language event constituting a discourse), the distinctiveness of discourse analysis and the concern of discourse analysts is to be able to provide as comprehensive a description as possible of the various components of a given discourse, including its meaning and structure, and the means by which these are created and conveyed.

Although many of the major tenets of discourse analysis appear to have had precursors in thought about language from the Greeks and Romans down through the Middle Ages and Renaissance on into the nineteenth century, it is Harris who is frequently cited as one of the earliest proponents of a theory of language units larger than the sentence.[19] Perhaps because his theory did not integrate form and function or syntax and semantics, or possibly simply because a sufficient foundation had not been laid in all of the various component disciplines necessary for discourse analysis, Harris's comments did not spark sufficient interest to lead to its widespread acceptance and immediate development. A number of other linguists from varying theoretical perspectives contributed to the development of the historical and intellectual atmosphere that made this new area of research possible, although few of these (if any) were using the terminology of what is now known as discourse analysis. A good number of these came from functional schools of linguistic thought,[20] including what has come to be known as tagmemics,

19. See Z. Harris, 'Discourse Analysis', *Lang* 28 (1952), pp. 1-30. One could speculate that the ensuing Chomskian revolution in linguistics did much to delay the appearance of a model concerned with units larger than the sentence.

20. For a brief introduction to functionalism, see J. Lyons, *Language and Linguistics: An Introduction* (Cambridge: Cambridge University Press, 1981), pp. 224-28; and S. Dik, *Functional Grammar* (North-Holland Linguistic Series; Amsterdam: North-Holland, 1978), esp. pp. 4-5.

stratificational grammar and, most of all, systemic linguistics.[21] What unites these disparate functional models together and makes it possible for their work to have had a formative influence upon the development of discourse analysis is that each defines language usage in terms of its social-semiotic function. In other words, language is seen as an instrument or tool for communication and social interaction. Within a framework of actual usage, language establishes a reciprocal relationship with its setting or context. Other influences on the development of discourse analysis from related social-scientific and literary disciplines include anthropology, sociology, literary and rhetorical analysis, psycholinguistics, computational linguistics, sociolinguistics and philosophical linguistics.

According to Beaugrande's useful analysis of the development of discourse analysis, in the 1960s and especially the 1970s, it was more properly understood as 'text grammar', since the methods used were essentially an extension of sentence grammars, often based upon generative models. In the late 1970s, however, the limitations of such a model began to be realized, and qualitative differences between the elements of sentences (such as noun and verb phrases) and the categories necessary for the analysis of texts were recognized. One of the major results was the kind of integrative method delimited above, in which there was concern for how elements of discourse are related to each other rather than attempting to analyse them in isolation. There was a corresponding development away from mere theorizing about language to the analysis of texts as they actually occurred, and various schools of text-linguistics came into their own. This period—the 1980s—was also the most prolific for discourse analysis. Current research continues to attempt to develop discourse analysis or text-linguistics as an 'empirical text science'[22] with its own data-gathering, methods and principles of analysis. Whether

21. On tagmemics, see K.L. Pike, *Language in Relation to a Unified Theory of the Structure of Human Behavior* (The Hague: Mouton, 1967) (though originally published in three parts between 1954–60); on stratificational grammar, see S.M. Lamb, *Outline of Stratificational Grammar* (Washington, DC: Georgetown University Press, 1966); and on systemics, see the early work by T.F. Mitchell, 'The Language of Buying and Selling in Cyrenaica: A Situational Statement' (*Hespéris* 44 [1957], pp. 31-71), reprinted in his *Principles of Firthian Linguistics* (London: Longman, 1975), pp. 167-200; and the numerous works by M.A.K. Halliday, especially the essays collected by G. Kress (ed.), *Halliday: System and Function in Language* (Oxford: Oxford University Press, 1976).

22. Beaugrande, 'Text Linguistics', p. 16.

success will be found still waits to be seen. In the 1990s the pace of production has slowed, since a number of early proponents, such as van Dijk, have become interested in related fields of study while the discipline of linguistics as a whole has entered a different phase. Beaugrande has characterized this as a period of stagnation,[23] although a more charitable view might be that it is a period of reflection and consolidation, as the discipline takes stock of its gains. Regarding the progress of discourse analysis, in 1968 Gleason could state that 'discourse analysis is really just getting underway. There are as yet very few firm substantive results',[24] and in 1983 Stubbs could similarly claim that 'no one is in a position to write a comprehensive account of discourse analysis. The subject is at once too vast and too lacking in focus and consensus.'[25] The same cannot be said in the 1990s, at least so far as Beaugrande is concerned. Not only was he a contributor to the two journal volumes devoted to discourse analysis cited above, but his latest book, *Linguistic Theory: The Discourse of Fundamental Works*, is an analysis of the discourse of those who have been what he considers the most significant linguistic figures in this century. What may appear to be simply clever literary introspection is probably better seen as a sign that discourse analysis has gained sufficient status as a method that it can be used as a heuristic tool to decipher its own founders and formulaters.

The use of discourse analysis in biblical studies is more recent still, and thus is even less well established in terms of theoretical foundations and application to the reading of texts. Part of the resistance to some of the newer methods of linguistic analysis may stem from disappointment at the perceived lack of productive new readings put forward by other experimental methods, such as the structuralism of the 1970s. It is unfortunate that a method of interpretation is judged for the most part on the novelty or lack of novelty (it depends upon one's perspective) of its interpretations, since the theoretical questions raised may well be every bit as—if not more—valuable than the answers, or at the least the answers will never be found if the questions are not first raised. However, it is also the case that theory without some form of application is probably doomed to fade sooner or later, since—at least in New

23. R. de Beaugrande, *Linguistic Theory: The Discourse of Fundamental Works* (London: Longman, 1991), p. 2.

24. H.A. Gleason, 'Contrastive Analysis in Discourse Structure', *Georgetown University Monograph Series on Languages and Linguistics* 21 (1968), p. 41.

25. Stubbs, *Discourse Analysis*, p. 12.

Testament studies—confrontation with the text must be the ultimate test of any approach. Nevertheless, in 1989 Beardslee recognized the possible potential for application of discourse analysis to study of the New Testament:

> It may well turn out to be the case that another type of linguistic interpretation [discourse analysis], making much less extensive hermeneutical claims, will come to be even more fruitful for actual exegesis than structuralism or Güttgemanns's generative poetics.[26]

Perhaps these words were written too recently to have had much impact, but for whatever reason, one could hardly claim that discourse analysis is a recognized interpretative method among anything approaching a sizeable number of biblical scholars today. This is especially true of those who study the New Testament.

Although many scholars may have heard the term discourse analysis, few know its methods or employ them in their research. In some ways it is surprising that this area of research has been so slow in arriving in New Testament studies, because there have been a few noteworthy scholars who have employed its methods. Perhaps the best known of these is Louw, who already wrote an insightful article introducing the topic in 1973.[27] He has been instrumental both in the development of a form of discourse analysis and in applying it to numerous texts. But his article, and many subsequent publications, appeared in work related to Bible translation, an arena where many who employ discourse analysis work, and they are, to a large extent because of their own choice, not part of mainstream biblical scholarship. How to account for this widespread disregard, when the discipline of New Testament studies is (or at least is supposed to be) so text-oriented and so given to drawing upon various models from literary and social-scientific disciplines, is difficult to ascertain.

Perhaps, as suggested above in the discussion of the development of discourse analysis, the failure to adopt it as an interpretative tool is to some degree the fault not of New Testament scholars but of the discipline of discourse analysis itself. It is perceived to be a discipline in the state of development, so much so that it is difficult for an outsider to

26. W.A. Beardslee, 'Recent Literary Criticism', in E.J. Epp and G.W. MacRae (eds.), *The New Testament and its Modern Interpreters* (Atlanta: Scholars Press, 1989), p. 188.

27. J.P. Louw, 'Discourse Analysis and the Greek New Testament', *BT* 24 (1973), pp. 101-18.

grasp what is essential and what is superfluous to the method. This gives biblical scholars, who as noted above have a tendency to conservatism, an unwarranted excuse for holding the method at arm's length. In their 1989 work on linguistics and biblical interpretation Cotterell and Turner offer characteristic criticism:

> We must at least comment on the tentative nature of this particular aspect of linguistics [discourse analysis]. The fact is that at the present there are no firm conclusions, no generally accepted formulae, no fixed methodology, not even an agreed terminology.[28]

If such criticism were taken as definitive, no discipline would ever develop. Nevertheless, this does not prevent Cotterell and Turner from adopting a model that is heavily influenced by one particular school of thought, the South African model advocated by Louw (see below). The kind of diversity that Cotterell and Turner speak of is not unknown to many disciplines, including the literary and sociologically-based ones so prevalent in biblical studies at this time. It is in the nature of humanistic and social-scientific investigation to be in the constant process of model-building and modification, while at the same time engaging in analysis of the data, allowing the data to influence the theory. It seems more like an example of special pleading to allow the state of flux of a discipline to constitute an insuperable barrier to using a method. Cotterell and Turner illustrate this well themselves in the two chapters they devote to discourse analysis.

It seems far more likely that the difficulty with discourse analysis being adopted by New Testament scholars may rest with the scholars themselves. Even though they may be willing to accept or at the least to try a variety of what might be called secondary models, that is, models that help them to categorize the data once they have been accumulated, there is much less apparent willingness to accept primary models, that is, models that directly affect the determination of primary data. One's model of the nature and structure of Greek affects one's primary model, that is, one's view of the workings of the very language in which the text is written. Whereas many New Testament scholars continue to study or at least read New Testament Greek through older philological and grammatical models (such as those found in Robertson, BDF and Turner), discourse analysis of the New Testament should be hand in glove with many of the contemporary theoretical developments of

28. Cotterell and Turner, *Linguistics*, p. 233.

modern linguistics, in particular what it is saying regarding the Greek of the New Testament. If it is to have the kind of impact upon New Testament studies as it is having within the field of modern linguistics, New Testament scholars will have to come to terms with the recent developments in Greek language theory and modify their view of Greek grammar and language in general.[29]

Although discourse analysis is in many ways still in its primary development, to aid in getting a feel for its state of play and to help in understanding the essays that follow, it may be wise to survey the four major schools of thought that have come to be used in New Testament studies. Before doing that, however, several caveats must be registered. First of all, this analysis is strictly preliminary. In the light of what has been said above, it must be seen that this differentiation is a rough and ready one designed to give some guidance in reading a particular author. The lines being drawn are along broad boundaries and are not meant as prescriptive of any given scholar or the school of thought. Secondly, several of the major figures can be identified with several of the schools of thought, since they have worked or their work is utilized in various places. Perhaps this illustrates that there is more commonality in methods than has been realized, or at least that there is a fluidity to boundaries indicating some commonly held presuppositions. Thirdly, there is not much theoretical literature that has actually emerged from New Testament scholars themselves on discourse analysis. Most of the work that has appeared has been interpretative in nature, applying a model to the text of the New Testament, making what is perceived to be necessary modifications in the light of the exigencies of dealing with an epigraphic language. Fourthly, not all of these schools of thought have been equally productive in the study of the New Testament as they have been in non-biblical discourse analysis, so that the numbers associated with each do not necessarily represent their popularity in the larger arena of the entire field of discourse analysis.

The first discourse analytical school of thought in New Testament studies to be examined here is the North American model employed by the Summer Institute of Linguistics or SIL. Heavily influenced in the past by the work of a number of well-established linguists, including Nida, Pike and Lamb,[30] as well as that of Louw (see above, and below

29. See above nn. 6-13 for recent work in linguistics.

30. Significant work by E.A. Nida includes *Toward a Science of Translating: With Special Reference to Principles and Procedures involved in Bible Translating*

under the South African school), SIL has tended to concentrate upon issues of Bible translation. The two major models informing recent discussion are Pike's tagmemics, especially as used by Longacre, and Lamb's stratificational grammar. Both of these functional models work on the principle of levels and layers of language, proceeding from what they see as the smallest parts of the language (whether phonetically or morphologically) to increasingly larger structures. Their models do not depend upon hidden rules or phrase-structures. Thus there is a rather straightforward connection between phonetic substance and semantic structures, and even further beyond in Pike's model (e.g. behavioural features). It is this kind of framework that has apparently influenced the development of SIL discourse analysis.

Although their contribution is rather recently known, various scholars connected with SIL have a long history of using it. For example, in 1974 K. Callow published *Discourse Considerations in Translating the Word of God*.[31] What characterizes this model is attention to larger units of meaning. Claiming that there has been much work done on units smaller than the paragraph, she assembles these kinds of data into larger meaning-structures. Consequently, she discusses the organization of discourse, elements of cohesion, and how prominence is established in a discourse, and gives attention to the information structure. Although the book is a small one, and does reflect many elements of sentence grammar in its method, much of this information is still useful.

In some ways it is surprising that a good portion of the work done by SIL in more recent years has apparently rejected Callow's idea that much has already been done on the smaller units and has taken up investigation of these kinds of units again, thus returning to the level of sentence grammar. For example, in S.H. Levinsohn's recent book,

(Leiden: Brill, 1964); with C.R. Taber, *The Theory and Practice of Translation* (United Bible Societies; Leiden: Brill, 1974); *Componential Analysis of Meaning: An Introduction to Semantic Structures* (The Hague: Mouton, 1975); besides the Lexicon with Louw. For the work of Pike and Lamb, see n. 21 above. On Longacre, besides his discourse grammar (see n. 16 above), see his 'Some Fundamental Insights of Tagmemics', *Lang* 41 (1965), pp. 65-76; 'The Paragraph as a Grammatical Unit', in T. Givón (ed.), *Discourse and Syntax* (Syntax and Semantics, 12; New York: Academic Press, 1979), pp. 115-34.

31. Grand Rapids: Zondervan, 1974. See also J. Beekman, J. Callow and M. Kopesec, *The Semantic Structure of Written Communication* (Dallas: Summer Institute of Linguistics, 5th edn, 1981).

Discourse Features of New Testament Greek: A Coursebook,[32] almost two-thirds of the chapters are concerned essentially with elements at the level of the sentence. Levinsohn's work is distinguished by trying to come to terms with patterns of usage for particular linguistic elements or phenomena (such as certain conjunctions, etc.), but there is a tendency to focus upon idiolect, or even the language of a single book, such as Galatians. This tendency continues to be seen in the essays in *Linguistics and New Testament Interpretation: Essays in Discourse Analysis*.[33] Although part one is entitled 'New Methodological Approaches', apart from Louw's first essay (which is not new in method) and Black's last essay (which does not fit well in the book), the other three essays discuss the sentence and paragraph. The second part, on 'Applications to Specific Texts', actually has some insightful contributions that are concerned with the kinds of questions that Callow discussed in her volume on discourse in translation (e.g. Van Dyke Parunak on 'Dimensions of Discourse Structure'), but most of the essays are concerned with connecting words, use of the participle and the like. A recent exception to this trend is an essay by Allen on Philemon,[34] in which, using Longacre's tagmemic model, he concentrates upon the 'paragraph' as a primary unit of analysis, appreciating the texture and profile of the text, that is, its information and thematic development. The result is an informative analysis of a complete discourse.

In brief, SIL is to be applauded for the work that it has done in Bible translation and in terms of a large number of language varieties that have been investigated through their fieldwork. Although some of the SIL work early on promised a major contribution and in fact foreshadowed non-biblical development of discourse analysis, the major recent contribution of SIL to discourse analysis is not a theoretical one but is a return to sentence grammar, with very focused and specialized studies on particular linguistic phenomena, often within a particular author or biblical book. The result is that while one may end up with a

32. Dallas: Summer Institute of Linguistics, 1992.

33. Ed. D.A. Black with K. Barnwell and S. Levinsohn; Nashville: Broadman, 1992.

34. D.L. Allen, 'The Discourse Structure of Philemon: A Study in Textlinguistics', in D.A. Black (ed.), *Scribes and Scriptures* (Festschrift J.H. Greenlee; Winona Lake: Eisenbrauns, 1992), pp. 77-96. See also G.T. Christopher, 'A Discourse Analysis of Colossians 2:16–3:17', *GTJ* 11 (1990), pp. 205-20.

theory regarding the Gospel of John's use of a particular connective, for example, one is still left wondering about how this might relate to larger issues of discourse within John and the rest of the New Testament. There is a failure to find a theory that is unique to discourse and does not appear to be an extension of the sentence-level of analysis. There are a number of other considerations regarding SIL as well. First, SIL has traditionally been quite insular in its work, speaking essentially to those interested in Bible translation. It is only in recent years that the organization and its participants have attempted to become more integrated into the mainstream of New Testament studies. This is to be welcomed. Secondly, although many of those in SIL are accomplished as linguists, the models that they employ in studying the grammar of Greek are not as informed as their language models. For example, none of the books cited above knows much of the recent discussions of Greek verb structure, relying upon the older grammars of Moulton, Robertson and BDF. Thirdly, to date no major theoretical work has been produced that has developed a theory in terms of the New Testament, even though there continues to be a significant amount of textual analysis. Callow's volume was the closest in many ways, but later writings have left a true theory of discourse analysis unstated and obscure.

The second school of thought to be considered here is the English and Australian model of discourse analysis. Inspired by the work of Firth,[35] Halliday along with Hasan have been the ones who have provided theoretical and applicational impetus for this school of thought.[36] In recent years, a so-called Birmingham school has developed as a particular application of Halliday's work to discourse analysis.[37] The basis of

35. His major papers are found in J.R. Firth, *Papers in Linguistics, 1934–51* (Oxford: Oxford University Press, 1951); *Selected Papers of J.R. Firth 1952–59* (ed. F.R. Palmer; London: Longman, 1968).

36. Among other works, see M.A.K. Halliday, *An Introduction to Functional Grammar* (London: Edwin Arnold, 1985); *idem*, 'Text as a Social Choice in Social Contexts', in T.A. van Dijk and J.B. Petofi (eds.), *Grammars and Descriptions* (Berlin: de Gruyter, 1977), pp. 176-202; M.A.K. Halliday and R. Hasan, 'Text and Context: Aspects of Language in a Social-Semiotic Perspective', *Sophia Linguistica* 6 (1980), pp. 4-91; *idem*, *Cohesion in English* (London: Longman, 1976); *idem*, *Language, Context, and Text: Aspects of Language in a Social-Semiotic Perspective* (Oxford: Oxford University Press, 1989).

37. Access to this material can be gained through M.A.K. Halliday and R.P. Fawcett (eds.), *New Developments in Systemic Linguistics*. I. *Theory and Description* (London: Pinter, 1987), esp. p. 5. The most significant work is found in

Halliday's model of language is that language is seen as a social semiotic consisting of networks of systems, that is, interconnected groupings of sometimes simultaneous and sometimes subsequent choices that establish the meaningful components of language. Regarding discourse, Halliday and Hasan delimit four categories of structure: experiential, interpersonal, logical and textual (logical is the least well-defined), each consisting of a number of networks of choices that are realized in the phenomena of the language. This model is by far the most integrative of the four discussed here, in the sense that it combines discussion of the discrete elements of language but in terms of the larger discourse structure, and it does these in terms of several terms of reference, including the correlation between grammatical forms and their meanings within particular linguistic contexts. Discussion begins with the discourse, rather than treating the discourse as merely an extended sentence. Various levels of analysis—such as the ideational, interpersonal and textual—are the starting point for considering the elements of text. The potential of the model can be seen in the fact that it is not merely an extension of sentence grammar but attempts to analyse discourse in context, with a reasoned and systemic link between meaning and instanciation in text.

In 1991 Porter and Reed gave a basic summary of discourse analysis as a way forward in New Testament studies,[38] followed by a chapter in Porter's *Idioms of the Greek New Testament*, the first attempt to integrate discourse analysis into New Testament Greek grammatical study.[39] Although Guthrie uses several categories from Halliday's model in his recent work on Hebrews (picked up by Lane in his commentary),[40] Reed's article in *Neotestamentica* on 1 Timothy is the most detailed to date.[41] Disputing the view that 1 Timothy is a random series of parenetic statements, he discusses various cohesive ties and the kinds of chains

M. Coulthard and M. Montgomery (eds.), *Studies in Discourse Analysis* (London: Routledge & Kegan Paul, 1981).

38. S.E. Porter and J.T. Reed, 'Greek Grammar since BDF: A Retrospective and Prospective Analysis', *FN* 4 (7; 1991), esp. pp. 156-62.

39. Porter, *Idioms*, pp. 298-307.

40. G.H. Guthrie, *The Structure of Hebrews: A Text-Linguistic Analysis* (NovTSup, 73; Leiden: Brill, 1994), pp. 45-75. See W. Lane, *Hebrews* (2 vols.; WBC, 47; Dallas: Word Books, 1991), esp. pp. xc-xcviii.

41. J.T. Reed, 'Cohesive Ties in 1 Timothy: In Defense of the Epistle's Unity', *Neot* 26 (1992), pp. 131-47; cf. also his 'To Timothy or Not? A Discourse Analysis of 1 Timothy', in Porter and Carson (eds.), *Biblical Greek Language and Linguistics*, pp. 90-118.

they form in the discourse, all pointing towards unity. The result is an analysis that draws attention to the primary participant structure consisting of that between Paul and Timothy.

In New Testament studies one of the major liabilities of this model, despite its widespread popularity in linguistic circles, is that it has not been adopted by very many scholars, and consequently there are not many applications of the model to the study of the New Testament beyond those cited above. The reasons for this are worth exploring in more detail. The first is that in many ways this model requires a complete re-thinking of how the language of the New Testament is viewed, a daunting task to one beginning the study of a discipline to say nothing of one who is already immersed in it. This re-thinking occurs at several levels, including both how a discourse is defined and thought of and how the various phenomena of the text count as data in the analysis. Apparently many are not willing to make the effort to re-think so much. A related limitation is the perceived need for a new vocabulary and new framework by which to discuss the findings. Even though they are similar to terms such as sense, denotation and reference, Hallidaian terms such as co-extension, co-classification and co-reference can be offputting.

A second perceived limitation of Halliday's model is the issue of return for effort involved. One must decide this for oneself, but the question is whether the effort of re-thinking the basics of the language all the way to the conception of discourse is worth the insights that one gains in the final analysis. For example, if Reed concludes that the primary participants in 1 Timothy are Paul and Timothy, and that the discourse indicates focus upon Timothy as recipient, how much force will this have in discussion of the context of the letter? Some may brand it as special pleading that relies upon an obscure method to defend a traditional position. This would be to miss the point of the exercise, however, since to arrive at this conclusion, a mass of evidence has been accumulated that enables the conclusion to be quantified and hence discussed on a firm basis. Nevertheless, it might still be thought that, with no radically new gain in understanding—although those who practice the Hallidaian method would dispute that this is all that has been accomplished—the resulting substantiation and formalization of evidence is not in itself worth the effort. At this stage in New Testament research, however, it might plausibly be asked whether there are many new conclusions to be found (although I would not want to preclude them), or whether any interpretative model is more likely only to support or defend previous theories, although perhaps on different and more substantial theoretical grounds.

The third model of discourse analysis to be discussed is by far the least cohesive, and the most far-ranging. This is the Continental European model, particularly focused upon the work of the Scandinavian school of New Testament studies.[42] Within this school there seem to be several important influences, although it is not altogether clear that these seminal thinkers are as well integrated systemically as they need to be. These influences seem to focus upon three different intellectual traditions, including some discourse analysts, such as Beaugrande, Dressler, Kinneavy, Gülich and Raible, and van Dijk, the communications model of Jacobson, and the modern rhetorical theory of Perelman.[43] The discourse analysts contribute an interest in and the terminology to discuss the macro-structure or superstructure of a text, in opposition to its micro-structure or the individual elements that make up this superstructure. The result is a division into discussion of syntax, semantics and pragmatics. The communications model of Jacobson appears to provide the larger communicative framework in which all of the elements of discourse are to be analysed, including establishing the basic communication functions. The interest in rhetoric is the most difficult to explain. Although there are perhaps historic precedents, the modern ones are less evident, except in two regards: the first is that there appears to be a commonly held presupposition regarding the need to determine the persuasive intent of a discourse, and the second is the apparent necessity to form a bridge from modern linguistic categories to the ancient world and vice versa.

Hellholm seems to have opened up this discussion in continental New Testament studies with his work on the *Shepherd of Hermas*, beginning with the outlining of a communications model that attempts to mediate

42. For a survey, see B. Olsson, 'A Decade of Text-Linguistic Analyses of Biblical Texts at Uppsala', *ST* 39 (1985), pp. 107-26.

43. On Beaugrande, Dressler, Gülich and Raible, and van Dijk, see above n. 16. On Kinneavy, see J.L. Kinneavy, *A Theory of Discourse* (New York: Norton, 1971); on Jacobson, see R. Jacobson, *Selected Writings* (4 vols.; The Hague: Mouton, 1967–71). On rhetorical theory, see C. Perelman and L. Olbrechts-Tyteca, *The New Rhetoric: A Treatise on Argumentation* (trans. J. Wilkinson and P. Weaver; Notre Dame: University of Notre Dame Press, 1969); and C. Perelman, *The New Rhetoric and the Humanities: Essays on Rhetoric and its Application* (Dordrecht: Reidel, 1979); *idem*, *The Realm of Rhetoric* (trans. W. Kluback; Notre Dame: University of Notre Dame Press, 1982).

the complex relationship between text and reader by means of the referential world.[44] This would appear to have been a very useful text to begin with, since it allows for the method to be tried on a relatively safe work. By contrast, in Schenk's commentary on Philippians[45] he utilizes discourse analysis in an attempt to gain insight into the question of unity, a vexing question for this letter. But the attempt is not altogether successful, perhaps because discourse analysis at least of written texts often (if not usually) works from the unstated assumption that the coherence of the text is assumed and can therefore be found, but that it is not the kind of thing that can be established by means of the method. Johanson has apparently taken it as far as this model has gone.[46] He has attempted to outline a theoretical framework that integrates the various discourse components of the method—including a range of work in discourse analysis by contributors from North America, Europe and South Africa—followed by discussion of 1 Thessalonians. There is a constant moving from large to small units, and an attempt to see their interconnections, thus utilizing the syntax–semantics–pragmatics model.

In the Continental European form of discourse analysis it is easiest to see the interdisciplinary and far-ranging approach of at least one form of the model. So much is included within this framework, that that may well become its single largest liability. Since the various facets are treated independently, it has not yet been established how these various elements coincide. This can be seen as recently as the article by Hellholm on Romans, in which he presents a complete macro-structural analysis of

44. D. Hellholm, *Das Visionenbuch des Hermas als Apokalypse: Formgeschichtliche und texttheoretische Studien zu einer literarischen Gattung*. I. *Methodologische Vorüberlegungen und makrostrukturelle Textanalyse* (ConBNT, 13.1; Lund: Gleerup, 1980), esp. pp. 1-10. Part II has not yet appeared. See also Hellholm's 'Amplificatio in the Macro-Structure of Romans', in S.E. Porter and T.H. Olbricht (eds.), *Rhetoric and the New Testament: Essays from the 1992 Heidelberg Conference* (JSNTSup, 90; Sheffield: JSOT Press, 1993), pp. 123-51. For an early attempt, see B. Olsson, *Structure and Meaning in the Fourth Gospel: A Text-Linguistic Analysis of John 2:1-11 and 4:1-42* (ConBNT, 6; Lund: Gleerup, 1974).

45. W. Schenk, *Der Philipperbrief des Paulus* (Stuttgart: Kohlhammer, 1984); see also 'Textlinguistische Aspekte der Strukturanalyse, dargestellt am Beispiel von 1 Kor 15.1-11', *NTS* 23 (1977), pp. 469-77; 'Hebräerbrief 4.14-16: Textlinguistik als Kommentierungsprinzip', *NTS* 26 (1980), pp. 242-52.

46. B.C. Johanson, *To all the Brethren: A Text-Linguistic and Rhetorical Approach to 1 Thessalonians* (ConBNT, 16; Stockholm: Almqvist & Wiksell, 1987).

the book, but one that also includes reference to its epistolary and rhetorical structures. Do they all fit so neatly together? The connections are all labeled to give some idea of how they are understood by the author, but there are larger questions begged by this method, such as how exactly these macro-structural relations are established, what the contribution of discourse analysis is if one is using rhetorical analysis, whether the two models are synonymous, or whether in fact rhetorical analysis can be used in this way. Secondly, it is not sufficiently appreciated that there are major questions about the syntax–semantics–pragmatics scheme for analysis of discourse. Not only are the terms themselves problematic as is the content that is subsumed under each, but the retention of them seems to imply that the method has not gone beyond the earliest stages of development of discourse analysis. If the goal is to provide a comprehensive analysis of discourse, it makes it difficult to consign a feature to a single category, whereas to recognize that an element of the text may function at several levels and in several ways tends to make the apparently facile division redundant. Thirdly, it is not altogether clear whether this method provides sufficient objective criteria to shed light on passages acknowledged to be difficult. For example, is Schenk in his commentary on Philippians appealing to objective data or a scholarly consensus? What is the presupposition regarding discourse that is present here, in terms of cohesion? Is cohesion a presupposition of discourse analysis, a presupposition regarding the text by its very nature, a concept applied after determination of discourse boundaries established by other means, or what?

The fourth and final school of thought regarding discourse analysis to be examined here is the South African school. In many ways the South African school has perhaps had the most far-reaching influence on both the theoretical and applicational developments of discourse analysis of the New Testament. As mentioned above, Louw's 1973 article was instrumental in introducing the topic to a larger audience in New Testament studies. His article was followed soon after by an article by du Toit.[47] There have been many works produced since that time, including several important ones in which Louw has had an influence, including his *Semantics of New Testament Greek*, in which the final, lengthy chapter extends the concept of semantics beyond the sentence

47. A.B. du Toit, 'The Significance of Discourse Analysis for New Testament Interpretation and Translation: Introductory Remarks with Special Reference to 1 Peter 1:3-13', *Neot* 8 (1974), pp. 4-79.

level, that is to the level of discourse; *Style and Discourse* a volume in which stylistic figures of speech are analysed in terms of their effect on rhetoric; and, most importantly, *A Semantic Discourse Analysis of Romans*, in which Louw demonstrates his method on the entire book of Romans.[48]

Louw's method of colon analysis, apparently inspired by Nida's work in Bible translation theory, has come to distinguish the South African approach and beyond. Colon analysis consists of breaking the text down into its constituent cola. A colon is a unit that is formed around a nominative and predicate structure. These cola are first isolated and then their interconnections are re-established in diagrammatic form, illustrating the semantic relations among them as increasingly larger semantic units are formed. Thus there is at least a theoretical relation between form and meaning, extending beyond the smallest unit of meaning, the colon. In his analysis of Romans, Louw begins with a basic syntactical analysis that results in a series of cola, and he then begins to unite these together, establishing textual coherence. Volume 1 of the work is the schematized display of Romans, with lines representing the linkages between cola as increasingly larger units are formed into paragraphs, pericopes and the like. Volume 2 is his commentary, which defends his diagrammatic analysis.[49]

In many ways this is the most well-coordinated school of thought in discourse analysis. The widespread influence of the model has been noteworthy, including the invitation of people such as Louw to be active participants in conferences and symposia focusing upon other models. Despite the amount of productive work, there are several limitations to the method, however. The first is its failure to establish a comprehensive

48. J.P. Louw, *Semantics of New Testament Greek* (Philadelphia: Fortress Press; Chico, CA: Scholars Press, 1982); E.A. Nida, J.P. Louw, A. Snyman and W.J. Cronje, *Style and Discourse, with Special Reference to the Text of the Greek New Testament* (Roggebaai: Bible Society, 1983); J.P. Louw, *A Semantic Discourse Analysis of Romans* (2 vols.; Pretoria: Dept. of Greek, University of Pretoria, 1987). See also his 'A Semiotic Approach to Discourse Analysis with Reference to Translation Theory', *BT* 36 (1985), pp. 101-107; *idem*, 'The Function of Discourse in a Sociosemiotic Theory of Translation: Illustrated by the Translation of *zeloute* in 1 Corinthians 12:31', *BT* 39 (1988), pp. 329-35.

49. See also Snyman, 'Semantic Discourse Analysis', pp. 89-98 and bibliography; Cotterell and Turner, *Linguistics*, pp. 230-92; P. Cotterell, 'The Nicodemus Conversation: A Fresh Appraisal', *ExpTim* 96 (1985), pp. 237-42; and D.A. Black, 'Hebrews 1:1-4: A Study in Discourse Analysis', *WTJ* 49 (1987), pp. 175-94.

theory. Although early on there was a tendency to think that the structure of cola established by an interpreter was the only possible structure of these particular cola, more recent work recognizes the subjective and interpretative element involved. The question, however, is how one establishes criteria for judging which analysis is the most convincing. In some of the literature there is the apparent endorsement of relying upon the results of conventional exegesis. This would seem to defeat the purpose of developing the model, if it is designed only to ratify or respond to what can be derived through other means. Secondly, the concept of the colon itself needs to be assessed. Does the colon have some sort of relation to an underlying deep structure, and hence does it simply serve as a surface-structure manifestation, or is the colon itself the smallest unit of meaning, with meaning confined to surface structure? What about nominal sentences (a common and regular occurrence in Greek), are they cola? How does syntax of the Greek language affect colon analysis? It is increasingly being realized that word order affects meaning, and this perhaps ought to be reflected in the cola analysis. Thirdly, the nature of the semantic relations needs to be analysed to determine their status. Whereas it is a relatively simple task to assign a label to two cola, defending the merits of the label is more difficult. More explicit criteria need to be developed so that various interpreters can discuss the merits of a given analysis and find a common ground of appeal. The alternative is that textual coherence will remain simply an imposed construct.

It is too soon to know if Beardslee's optimistic statement quoted above will be fulfilled or if discourse analysis will disappear from the repertoire of New Testament interpretative models. To be sure, there are a growing number of scholars attempting to demonstrate its worth by producing analyses of various kinds of texts. It is probably fair to say that for discourse analysis to continue to prove viable it will need not only to continue to look at texts in productive and creative ways, but to develop explicit and accessible theoretical models. This does not mean that there cannot be a variety of competing interpretative models, but it does mean that those approaching from the outside will need to be able to grasp the particulars of the methods. The essays that follow demonstrate one recent discussion of discourse analysis as applied to an agreed-upon issue and text, the issue of unity in Philippians. Five essays are included. The first three are major papers representing positive proposals regarding the use of discourse analysis. In many ways, the panel is a fair representation of the field of study, since all three represent different perspectives. The first, George Guthrie, uses an eclectic method, drawing upon several of the schools of thought mentioned above. The second and third are devotees of their particular methods. Stephen Levinsohn is a consultant for the Summer Institute of Linguistics, and Jeffrey Reed follows the method of Halliday, although each is aware of the other schools of thought. The first respondent, Moisés Silva, is non-committal in his endorsement of discourse analysis, although he has in some of his recent work on Philippians demonstrated his sensitivity to matters of discourse. I, as the second respondent, also tend to follow Halliday's method. The design of the symposium was not necessarily to bring all of the various models to the fore but to see discourse analysis at work. The fact that several methods are represented and critiques are offered would provide basis for seeing this goal as having been accomplished. On the basis of the presentations and their responses it must now be for others to judge whether the results are sufficient to warrant further theoretical and practical work.

COHESION SHIFTS AND STITCHES IN PHILIPPIANS*

George H. Guthrie

The widely published question concerning the integrity of Philippians has raised a resounding 'no' from a majority of commentators in this century. Against this 'crescendo of voices' David E. Garland offered his 1985 article, 'The Composition and Unity of Philippians: Some Neglected Literary Factors'.[1] Having thoroughly rehearsed the current state of investigation, Garland pointed to Paul's uses of *inclusio*, which mark certain units in the book, as well as to the cohesive argument running from 1.27 to 4.3. In the opinion of several recent commentators Garland's argument offers compelling evidence for the book's unity and moves the debate out of stagnation and into a more careful consideration of the text.[2]

Garland has been joined by others attempting whole-discourse analyses of Philippians. For example, Duane F. Watson offers an examination of Philippians based on rhetorical analysis, suggesting that the book was crafted according to the conventions of the oratorical schools.[3]

On the whole, while debates concerning the structures of New Testament books have been going on for centuries, coherent methodologies for assessing those structures are just beginning to be set forth. These promise to help in moving debates beyond the sentence level to broader discourse concerns. Literary criticism, as practiced by David

* Appendixes 5 and 6 previously appeared in G.H. Guthrie, *The Structure of Hebrews: A Text-Linguistic Analysis* (NovTSup, 73; Leiden: Brill, 1994).

1. D.E. Garland, 'The Composition and Unity of Philippians: Some Neglected Literary Factors', *NovT* 27 (1985), pp. 141-73.

2. E.g., P.T. O'Brien, *The Epistle to the Philippians: A Commentary on the Greek Text* (NIGTC; Grand Rapids: Eerdmans, 1991), pp. 10-18; M. Silva, *Philippians* (Grand Rapids: Baker, 1992), pp. 14-15.

3. D.F. Watson, 'A Rhetorical Analysis of Philippians and its Implications for the Unity Question', *NovT* 30 (1988), pp. 57-88.

Garland, and rhetorical criticism, as practiced by Duane Watson, both have something to say, although in my opinion the latter tends to be reductionistic when applied on the macro-discourse level of New Testament texts.[4]

It may be suggested that both literary criticism and rhetorical criticism work well as important sub-methodologies within text-linguistic analysis, or 'discourse analysis' as it is commonly called in North America. The use of discourse analysis in biblical studies must be ever sensitive to the literary and rhetorical conventions of the first century in order to be effective. At the same time, discourse analysis attempts to understand broader dynamics in language use and discourse development, and thus offers other vantage-points from which a text may be read. Yet, the discipline is in its infancy and in need of development and integration by those involved in biblical studies.

I would like to accomplish two primary objectives in this essay: (1) to suggest a possible approach to discourse analysis; and (2) to present examples of how discourse analysis offers insights which add to the discussion concerning the integrity of Philippians.

The Method

Methodological details are provided in the appendixes; for an overview readers are referred to Appendix 1.

Step One: Grammatical Analysis

Step one, of course, needs little explanation. I begin with depicting syntax relationships in a block diagram form. The method of block diagramming I use is explained and illustrated, employing Jas 1.2-5, in Appendix 2. I prefer this method since, for the most part, it maintains word order as it occurs in the text.

Step Two: Constituent Analysis on the Micro-discourse Level

By constituent analysis I mean evaluating relationships between the various clauses and groups of clauses in a text. These clauses are normally

4. As far as the macro-discourse level of New Testament letters is concerned, it seems that studies on Hellenistic letter-forms (e.g., L. Alexander, 'Hellenistic Letter-Forms and the Structure of Philippians', *JSNT* 37 [1989], pp. 87-101), though also open to reductionism, prove *more* helpful than the forcing of New Testament works into oratorical patterns. Rhetorical criticism seems to behave itself better under consideration of style conventions on the micro-discourse level.

grouped to form cola, to use J.P. Louw's terminology, which in turn are grouped to form paragraphs. To understand the function of a paragraph unit in the broader discourse one must first understand the various functions of the clauses that make up the paragraph. Appendix 3 provides a depiction of possible coordinate and subordinate clausal relationships and an example of how constituent analysis might be applied to Jas 1.2-4. Here I must add one word of caution. A clause may be *grammatically* subordinate to another yet *semantically* of equal, or even greater, prominence. For example, verbal aspect, repetition of lexical or pronominal forms, word order, clause structure, and the peaks of chiasmus structures may all serve to mark an element in the text as prominent. The method for diagramming grammatical over against semantic prominence is described in detail in Appendix 3.

Step Three: Identifying Unit Boundaries
1. Tracking Cohesion Dynamics in the Discourse[5]
The Concept of Cohesion. Cohesion, as used in linguistic investigation, may be defined as a semantic property of a text which gives the text unity.[6] Any discourse unit has a network of relationships, some grammatical and others lexical, which make that unit of text cohesive. Genre, topic(s), conjunction, logical relationships between parts of an argument or narrative, consistency of grammatical subject, verb tense, person and number, various types of lexical repetition, consistency of reference to a main 'actor', or consistency of reference utilizing the same pronominal items, all may affect the level of cohesion in a discourse.

5. For a more detailed explanation of cohesion analysis and an example of how it may be applied to an extensive text, see Guthrie, *The Structure of Hebrews*, pp. 49-54, 59-75.

6. R.-A. de Beaugrande and W. Dressler use the term 'cohesion' to refer to dynamics on the surface structure of the text, while using 'coherence' to refer to dynamics on the notional level. What K. Berger, T. van Dijk, P. Cotterell and M. Turner refer to as 'coherence' is roughly synonymous to the definition of 'cohesion' found in Halliday and Hasan. Use of the term 'cohesion' in the present study follows the definition of Halliday and Hasan and may be used interchangeably with the concept of coherence as used by Berger *et al.* See R.-A. de Beaugrande and W.U. Dressler, *Introduction to Text Linguistics* (LLL; New York: Longman, 1981), ch. 4; K. Berger, *Exegese des Neuen Testaments: Neue Wege vom Text zur Auslegung* (Heidelberg: Quelle & Meyer, 2nd edn, 1984), pp. 12-17; T. van Dijk, *Text and Context* (New York: Longman, 1977), ch. 4; P. Cotterell and M. Turner, *Linguistics and Biblical Interpretation* (Downers Grove, IL: IVP, 1989), pp. 230-31.

Cohesion Analysis. Concentration of these cohesive dynamics makes the highest level of cohesion in a discourse occur at the paragraph level. Cola of the same paragraph have a higher level of cohesiveness when considered together than with cola outside that paragraph because so many features providing cohesion are brought to bear. The cohesive dynamics provide each paragraph with a unique semantic program. Furthermore, paragraphs of the same embedded discourse have a higher level of cohesiveness when considered together than with paragraphs outside that embedded discourse. This cohesiveness gives distinction to each embedded discourse unit.

In a paragraph that has a high level of cohesion, there should be relative consistency in several of the 'cohesion fields' of genre, topic, subject, actor, verb tense, person and number, as well as temporal and local frames of reference. A repetition of lexical, or reference, items may also be present. While shifts in the cohesion fields will occur throughout even the most cohesive discourse unit (e.g., the author may make a change in subject or verb tense) there should be corresponding shifts in several of the cohesion fields when the discourse moves from one paragraph to the next. Corresponding shifts occur because, with the change to a new unit, the cohesive dynamics change. Identification of these corresponding cohesion shifts may be accomplished by careful colon-by-colon analysis of the text. Such analysis, referred to in the present study as 'cohesion shift analysis', offers a starting point for the delimitation of discourse units by identification of unit boundaries. The chart in Appendix 4 may be used for this type of investigation.

At the same time, cohesion analysis helps identify the cohesive ties binding unit to unit, demonstrating aspects of the text which function for continuity. For example, the author may start a new unit by changing the temporal frame of reference, the main actor, and so on, yet continue to utilize lexical and reference items which were common to the unit just completed. Development in a discourse will normally involve a certain amount of both discontinuity and continuity. The elements which affect each must be analyzed to understand how the discourse develops.

2. *Identification of Inclusions*

The identification of inclusions offers a second means by which unit boundaries in a discourse may be isolated. The *inclusio* was a commonly used device in ancient literary and oratorical traditions, clear examples of the device being found in both biblical and extra-biblical sources.[7] Through use of *inclusio* an author marked the beginning and ending sections of a block of text by utilizing distant lexical parallels. While these parallels may involve the same elements, synonymous or complementary elements may be utilized as well. The elements used to form an *inclusio* may reside near the beginning or ending of a unit, rather than at the exact initiation or termination points. The lexical column of the cohesion analysis chart makes the analyst cognizant of special uses of reiterated items.

3. *Special Uses of Connectives or Repeated Phrases*
An author may also utilize certain connectives or types of parallelism other than inclusions to mark turning points in his discourse. For example, the author of Hebrews consistently uses γάρ as a 'next main point' marker in his discourse. He also utilizes 'parallel introductions' at 5.1 and 8.3 to mark the beginnings of the two embedded discourses which make up the central section of exposition in the sermon. Parallel introductions comprise a special type of transitional device which involves the repeating of a phrase stated earlier in the discourse.[8]

4. *Reassessment of Unit Constituent Structures and Unit Topics*
At this point in the process it is helpful to re-evaluate one's understanding of the main point of each unit, as well as the constituent structures within each unit, based on insights from cohesion dynamics, uses of *inclusio*, and other discourse markers.

Step Four: Analysis of the Interrelatedness of Units in the Discourse
There are several ways one may discern the interrelatedness of smaller units of discourse. First, one must note uses of *inclusio* that tie together

7. For use of *inclusio* in ancient Greek literature, see H. Lausberg, *Handbuch der literarischen Rhetorik: Eine Grundlegung der Literaturwissenschaft* (Munich: Max Hueber, 1960), I, p. 317. R. Volkmann, *Die Rhetorik der Griechen und Römer in systematischer Übersicht* (Leipzig: B.G. Teubner, 1985), p. 471. For its use in biblical literature, see, e.g., J. Jackson and M. Kessler (eds.), *Rhetorical Criticism: Essays in Honor of James Muilenberg* (Pittsburgh, PA: Pickwick Press, 1974), p. 24; P. Borgen, *Bread From Heaven: An Exegetical Study of the Concept of Manna in the Gospel of John and the Writings of Philo* (NovTSup; Leiden: Brill, 1965), pp. 34-38; Guthrie, *The Structure of Hebrews*, pp. 76-89.

8. Guthrie, *The Structure of Hebrews*, pp. 104-105.

larger embedded discourse sections. This, for example, is a key aspect of David Garland's helpful study mentioned earlier. Garland notes an *inclusio* that marks a broad section of the discourse running from Phil. 1.27 to 4.3. Discourse units embedded within this broader section are also marked by uses of *inclusio*.

Secondly, it is useful to identify lexical items that play key roles in two or more units. Semantic threads in a discourse are woven most often with the same, or related, lexical items.[9] These threads may relate structurally aligned units, but also may relate two or more non-structurally aligned units of text. Once again the lexical column of the cohesion analysis chart can highlight semantic threads as the analyst is forced to consider previous uses of a lexical item.

Thirdly, one must identify transitional techniques that facilitate movement from unit to unit and section to section. Ten such transitional techniques are depicted and briefly explained in Appendix 5. This constitutes one of the most neglected aspects in structural assessments of New Testament books.

Fourthly, depicting the embedding of units in the discourse can be helpful. This may be done by utilizing diagrams such as the one provided in Appendix 6.

Step Five: Analysis of the Means of Discourse Progression from Unit to Unit

The final step in this method involves scrutinizing the means by which the author advances his or her discourse. Several are possible and some may be used conjointly. The discourse may, for example, advance through logical association of two or more discourse units. These logical relations are similar to the logical relations possible between clauses mentioned above under Step Two. Thus, one paragraph may set forth a proposition and the next provide an extensive illustration of that proposition. One paragraph may be hortatory and the next provide the grounds for the exhortation. The discourse may also advance through a change in the temporal sphere, spatial sphere, the main actor or the main referents. This is especially prevalent in narrative. A third possibility is that the discourse may move forward by a paragraph functioning to reiterate a main theme dealt with earlier in the discourse. Finally, a discourse may advance on the basis of the transitional techniques

9. Lexical items may relate through collocation, reiteration, synonymy, antonymy, hyponymy or metonymy.

mentioned in Step Four. In concluding my discussion of the method I should say that all the above steps should be accompanied by multiple readings of the whole discourse.

The Method Applied

I would now like to suggest several points at which the method detailed above proves helpful in examining a discourse like Philippians. These suggestions are provisional and intended to be illustrative rather than a comprehensive analysis of the book's structure. I will first deal with important inclusions and transitional devices in Philippians and then discuss cohesion dynamics at the alleged interpolation points in the discourse.

Inclusions and Transitions

As mentioned above under Steps Three and Four, identification of inclusions offers an important means of isolating unit boundaries in some ancient discourses. David Garland's pinpointing uses of this device in Philippians stands at the heart of his important article. I believe Garland is correct concerning the inclusions bracketing 1.12-26 and 1.27–4.3.[10] However, I believe further elements crafting inclusions may be detected within these sections.

Sections within 1.12-26. It may be that the references to Christ in 1.13 and 18, and imprisonment in 1.13-14 and 17, and the uses of the attributive pronominal adjectives in 1.13 and 18 are intended to mark 1.12-18 as a unit. This unit coheres around the topic of the gospel's proclamation. Phil. 1.19-26 then turns to the subjects of Paul's possible release from prison and his attitude concerning his plight. This unit may also be seen as marked by an *inclusio*. In 1.19 Paul writes that he *knows* (οἶδα) that *this* (τοῦτο, i.e. the imprisonment) shall ultimately result in his deliverance due to their prayers and the support of the Spirit of Jesus Christ (Ἰησοῦ Χριστοῦ).

In vv. 25-26 these elements are echoed. Paul is convinced of τοῦτο (i.e., that his remaining in the flesh is necessary) and *knows* (οἶδα) that he shall remain with them, which will result in their progress, joy and the abounding of their confidence ἐν Χριστῷ Ἰησοῦ. The isolation of these

10. Garland, 'The Composition and Unity of Philippians', pp. 159-62.

two embedded discourse units finds further support in the parallel introductions noted in vv. 12 and 19.[11]

What then of the break between these two units? The break between the two uses of χαίρω, suggested in the Nestle–Aland text, is preferable for three reasons. First, the progressive nature of the ἀλλὰ καί construction may be seen as marking the next step in the discourse.[12] Secondly, the future tense form χαρήσομαι finds cohesiveness with the future tense forms in the following verses. Thirdly, χαρήσομαι could also be seen as taking part in the *inclusio* marking 1.18b-26, finding its complement in the reference to χαράν in v. 25.

If this assessment of the break between these two units is correct, the dual reference to rejoicing in Phil. 1.18 should be seen as a hook word transition effecting a smooth passage from the first unit to the second.[13]

Garland's Identification of an Inclusio *Marking 2.1-18.* Garland briefly mentions the dual appeal to joy in 2.2 and 2.17-18 as marking 2.1-18 as a unit.[14] Upon careful consideration, however, four problems arise from this proposition. First, 2.12-16 coheres around the topic of work/toil, reiterating a number of elements from 1.27-28.[15] There seems to be at least a minor topical shift with 2.17 from the exhortations to unity and humility (1.27–2.16) to Paul's potential martyrdom. Secondly, the ἀλλὰ καί construction has already been shown to play a role in marking the beginning of a new unit in 1.18. It occurs again in 2.17 and may, as in 1.18, indicate progression to a new unit. Thirdly, elements in 2.1-4 parallel 2.17-21. Here we may add to the χαράν of 2.2 the dual references to encouragement (2.1, 20) and unity of spirit (σύμψυχοι in 2.2

11. Silva, *Philippians*, p. 76. See Appendix 5 for an explanation of parallel introductions.

12. G.F. Hawthorne, *Philippians* (WBC; Waco, TX: Word Books, 1983), p. 39. In the vast majority of cases in the New Testament an ἀλλὰ καί construction is preceded by and used in conjunction with οὐ μόνον as at Phil. 1.29, 2.4 and 2.27. It may be argued that at 1.18, 2.17 and 3.8, cases in Philippians where the ἀλλὰ καί construction is used without being preceded by a negative, the discourse progresses to the next thought.

13. On the use of hook word transitions, see Appendix 5 and Guthrie, *The Structure of Hebrews*, p. 96.

14. Garland, 'The Composition and Unity of Philippians', p. 160.

15. Including the ideas of work, Paul's presence or absence, salvation, unity, right conduct, being in the midst of those opposed to the gospel, sharing the gospel, and references to Christ and God.

and ἰσόψυχον in 2.19) as well as the τὸ αὐτό (2.2, 18) and τὰ ἑαυτῶν (2.4, 21) constructions. Fourthly, a pronounced parallelism exists between 2.17-18 and 2.29–3.1. At both 2.17-18 and 2.29–3.1 Paul (a) balances a reference to his service (λειτουργίᾳ) to them with a reference to their service (λειτουργίας) to him; (b) exhorts his readers to rejoice (χαίρετε), and (c) uses a τὸ αὐτό construction in the same sentence with personal pronouns referring to himself and the hearers. A further parallel may exist between the risk to Paul's life and the life-threatening situation of Epaphroditus. If these parallels craft an *inclusio*, the unit marked runs from 2.17 to 3.1.

It could be that the τὰ αὐτά of 3.1b refers to the need to rejoice and the need to honor men like Epaphroditus (see the references to rejoicing related to the coming of Epaphroditus in 2.28-29). Notice that in 3.1b Paul speaks of safeguarding his hearers. This finds cohesion with his expressions of concern in 2.19-20, 28. Regardless of one's interpretation of this difficult statement, the occurrence of elements in 3.1b which, along with elements in 2.29–3.1a, parallel 2.17-18, offers at least one objective reason for suggesting that the first verse of ch. 3 concludes the unit.

No harsh break exists between 2.16 and 2.17 since Paul effects the transition by mentioning his ministry in both verses. Yet 2.17–3.1 may be seen as a unit, with an introduction (2.17-18), two embedded units dealing with Paul's associates (Timothy in 2.19-24 and Epaphroditus in 2.25-30), and a closing (3.1).[16] The extensive parallels between 2.1-4 and 2.17-21 represent parallel introductions to the first two main movements within 1.27–4.3, the first running from 2.1 to 2.16 and the second from 2.17 to 3.1. The much discussed τὸ λοιπόν of 3.1a would then be seen as summing up a brief series of exhortations, as it does at 4.8.

The Inclusio *Marking 1.27–4.3.* Identification of the extensive verbal parallels between Phil. 1.27-30 and 3.20–4.3 is perhaps the most important insight in David Garland's study. Garland interprets these parallels to indicate an *inclusio* marking 1.27–4.3 as a unit. Duane Watson challenges this conclusion, suggesting that 4.1-3 be seen as the 'beginning of the *repetitio*, the summing up section of the *peroratio*'.[17]

Although I side with Garland on the function of these parallels, I

16. Garland notes the inclusions marking the units dealing with Timothy and Epaphroditus. See 'The Composition and Unity of Philippians', p. 160.

17. Watson, 'A Rhetorical Analysis of Philippians', p. 84.

believe that he and Watson both have failed to mark properly the ending of the unit begun at 3.2. Garland extends the digression through 3.21, even though he earlier notes that parallels with 1.27-30 occur at 3.19-20 (ἀπώλεια in 3.19, πολίτευμα and σωτῆρα in 3.20) and continue through 4.3.[18] Conceptual parallels with 1.27-30 may also be seen in the references to right conduct (3.17-18) and the references to 'enemies' of the Christian movement (3.18).

Phil. 4.4-9 also evidences certain parallels with 1.27-30, although the admonitions in this section are more general in nature. References to anxiety (1.28 // 4.6), God's provision (1.28 // 4.7), and the 'seeing/hearing' motif (1.27, 30 // 4.9) all find expression in both units.[19]

Furthermore, the section beginning with 3.17 and continuing through 4.9 is marked with an *inclusio*. Paul opens and closes the section with exhortations to follow his example.

Therefore, it may be suggested that Phil. 3.17–4.9 forms the conclusion of the letter's main hortatory mid-section. The concluding exhortation to follow the example of Paul and his associates, found in 3.17-21, sums up 2.17–3.1. Phil. 4.1-3 exhorts individuals in the church to be unified, giving specific application to 1.17–2.16. Notice that these two concluding units are presented in inverted order to the sections with which they correspond. Finally, Paul closes the main hortatory mid-section with a series of general exhortations in 4.4-9.

This leaves us with a layout of the discourse depicted in Appendix 7. Notice first that the mid-section of the letter is bracketed by sections dealing with Paul's circumstances. Secondly, the digression at 3.2 occurs at the center point of the four primary divisions of the mid-section. Thirdly, the dual uses of τὸ λοιπόν, the first at 3.1a and the second at 4.8, occur at the end of each of the two halves of the mid-section. This understanding of the discourse's structure has obvious implications for the unity question.

Furthermore, by this point in the discourse the 'rejoice' motif has already occurred at three transition points: 1.18, 2.17-18 and 3.1. We again find the motif at the beginning of the last unit in the body proper (4.4) and the beginning of the final section on Paul's circumstances (4.10). I propose that these final two uses form a parallel introduction

18. Garland, 'The Composition and Unity of Philippians', pp. 161-73.

19. Watson suggests ἐπιεικές in 4.5 'summarizes...standing firm (στήκω), striving (συναθλέω), and struggling (ἀγών)' in 1.27-30. See Watson, 'A Rhetorical Analysis of Philippians', p. 77.

transition by which Paul moves from the main body back to a consideration of his circumstances.

One plausible answer to the question concerning Paul's waiting until the end of the letter for his 'thank you' may be suggested. Paul ends the description of his present, difficult situation, found in 1.12-26, with the possibility of his deliverance and coming to the Philippians (1.19-26). He then launches his hortatory material by placing their conduct in the context of his possible coming (1.27). The 'coming' theme carries on through the section on Paul's associates, still being related to the conduct of the Philippians (2.12, 19-30). This builds a certain amount of healthy tension into the exhortation. Having accomplished his exhortation with 4.9, he ends the letter on a positive note by thanking the Philippians for their gift and assuring them of his well-being. This may be seen as a form of mitigation by which the apostle softens the blow of the sustained exhortation and leaves the hearers with words of encouragement.

Cohesion Dynamics

Further insights on the question of Philippians' unity may be had by addressing the cohesion dynamics present at alleged interpolation points.

The abrupt shift at Phil. 3.2 has been a primary concern of those arguing against the book's unity. If 3.2 indeed launches a digression, the abruptness presents no problem but rather would be expected.[20] Furthermore, the elements of continuity in 3.2-16 which provide cohesion with what has preceded must be taken into consideration (see Appendix 8).

In 3.2 Paul warns his readers of 'evil workers' (κακοὺς ἐργάτας), which follows quite nicely from his discussion of his fellow workers. Note especially the use of συνεργόν in 2.25. The Philippians are to hold men like Epaphroditus in high regard (2.29) and to beware of bad men (3.2).

Cohesion between the two units also may be seen by the continuing uses of pronouns having Paul and the Philippians as referents. If 3.2-16 was not part of the original composition, then the pronouns used at the beginning of this unit have no identifiable referents. Cohesion between the two units also finds evidence in the verb, actor and subject columns as a glance down those columns of the cohesion chart suggests.

20. Garland, 'The Composition and Unity of Philippians', p. 173.

Therefore, while the abrupt shift at 3.2 fulfills its role in marking a digression, the elements which provide discourse cohesion between Phil. 3.2-16 and the previous unit offer further evidence against an interpolation theory.

Cohesion analysis displays Phil. 4.4 as the beginning of a new unit, which has already been suggested above. Cohesion shifts would be expected since Paul moves from an exhortation to specific workers (4.1-3) to general exhortations addressed to the whole church (4.4-9). Yet, the τὸ ἐπιεικὲς ὑμῶν γνωσθήτω of 4.5 may be seen as following from the relational conflict reflected in 4.1-3. Also, the ἐν κυρίῳ of 4.4 harkens back to the same phrase in 4.1.

Upon considering the cohesion dynamics at Phil. 4.10 numerous shifts are apparent, continuity being provided primarily in the referent column and by the parallel introduction transition mentioned above. Yet would this not be expected if Paul was moving out of the main body of his letter and moving into a section corresponding to Phil. 1.12-26.

Conclusion

In closing, questions surrounding the integrity of Philippians are certainly difficult and worthy of continued investigation. Although one can never speak dogmatically concerning the presence or absence of interpolations in a text, the discourse dynamics evidenced in Philippians seem to work against those skeptical of the book's unity. Hopefully the insights offered above will further discussion and understanding of this New Testament letter.

The methodology detailed and applied in this presentation is offered as one possible approach to analyzing discourses. Inclusions, transitions and cohesion dynamics constitute three of numerous factors which may be considered when dealing with discourses such as Philippians. Discourse analysis is just now making its way into New Testament critical methodology and is in great need of methodological and terminological development. It is hoped that this discussion will further that cause.

Appendix 1

OVERVIEW OF THE METHOD

Step One: Perform Basic Grammatical Analysis

Step Two: Perform Constituent Analysis at the Micro-discourse Level (i.e., trace the semantic relationships between clauses)
Diagram coordinate and subordinate clause relationships.
Analyze prominence features in the text.

Step Three: Identify Unit Boundaries
Track cohesion dynamics.
Note devices such as *inclusio* (utilizing insights from the lexical cohesion column of the Cohesion Analysis chart).
Note special uses of connectives or repeated forms (e.g., parallel introductions).
Reassess unit constituent structures and unit topics.

Step Four: Analyze the Interrelatedness of Units in the Discourse
Note uses of *inclusio* which tie together larger embedded discourse sections.
Note lexical items used to give cohesion to larger sections.
Depict the embedding of units in the discourse.
Identify transitional techniques which facilitate movement from unit to unit and section to section.

Step Five: Analyze the Method of Progression from Unit to Unit (e.g., logical, spatial, etc.)

Appendix 2

DIAGRAMMATIC METHOD FOR SYNTACTIC ANALYSIS

The method was developed by Lorin L. Cranford and has been altered slightly by G.H. Guthrie and J.S. Duvall.

1. The sequential order of each verse in the Greek text is followed for the most part. Exceptions to this rule include the positioning of postpositive conjunctions and times when an adverbial or adjectival clause needs to be pulled out of order (in which case ellipsis points may be used to indicate where the clause had been in the verse). It seems best to try to keep all of the main clause on the same line.

2. All main clause statements begin on the far left margin.

3. All coordinate conjunctions that link together main clause statements are indented five spaces from the far left margin. When coordinate conjunctions join subordinate expressions they are indented five spaces from the beginning margin established by the subordinate expression.

4. All modifying elements are indented three spaces to the right of the first letter of the word they modify. This includes all words, phrases, and clauses serving either adjectival or adverbial purposes. Appositional elements, however, are indented only one space on the word they delimit. When modifiers occur in the prefield, they are diagrammed on the line above. When modifiers follow, they are diagrammed on the line below. Predicate nominatives remain on the same line with the subject and linking verb.

5. Direct and indirect objects are located on the line above or below the main clause and one space off the end of the main clause. The exception here is when the main clause and direct object are separated by intervening, modifying material, which is positioned on the line below the main clause and extends beyond the end of the main clause. In this case the direct object is placed one space off the end of the main clause on the second available line. A line is skipped to show that the direct object is not directly related to the modifying material. (This is, perhaps, the least 'tidy' aspect of this method. However, the color-coding detailed below helps clarify direct objects which are far removed from the main elements of the main clause.)

6. Two lines are skipped after a major break in the punctuation. A line may also be skipped in cases where the diagram does not clearly depict whether a modifying element belongs with the material on the line above or the line below.

7. Color Code: (one could use colors to highlight syntax distinctions)
purple = conjunctions
pink = main clause
blue = adjectival elements
orange = adverbial prepositional elements
yellow = all other adverbial elements
green = direct and indirect objects

An Example of the Diagrammatic Method

πᾶσαν χαρὰν
ἡγήσασθε
ἀδελφοί μου
ὅταν . . . . . περιπέσητε
πειρασμοῖς
ποικίλοις
γινώσκοντες
ὅτι τὸ δοκίμιον . . . κατεργάζεται
ὑμῶν τῆς πίστεως ὑπομονήν

δὲ
ἔργον
τέλειον
ἡ . . . ὑπομονὴ . . . ἐχέτω
ἵνα ἦτε τέλειοι
καὶ
ὁλόκληροι
ἐν μηδενὶ
λειπόμενοι

δὲ
σοφίας
εἰ . . . τις ὑμῶν λείπεται
αἰτείτω
παρὰ . . . θεοῦ
τοῦ διδόντος
(σοφίας) πᾶσιν
ἁπλῶς
καὶ
μὴ ὀνειδίζοντος

καὶ
δοθήσεται
αὐτῷ

Appendix 3

SEMANTIC OR CONSTITUENT ANALYSIS

The following was developed by Bruce Corley and has been slightly adjusted by G.H. Guthrie.

I. *Parataxis (Coordinate)*

A. *Types of Nuclear Sentence Utterances*

1. Declarative (thesis, reportorial)
2. Interrogative (deliberative)
3. Imperatival (command, exhortation)
4. Exclamatory (wish)

B. *Additive Relationships*
(These combinations are effective ways of emphasis, parallelism, and raising expectancy.)

1. Simultaneous
2. Equivalent
3. Sequential
4. Conjoined

C. *Dyadic Relationships*
(These are paired thoughts that serve to define, eliminate and clarify.)

1. Alternative (Disjunctive)
2. Contrastive
3. Corrective
4. Question/Answer
5. Positive/Negative

II. *Hypotaxis (Subordinate)*

A. *Substantival Relationships*

1. Explanatory
2. Comparative
3. Illustrative
4. Generic-Specific (Restatement)
5. Appositional
6. Reinforcement

B. *Circumstantial Relationships*

1. Temporal
2. Local
3. Modal (How?)
4. Situational (What else in the event?)

C. *Logical Relationships*

1. Ground
2. Inference
3. Result
4. Purpose
5. Concession
6. Condition

An Example of Constituent Analysis

This is performed after the grammatical analysis explained in Appendix 2.

Lines show equal prominence by proceding out from the first clause making an 'L' down and then making another 'L' to the edge of the next clause.

A clause that is semantically subordinate branches off ('T') of the line proceding from the clause to which it is subordinate.

Constituent functions are in parentheses on the vertical lines nearest the clause or phrase they identify.

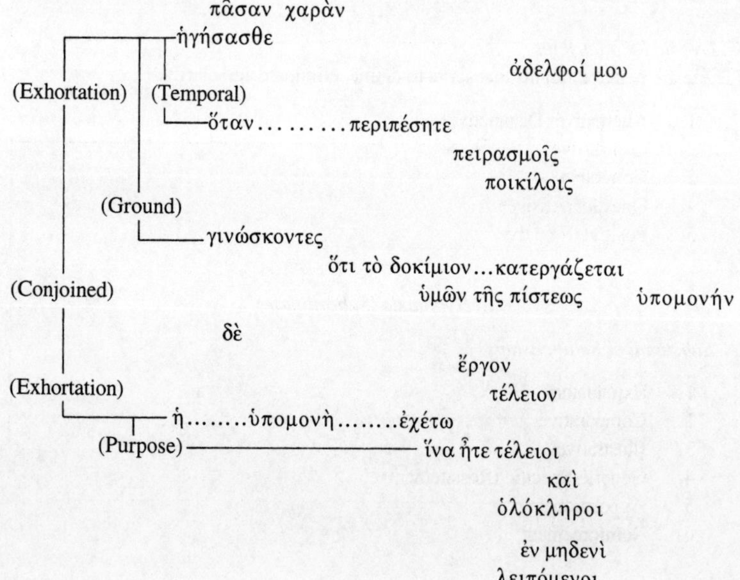

Appendix 4

COHESION ANALYSIS CHART

							Verb					
Colon	Genre	Topic	Temp./Loc.	Actor	Subject	Tns.	V	M	P	N	Reference	Lexical

Appendix 5

TRANSITIONAL DEVICES

The suggestions here are based partly on an article by H. Van Dyke Parunak entitled 'Transitional Techniques in the Bible', *JBL* 102 (1983), pp. 525-48. Here the techniques are given different designations and several not covered by Parunak are added.

Constituent Transitions

Constituent Transitions are those in which the transitional element is located in one or more of the constituents at the beginning or ending of the two units being joined together by the transition.

Hook Words

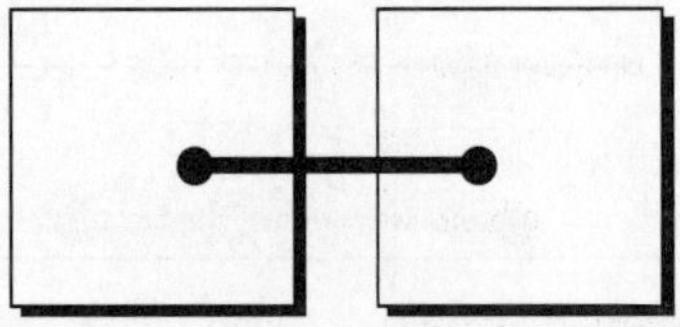

By use of a common word(s) at the end of one section and at the beginning of the next the author generated a transition between the two.

Distant Hook Words

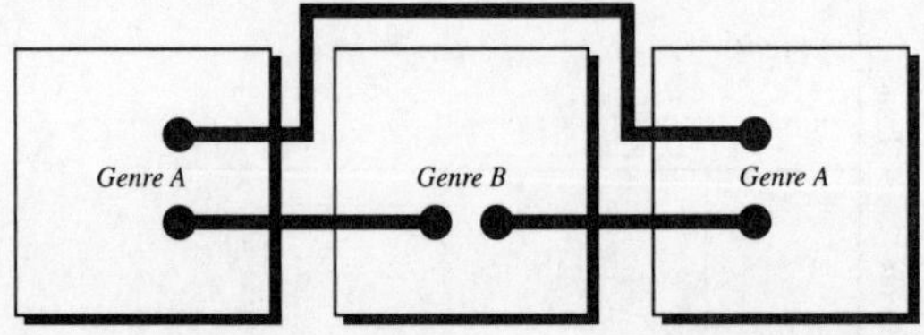

Where a unit of genre A is followed by a unit of genre B, which in turn is followed by another unit of genre A, the author could use two sets of hook words—one to attach the first unit of genre A to the unit of genre B and another to attach the first unit of genre A to the next unit of genre A.

Hooked Key Words

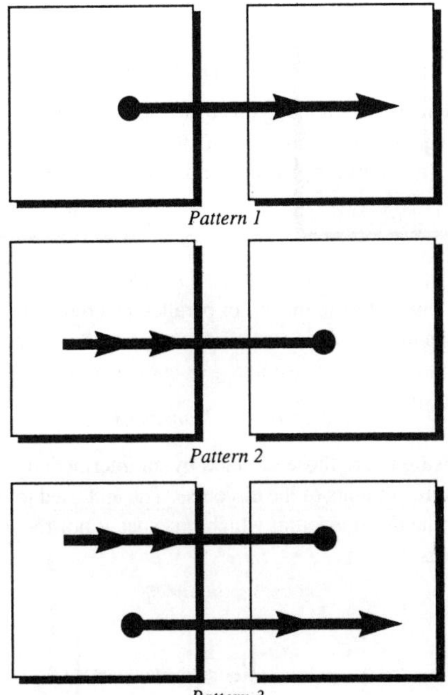

Pattern 1

Pattern 2

Pattern 3

The transition is effected either by (1) a characteristic term being used in the second unit which had been introduced in the conclusion of the first unit, (2) a characteristic term in the first unit being used in the introduction to the next, or (3) a combination of the two.

Overlapping Constituents

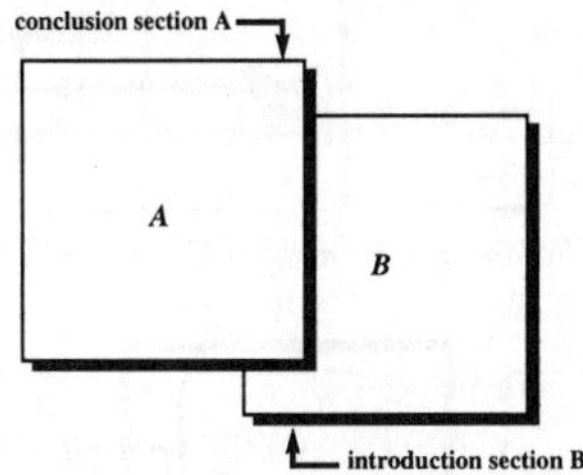

A passage is used simultaneously as the conclusion of one block of material and the introduction to the next.

Parallel Introductions

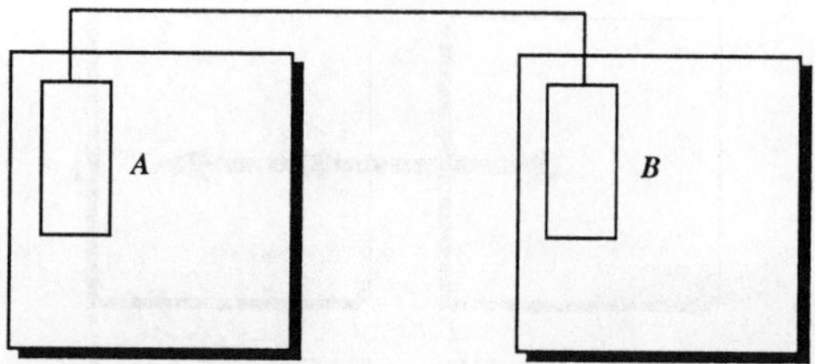

'Parallel Introductions' refers to the use of parallel material at the beginnings of two successive discourse units.

Intermediary Transitions

Intermediary Transitions are those effected by an intermediary unit of text which stands between two larger units of the discourse. The unit used to make the transition belongs to neither the discourse unit which precedes it nor the one which follows, but contains elements of both.

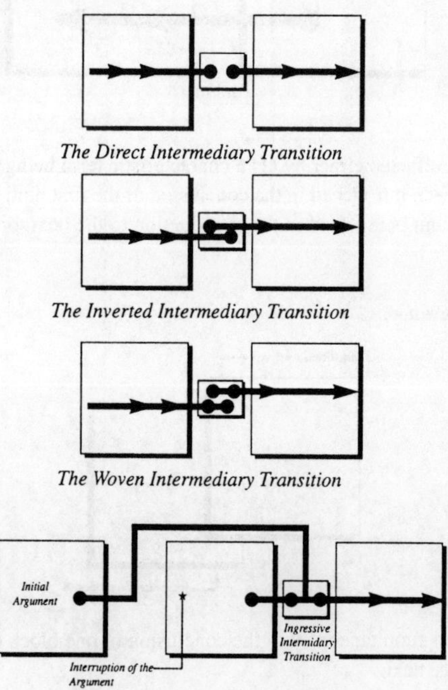

The Direct Intermediary Transition

The Inverted Intermediary Transition

The Woven Intermediary Transition

The Ingressive Intermediary Transition

Appendix 6

Diagramming Embedded Discourse Units

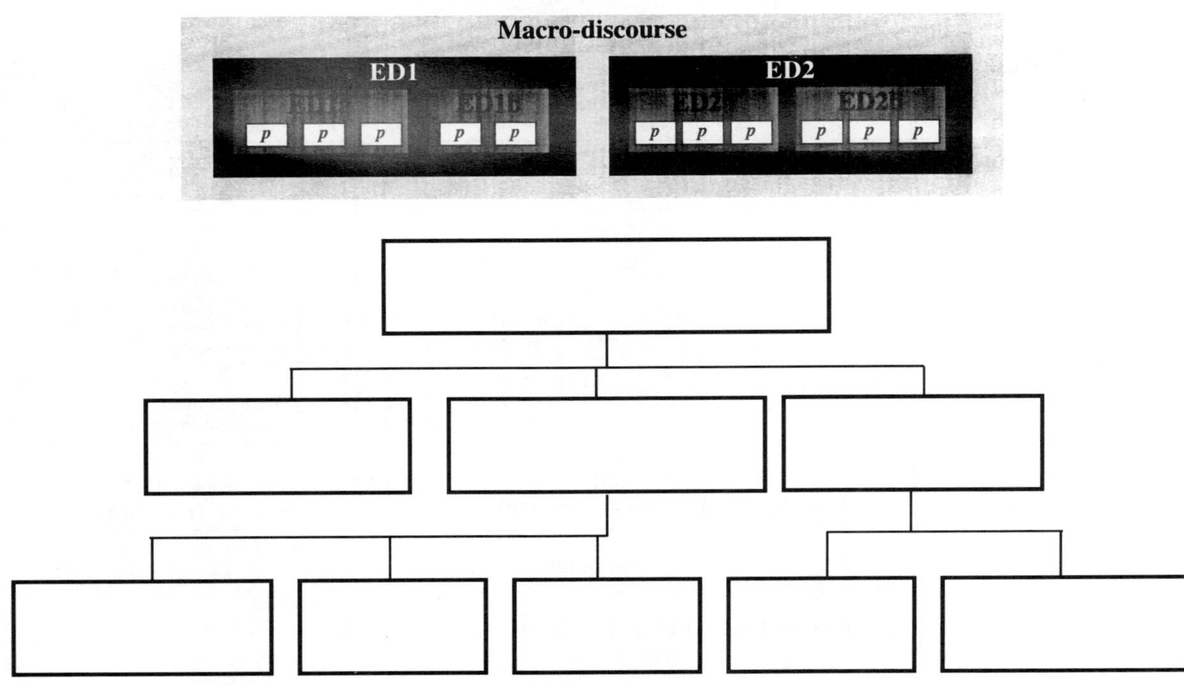

Appendix 7

A Proposal on the Structure of Philippians

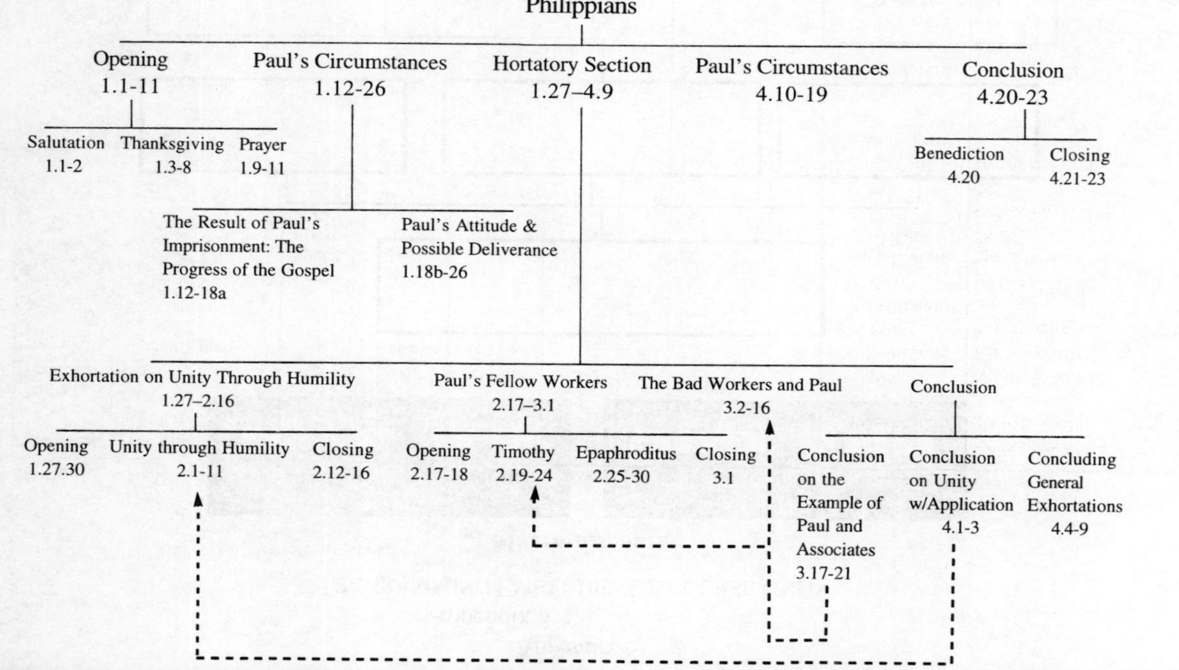

Appendix 8

COHESION ANALYSIS OF ALLEGED INTERPOLATION POINTS AT PHILIPPIANS 2.29–3.2

Colon	Genre	Topic	Temp./Loc.	Actor	Subject	Tns.	Verb V	Verb M	Verb P	Verb N	Reference	Lexical
2.29a	Epis./Hort.	The Coming of Epaphroditus	–	the hearers	2 P Pron. (vb)	Pres.	M	M	2	P	2 P Pron. (vb)→hearers αὐτόν→Epaph.	ἐν κυρίῳ→2.24 χαρᾶς→2.28
2.29b-30	Epis./Hort.	The Coming of Epaphroditus	–	the hearers	2 P Pron. (vb)	Pres.	A	M	2	P	2 P Pron. (vb)→hearers 3 S Pron. (vb)→Epaph.	Χριστοῦ→2.21 ἔχετε→2.20 λειτουργίας→2.17, 25
3.1a	Epis./Hort.	Rejoice	–	the hearers	2 P Pron. (vb)	Pres.	A	M	2	P	2 P Pron. (vb)→hearers μοῦ→Paul	ἀδελφοί→2.25 χαίρετε→2.17-18, 28-29 ἐν κυρίῳ→2.19, 24, 29
3.1b	Epis./Hort.	The need to rejoice and honor men like Epaphroditus?	–	Paul	inf.	–	–	–	–	–	ἐμοί→Paul ὑμῖν→hearers	τὰ αὐτά→2.18
3.2a	Epis./Hort.	Evil Workers	–	the hearers	2 P Pron. (vb)	Pres.	A	M	2	P	2 P Pron. (vb)→hearers	
3.2b	Epis./Hort.	Evil Workers	–	the hearers	2 P Pron (vb)	Pres.	A	M	2	P	2 P Pron. (vb)→hearers	ἐργάτας→ συνεργόν (2.25)
3.2c	Epis./Hort.	Evil Workers	–	the hearers	2 P Pron. (vb)	Pres.	A	M	2	P	2 P Pron.(vb) →hearers	and ἔργον (2.30)

A Discourse Study of Constituent Order and the Article in Philippians

Stephen H. Levinsohn

This essay[1] has two primary goals. The first is to argue that the linguistic concepts of topicality and focality, as defined below, are important for understanding the significance of constituent order in Koine Greek. The second is to show that the presence versus absence of the article, in connection with a noun whose referent is known and particular, relates to the distinction between topicality and focality.

The paper further shows that the topicality/focality distinction, together with the principles of constituent order which lead from it, helps in the resolution of certain exegetical issues, as well as contributing to the discussion of the integrity of the book of Philippians.

Linguist Simon Dik recognises two distinct 'clause-internal pragmatic functions',[2] topicality and focality. These functions he defines as follows: 'Topicality characterises those elements "about" which information is provided or requested in the discourse'.[3] Focality characterizes 'the most important or salient parts of what we say about the topical things'.[4]

Dik goes on to say that a language may give 'special distinctive treatment to some topical or focal element'.[5] One such treatment, in Koine Greek as in many languages, is to place the element concerned towards the beginning of the clause or sentence. In particular, to give special treatment to a topical element, Greek topicalizes it—places it at

1. I would like to thank John Callow and John Banker for their valuable comments on an earlier draft of this essay. I am grateful, too, for observations made by Stanley E. Porter and Moisés Silva on the version presented at the SBL Annual Meeting of November 1993.

2. S.C. Dik, *The Theory of Functional Grammar*. I. *The Structure of the Clause* (Dordrecht: Foris Publications, 1989), p. 265.

3. Dik, *Functional Grammar*, p. 266.

4. Dik, *Functional Grammar*, p. 264.

5. Dik, *Functional Grammar*, p. 264.

the beginning of the clause or sentence concerned.[6] To give special treatment to a focal element, that is, to mark it as salient, Greek places it at the beginning of the clause or sentence, though after any topicalized element.

The above principles, together with the others presented in this essay, are illustrated from that part of Philippians which is typically labeled 'B' (1.1–3.1 and some verses from ch. 4). Examples from parts 'C' (approximately 3.2–4.1) and 'A' (4.10-20 or 23), plus, where possible, 2.19-24, are then cited to show that, in general, the principles apply to all the parts. However, it has not been possible to demonstrate whether or not principle 4 applies to part A or to 2.19-24. More significantly, it appears likely that principle 5 does *not* operate in A.[7]

Principle 1

The first functional principle affecting constituent order in Philippians (as well as Koine Greek in general and numerous other languages) may be expressed as follows:

> (1) To provide a new point of departure for what follows, place the element which expresses that point of departure at the beginning of the clause or sentence concerned.

This first principle concerns topical elements and the giving of special treatment to such elements by topicalizing them. In addition, it addresses why certain topical elements are given special treatment, viz., to provide a 'point of departure for the communication'[8] or, as Chafe puts it, to set

6. Linguists employ a variety of terms to refer to topical elements that have been moved to the front of a clause or sentence. Terms such as 'basis' (E. Beneš, 'Die Verbstellung im Deutschen, von der Mitteilungsperspektive her betrachtet', *Philologica Pragensia* 5 [1962], p. 6) or 'point of departure' (Beneš, 'Die Verbstellung', p. 6; S.H. Levinsohn, *Discourse Features of New Testament Greek: A Coursebook* [Dallas: Summer Institute of Linguistics, 1992], p. 16) are to be preferred over ones that contain the element 'topic'; if the point of departure is not the subject, it is often the topic neither of the clause or sentence concerned, nor of the wider context. Greek grammarians commonly describe both topical and focal elements which have been so treated as 'emphatic'.

7. D.E. Garland ('The Composition and Unity of Philippians: Some Neglected Literary Factors', *NovT* 27 [1985], p. 155) provides a summary of different divisions of Philippians into three 'letters'.

8. Beneš, 'Die Verbstellung', p. 6, as translated by P.L. Garvin, 'Czechoslovakia', in T.E. Sebeok (ed.), *Current Trends in Linguistics* (The Hague: Mouton, 1963), p. 508.

a 'domain within which the main predication holds'.[9]

Thus, in Phil. 2.22, τὴν...δοκιμὴν αὐτοῦ provides the point of departure for the communication about Timothy's character. It is within the domain 'his character' that the predication 'you know that, as a son with a father, he has served with me in the Gospel' (see RSV) holds; the assertion is made about 'his character', in contrast with the 'all' of v. 21.

However, there is a second side to topicalized elements, which gives them a 'bi-directional function'.[10] This stems from why it is necessary to provide a point of departure at all. A point of departure for what follows needs to be stated when it differs from the point of departure for what has preceded.[11]

In the case of 2.22, for example, the previous verse has as its point of departure οἱ πάντες. Since the point of departure for v. 22 is different, the verse begins with a topicalized element.

The element which is topicalized is frequently the subject. In 2.21, for example, οἱ τάντες provides the point of departure for the communication about 'they all' (viz., 'look after their own interests, not those of Jesus Christ', RSV). This point of departure is necessary because it is different from the domain ('I') in which the assertions of vv. 19-20 have been made.

The overall domain for the book of Philippians is established in the opening salutation (vv. 1-2), which names the author(s) and addressees. Points of departure in Philippians tend to apply only to the immediate communication. In the absence of further topicalization, the domain for further communications reverts to that of the wider context (except that 'Paul and Timothy' [v. 1] becomes 'I' in v. 3 and remains singular for the rest of the book; see further below). This is illustrated in 1.9b:

(1.9a) καὶ τοῦτο προσεύχομαι,
(1.9b) ἵνα ἡ ἀγάπη ὑμῶν ἔτι μᾶλλον καὶ μᾶλλον περισσεύῃ ἐν ἐπιγνώσει καὶ πάσῃ αἰσθήσει,
(1.10a) εἰς τὸ δοκιμάζειν ὑμᾶς τὰ διαφέροντα.

9. W.L. Chafe, 'Givenness, Contrastiveness, Definiteness, Subjects, Topics and Point of View', in C.N. Li (ed.), *Subject and Topic* (New York: Academic Press, 1976), p. 50.

10. Levinsohn, *Discourse Features*, p. 17.

11. A point of departure may also reiterate a previous one; see Levinsohn, *Discourse Features*, pp. 19-20. τοῦτο in 1.19 may provide an instance of a reiterated point of departure if, as H. Alford (*The Greek Testament* [London: Rivingtons, 1865], III, p. 159) proposes, its referent is considered to be the same as that of ἐν τούτῳ in 1.18.

ἡ ἀγάπη ὑμῶν provides the point of departure for the predication 'may abound more and more, with knowledge and all discernment' (RSV), as the domain changes from 'I' and 'you' to 'your love'. Following that predication, the domain immediately reverts to 'you'; see the post-verbal ὑμᾶς in the infinitival clause of v. 10a.

Typically, then, an element is topicalized only when it is necessary to provide a new point of departure. In this regard, 1.3 (the beginning of the body of the letter) is instructive. In some manuscripts ἐγώ is topicalized, reflecting a shift of attention from Paul and Timothy in vv. 1-2 to a singular first person thereafter. In most manuscripts, however, no element is topicalized, suggesting that the overall domain established in the opening salutation is assumed still to apply:[12]

(1.1) Παῦλος καὶ Τιμόθεος...πᾶσιν τοῖς ἁγίοις ἐν Χριστῷ Ἰησοῦ τοῖς οὖσιν ἐν Φιλίπποις...

(1.3) εὐχαριστῶ τῷ θεῷ μου ἐπὶ πάσῃ τῇ μνείᾳ ὑμῶν.

Phil. 1.8 illustrates a change of subject without topicalization. This is appropriate because the purpose of the verse is not to make a comment about God as topic, but to provide support (see γάρ) for the assertions made in previous verse(s), both of which have the wide domain of 'I' and 'you':

(1.7) ...διὰ τὸ ἔχειν με ἐν τῇ καρδίᾳ ὑμᾶς...

(1.8a) μάρτυς γάρ μου [ἐστιν] ὁ θεός,[13]

(1.8b) ὡς ἐπιποθῶ πάντας ὑμᾶς ἐν σπλάγχνοις Χριστοῦ Ἰησοῦ.

The points made above concerning topicalization apply not only to part B of Philippians (including 2.19-24), but also to C and A. For example, topicalization in connection with the provision of a new point of departure occurs in 3.4 (a shift from 'we' to 'I') and 4.19 (a shift from 'I' to 'my God'). Overt subjects which are not topicalized occur in 3.21 (αὐτόν) and 4.15 (καὶ ὑμεῖς); in both instances, the subject remains the same as before, and no change in the point of departure is appropriate.

Of particular interest is the establishment of 'I' as the point of departure for 4.11b-13; although the subject of both parts of v. 11 is the same, previous verses have been concerned with 'you' as subject, so it is

12. As J.H. Greenlee observes (*An Exegetical Summary of Philippians* [Dallas: Summer Institute of Linguistics, 1992], p. 9), 'Although Timothy is spoken of as a joint writer... all commentators agree that Paul is the sole author of the letter'.

13. In this and other examples, no mention is made of variants which are not pertinent to the topic of this paper.

appropriate to mark the switch to 'I', as the ground is given for Paul's claim, 'Not that I speak in respect of want' (the passage reverts back to 'you' in v. 14).

Turning to the boundaries between the proposed parts of Philippians, the absence or presence of a topicalized element in each case is consistent with the principle outlined in this section.

Following several of the proposed boundaries, the addressee is subject (3.2; 4.4, 10, 21; see also 3.1a, following τὸ λοιπόν and a vocative), and topicalization does not occur. In 2.19 the subject reverts to 'I', after a brief switch to the addressees in v. 18, and topicalization does not occur until the next clause (Τιμόθεον). In each case, the absence of topicalization is consistent with reversions to the wider domain of the passage, following clauses with a different point of departure (in the case of 3.2, ὑμῖν was also the point of departure of the previous clause).

Phil. 4.2, in contrast, necessitates the provision of new points of departure (Εὐοδίαν, Συντύχην), as attention switches from the wide domain of the addressees in general (4.1) to these particular individuals. In 3.1b τὰ αὐτὰ γράφειν ὑμῖν provides a point of departure for two verbless clauses, before the passage reverts to the wider domain in which the addressees are subject. Finally, in 4.8, again following τὸ λοιπόν and a vocative, a series of mostly verbless clauses provides the point of departure for the sentence, and is then summarized by ταῦτα.

Each part of Philippians, therefore, follows principle 1 in placing points of departure at the beginning of the clause or sentence concerned. Nevertheless, since this principle applies to Koine Greek in general, this conclusion is not surprising. Negatively, however, adherence to principle 1 throughout the book and, in particular, at the boundaries between the proposed parts of Philippians, provides no evidence against it being an integral whole.

Principle 2

The second functional principle affecting constituent order in Philippians (as well as Koine Greek in general and many other languages) may be expressed as follows:

> (2) To mark an element as salient, place it at the beginning of the clause or sentence concerned, immediately following any topicalized element.

This second principle concerns focal elements and the giving of special treatment to such elements by placing them early in the clause or sentence.

Phil. 1.9 (cited above) provides two examples of this principle in operation. First, in the clause which introduces the prayer, τοῦτο precedes προσεύχομαι. This τοῦτο is commonly recognized as 'emphatic',[14] to draw attention to the following prayer. The prayer itself then begins with ἡ ἀγάπη ὑμῶν, an element topicalized to provide the point of departure for what follows. This element in turn is followed by ἔτι μᾶλλον καὶ μᾶλλον, in a position which marks it as salient: 'that your love may abound *still more and more...*'

Phil. 1.17 (or 1.16, depending on the text followed) is a further illustration of an element placed before the verb to mark it as salient ('thinking *affliction* to add to my bonds'):

(1.17) ...(οἰόμενοι) θλῖψιν ἐγείρειν τοῖς δεσμοῖς μου.

The effect of placing an element towards the beginning of a clause or sentence is described here as *marking* it for salience because there are positions in which the element concerned may be *naturally* salient. A distinction between natural and marked salience is recognized by many linguists. Crozier, for example, distinguishes elements in positions of 'unmarked focus' and 'marked focus'.[15]

The concept of a naturally most salient position in the clause or sentence probably dates back to the work of Firbas, in the context of Prague School studies of constituent order in European languages. Firbas claims that, when elements are ordered naturally, the communication will begin with the topic (what he calls the 'theme') and finish (insofar as other constraints permit) with the most salient constituent of the comment (which constituent he calls the 'rheme').[16]

In line with this claim, I have maintained for Koine Greek that the unmarked position for the most salient constituents of the comment about a sentence topic is 'as far to the right of the sentence as is consistent with the core-periphery ordering constraint'.[17] The constraint concerned is that core constituents (loosely classified as those 'nominal constituents not preceded by a preposition')[18] normally precede

14. Cf., for example, J.J. Müller, *The Epistles of Paul to the Philippians and to Philemon* (NICNT; Grand Rapids: Eerdmans, 1955), p. 45 n. 1.

15. D.H. Crozier, 'A Study in the Discourse Grammar of Cishingini' (PhD thesis, University of Ibadan, 1984), pp. 119, 141.

16. J. Firbas, 'From Comparative Word-Order Studies', *BRNO Studies in English* 4 (1964), pp. 111-26.

17. Levinsohn, *Discourse Features*, p. 77.

18. Levinsohn, *Discourse Features*, p. 76.

peripheral ones (largely 'prepositional and adverbial phrases').[19]

Phil. 1.10-11 provides examples of unmarked constituent order. In each clause, the non-verbal constituents of the comment about the sentence topic 'you' (i.e., all the elements of the predicates) occur after the verb, with the core constituents (as defined above) preceding the peripheral ones. None of the elements is *marked* as particularly salient, relative to the others; rather, their relative salience is to be deduced by other means.[20]

(1.10a) εἰς τὸ δοκιμάζειν ὑμᾶς τὰ διαφέροντα,
(1.10b) ἵνα ἦτε εἰλικρινεῖς καὶ ἀπρόσκοποι εἰς [τὴν] ἡμέραν Χριστοῦ,
(1.11) πεπληρωμένοι καρπὸν δικαιοσύνης τὸν διὰ Ἰησοῦ Χριστοῦ, εἰς δόξαν καὶ ἔπαινον θεοῦ.

The points made above concerning salience apply not only to part B of Philippians, but also to C, A and 2.19-24. Elements are placed at the beginning of a clause or sentence to mark them as salient, for example, in 3.8 (Χριστόν), 4.11 (καθ' ὑστέρησιν) and 2.20b (γνησίως, following a relative pronoun). They follow a topicalized element in 3.20 (ἐν οὐρανοῖς), 4.11 (αὐτάρκης) and 2.21 (τὰ ἑαυτῶν).

Examples of unmarked constituent order, in which naturally salient elements follow the verb, include 3.6 (ἄμεμπτος), 4.17 (τὸν καρπὸν τὸν πλεονάζοντα εἰς λόγον ὑμῶν) and 2.23b (ἐξαυτῆς). Of

19. Levinsohn, *Discourse Features*, p. 76. The core-periphery ordering constraint may be broken when appropriate. In 1.7, for example, ὑμᾶς follows ἐν τῇ καρδίᾳ because the participial clause which follows takes up 'you' as its subject. See also 3.7 (discussed in §5); the notion of 'loss' is further developed in the next verse.

20. These means include whether the information has been given in the context or not and, in the case of known, particular referents, whether the constituent is arthrous or anarthrous; see §5. Thus, in 1.10b, the arthrous reading εἰ τὴν ἡμέραν Χριστοῦ would imply not only that the referent is known and particular, but also that it is supportive, rather than salient.

In 1.19b μοι is perhaps to be interpreted as a 'foil'—'a constituent that is presented for the purpose of being contrasted or added to in the following material' (Levinsohn, *Discourse Features*, p. 84), and which typically is marked as salient. In this case μοι would be the foil for ὑμῶν, later in the clause, which is forefronted within its phrase, as a switch is made from 'me' to the parts played by the readers themselves and by the Spirit of Jesus Christ (see H.A.W. Meyer, *Critical and Exegetical Handbook to the Epistles to the Philippians and Colossians* (trans. J.C. Moore and W.P. Dickson; Edinburgh: T. & T. Clark, 1875).

particular interest is 3.17c (καθὼς ἔχετε τύπον ἡμᾶς); it is normal for pronominal elements to precede nominal ones[21] but here ἡμᾶς, rather than τύπον, is the most salient element.

Phil. 3.3b provides an example of chiasmus involving salient elements: the first and third elements precede the verb (πνεύματι θεοῦ λατρεύοντες, ἐν σαρκὶ πεποιθότες), whereas the second follows it (καυχώμενοι ἐν Χριστῷ Ἰησοῦ).

Each part of Philippians, therefore, follows principle 2 in marking elements as salient by placing them at the beginning of the clause or sentence concerned, immediately following any topicalized element. Like principle 1, however, since principle 2 applies to Koine Greek in general, this conclusion is not surprising, and cannot be said to shed any positive light on the integrity of the book.

Principle 3

The third principle affecting constituent order is dependent on the operation of the previous two, and may be expressed as follows:

> (3) When a clause or sentence begins with a topicalized element followed by one marked for salience, a further non-verbal element may precede the verb, provided its referent is 'given' information[22] and is of a supportive nature.

This principle, which applies specifically to Philippians, rather than to Koine Greek as a whole,[23] may be illustrated by a comparison of 1.9b and 1.15b (for convenience, elements are separated by slash lines):

(1.9b) ἵνα ἡ ἀγάπη ὑμῶν/ἔτι μᾶλλον καὶ μᾶλλον/περισσεύῃ/ἐν ἐπιγνώσει καὶ πάσῃ αἰσθήσει,
(1.15a) τινὲς μὲν καὶ διὰ φθόνον καὶ ἔριν,
(1.15b) τινὲς δὲ/καὶ δι' εὐδοκίαν/τὸν Χριστὸν/κηρύσσουσιν.

In both cases, the clause begins with a topicalized element followed by one marked for salience. The remaining material in 1.9b (ἐν ἐπιγνώσει

21. Levinsohn, *Discourse Features*, pp. 75-76.

22. Dik points out (*Functional Grammar*, pp. 265-66) that what is 'given' and what is 'new' is 'mediated' through the author's 'estimate' as to the information available to the addressees at the time of speaking or writing.

23. A comparable principle for Galatians is proposed only for instances in which a clause or sentence begins with an element marked as salient; Levinsohn, *Discourse Features*, p. 83, following S.H. Levinsohn, 'Phrase Order and the Article in Galatians', *OPTaT* 3.2 (1989), pp. 56-58.

καὶ πάσῃ αἰσθήσει) is not 'given' information that has been mentioned or assumed in the immediate context; rather, it is a further salient, non-verbal constituent of the predicate, so follows the verb. In 1.15b, in contrast, τὸν Χριστόν is 'given' information, part of the supportive material which the two contrasting parts of the verse have in common (τὸν Χριστὸν κηρύσσουσιν reiterates τὸν λόγον [τοῦ θεοῦ] λαλεῖν from the previous verse; the arthrous nature of these elements also confirms their supportive role; see principle 5).

When an element marked for salience begins a clause or sentence because no element is topicalized, 'given' elements of the predicate usually are found after the verb. This is illustrated in 1.17; θλῖψιν is placed before the verb to mark it as salient, but the recurring phrase τοῖς δεσμοῖς μου follows the verb:

(1.17) ...(οἰόμενοι) θλῖψιν ἐγείρειν τοῖς δεσμοῖς μου.

Principle 3 suggests that the phrases in 1.4 and 1.7, which different commentators connect with either the following or the preceding material,[24] should both be interpreted as topicalized elements providing the point of departure for what follows. This is because, in both cases, a 'given' constituent of the predicate precedes the verb. Phil. 1.4 illustrates the point:

(1.3) εὐχαριστῶ τῷ θεῷ μου ἐπὶ πάσῃ τῇ μνείᾳ ὑμῶν,
(1.4) πάντοτε ἐν πάσῃ δεήσει μου ὑπὲρ πάντων ὑμῶν/μετὰ χαρᾶς/τὴν δέησιν/ποιούμενος.

Following the above interpretation, πάντοτε ἐν πάσῃ δεήσει μου ὑπὲρ πάντων ὑμῶν defines the point of departure for what follows, μετὰ χαρᾶς is placed before the verb to mark it as salient, while τὴν δέησιν is 'given', supportive information, relating back to ἐν πάσῃ δεήσει earlier in the verse.

Phil. 2.4 provides an example in which a 'given' element precedes the verb, even though the only other element preceding it is one marked as salient:

(2.4) μὴ τὰ ἑαυτῶν/ἕκαστος/σκοποῦντες...

However, the sentence is negative. In such sentences not only is it normal for a non-verbal element to be placed immediately after the

24. Cf. Greenlee, *Exegetical Summary*, pp. 15, 24 for a summary of the different positions.

negative to mark it as salient, but it is common also for other elements to come between the salient element and the verb.[25]

Principle 3 applies not only in part B of Philippians, but also in C, A, and 2.19-24. Thus, in 4.16, following the point of departure καὶ ἐν Θεσσαλονίκῃ and the salient element καὶ ἅπαξ καὶ δίς, the 'given' element εἰς τὴν χρείαν μοι also precedes the verb. In 3.15b, following the point of departure εἴ τι ἑτέρως φρονεῖτε and the salient element καὶ τοῦτο, two 'given' elements precede the verb (ὁ θεός and ὑμῖν). In 2.20, following the relative pronoun ὅστις (the equivalent of a point of departure) and the salient element γνησίως, the 'given' element τὰ περὶ ὑμῶν precedes the verb.[26]

Conversely, when the conditions for placing a 'given' element before the verb are not fulfilled, it follows the verb. See, for example, 3.9 (ἐν αὐτῷ) and 4.14 (μου τῇ θλίψει).

Each part of Philippians, therefore, follows principle 3 in placing 'given' elements before the verb, when the clause or sentence concerned already begins with a topicalized element plus one marked for salience. Since this principle does *not* apply to Koine Greek in general (see n. 23), this conclusion therefore has some bearing on discussions of the integrity of the book.

Principle 4

The fourth principle affecting constituent order is consistent with the naturally most salient position in a clause or sentence being as far to the right as possible, and may be expressed as follows:

> (4) When the verb is the most salient constituent of a clause, any non-verbal constituent of the predicate whose referent is 'given' information precedes it.

This principle, which again applies specifically to Philippians, rather than to Koine Greek as a whole,[27] thus places the verb at the end of its clause

25. Cf. Levinsohn, *Discourse Features*, pp. 86-87.

26. In 4.15, following initial elements that provide the point of departure for the clause introduced by ὅτι, the salient element οὐδεμία ἐκκλησία is interrupted by the 'given' element μοι. One reason for making such constituents 'discontinuous' is to show that their parts 'are of unequal importance' (Levinsohn, *Discourse Features*, p. 89). Applied to this instance, οὐδεμία would be more important (salient) than ἐκκλησία.

27. This principle does not hold for Galatians, for which 'articular elements of

when it is its most salient constituent. This is illustrated in 1.29; both the elements containing forms of αὐτός precede their verb because, in both instances, it is the verb which is most salient.[28]

(1.29a) ὅτι ὑμῖν ἐχαρίσθη τὸ ὑπὲρ Χριστοῦ,
(1.29b) οὐ μόνον τὸ εἰς αὐτὸν πιστεύειν,
(1.29c) ἀλλὰ καὶ τὸ ὑπὲρ αὐτοῦ πάσχειν.

Phil. 2.9a is an instance in which the clause begins with a topicalized element and ends with the verb. Again, αὐτόν precedes the verb because the latter is most salient:

(2.9a) διὸ καὶ ὁ θεὸς αὐτὸν ὑπερύψωσεν.

Phil. 3.8c illustrates the same principle in part C of Philippians; ἐζημιώθην is the most salient constituent of the clause, and τὰ πάντα (last referred to as πάντα in the previous clause) precedes it. No example or counter-example to principle 4 occurs in part A or in 2.19-24, however.

The fact that principle 4 does *not* apply to Koine Greek in general (see n. 27), but does apply to both part B and part C of Philippians, tends to confirm the position of those commentators who argue for the unity of these parts of the book.

Principle 5

This essay has claimed that elements are placed at or towards the beginning of a clause or sentence for two distinct reasons: (1) to topicalize them; (2) to mark them as salient. When both elements are present, there is little problem in distinguishing them: the topicalized one precedes the one marked as salient. When only one is present, however, the question arises as to how to distinguish points of departure from elements marked as salient.

One means of distinguishing the two in Koine Greek is often the presence versus absence of the article.[29] Dik notes a partial correlation

the predicate (and also pronominal elements) usually occur immediately after the verb if they present "known" information' (Levinsohn, 'Galatians', p. 51).

28. These elements occur in the same position as those marked as salient (principle 2). Consequently, the fact that the information concerned is 'given', rather than 'new', must again be taken into account in determining the relative salience of constituents.

29. For other means of distinguishing points of departure from elements placed

between the topicality/focality dimensions and the 'given'/'new' distinction.[30] Grammars of Greek, in turn, agree that one of the occasions for using the article is when the referent of the noun to which it is attributive is 'known, particular'.[31] In other words, the correlation between givenness and topicality, and the association of the article in Greek with givenness, together lead to the tendency for topicalized elements to be arthrous. Conversely, the tendency for elements marked as salient to be anarthrous follows from the correlation between newness and focality.

In fact, the absence of the article in connection with certain elements is more closely associated with salience than the above reasoning might suggest. This is because a noun whose referent is known and particular may still be anarthrous! The principle involved may be expressed as follows.[32]

(5) If a noun whose referent is known and particular is anarthrous, its referent is salient.

Phil. 1.15b and 1.18b provide a contrastive pair to illustrate this principle; both refer to Χριστός, and a semantically related verb is used in both.[33]

(1.15b) τινὲς δὲ καὶ δι' εὐδοκίαν τὸν Χριστὸν κηρύσσουσιν,
(1.18b) παντὶ τρόπῳ εἴτε προφάσει εἴτε ἀληθείᾳ, Χριστὸς καταγγέλλεται.

Phil. 1.15b has already been cited as a clause which begins with a topicalized element plus one marked for salience, followed by a supportive element that supplies 'given' information—hence the appropriateness of the arthrous nature of τὸν Χριστόν. Phil. 1.18b, in contrast, begins with a complex topicalized element (παντὶ τρόπῳ, εἴτε προφάσει εἴτε ἀληθείᾳ), and is followed by an element whose position before the verb marks it as salient—hence the appropriateness of the anarthrous nature of Χριστός.

It is perhaps necessary to point out that, for the presence versus absence of the article to be significant, the referent of the noun to which it is attributive *must* be known and particular. Thus, principle 5 cannot

before the verb for salience, see Levinsohn, *Discourse Features*, pp. 20-21.

30. Dik, *Functional Grammar*, p. 266.

31. BDF, §252.

32. Cf. Levinsohn, *Discourse Features*, p. 107.

33. This principle confirms that in 1.17 the arthrous variant τὸν Χριστόν is the preferred reading.

be applied when it is not clear that the referent is particular or known. For example, in 1.18b (cited above), the anarthrous nature of προφάσει, ἀληθείᾳ and even παντὶ τρόπῳ is due entirely to their referents being generic, rather than particular.[34]

Once it is clear from the context that the referent is both known and particular, however, the presence versus absence of the article is of significance, as far as salience is concerned. Thus, in 2.13, the anarthrous reading θεός is consistent with the NIV translation which brings God into focus: 'for it is God who works in you to will and to act according to his good purpose'. The arthrous reading, in contrast, would suggest a sentence with topic-comment articulation; in other words, 'is at work in you, both to will and to work for his good pleasure' (RSV) would be a comment about God!

(2.13) [ὁ] θεὸς γάρ ἐστιν ὁ ἐνεργῶν ἐν ὑμῖν καὶ τὸ θέλειν καὶ τὸ ἐνεργεῖν ὑπὲρ τῆς εὐδοκίας.

Similarly, principle 5 explains the arthrous nature of τῇ ταπεινοφροσύνῃ in 2.3b.[35]

(2.3a) μηδὲν κατ' ἐριθείαν μηδὲ κατὰ κενοδοξίαν,
(2.3b) ἀλλὰ τῇ ταπεινοφροσύνῃ ἀλλήλους ἡγούμενοι ὑπερέχοντας ἑαυτῶν.

τῇ ταπεινοφροσύνῃ is the first constituent of the clause, and is followed by an element, ἀλλήλους, which is marked as salient. Its arthrous nature is therefore consistent with it being the point of departure for what follows (suggested also by Kent's comment, 'In the exercise of humility, Paul instructed his readers to "consider others better than yourselves"').[36]

The presence versus absence of the article, in connection with known, particular referents, is relevant to the salience of the element concerned, not only when it precedes the verb, but also when it follows it. As noted earlier, in sentences with unmarked constituent order, non-verbal elements of the predicate occur after the verb, with the core-periphery constraint and other factors determining their relative order. In such

34. Nor, of course, can principle 5 apply to constructions in which the use of the article is obligatory, such as τὰ κατ' ἐμέ (1.12).

35. Cf. Greenlee, *Exegetical Summary*, p. 100 for a summary of commentators' suggestions as to why the phrase is arthrous.

36. H.A. Kent, 'Philippians', in F.E. Gaebelein (ed.), *The Expositor's Bible Commentary* (Grand Rapids: Zondervan, 1978), XI, p. 122.

sentences constituents are typically anarthrous if salient, and arthrous if of a supportive nature.

For example, the anarthrous nature of the final constituent of 1.8 (ἐν σπλάγχνοις Χριστοῦ Ἰησοῦ) is consistent with that element being salient. In contrast, as noted earlier, because the purpose of the verse is not to make a comment about God but to support the assertions made in the previous verse(s), the reference to God is part of the supportive material and, appropriately, is arthrous:

(1.8) μάρτυς γάρ μου [ἐστιν] ὁ θεός, ὡς ἐπιποθῶ πάντας ὑμᾶς ἐν σπλάγχνοις Χριστοῦ Ἰησοῦ.

In 1.27 the fact that the elements concerning oneness of spirit and soul are anarthrous, whereas τῇ πίστει τοῦ εὐαγγελίου is arthrous, indicates that the oneness is salient and 'the faith of the Gospel' is supportive.[37]

(1.27) ...ἀκούω τὰ περὶ ὑμῶν, ὅτι στήκετε ἐν ἑνὶ πνεύματι, μιᾷ ψυχῇ συναθλοῦντες τῇ πίστει τοῦ εὐαγγελίου.

Principle 5 applies without reservation to part C of Philippians. For example, the references to Christ as the salient element of a clause or sentence, which were cited earlier in the paper (3.3b, 8 [Χριστόν]), are both anarthrous. In 3.7, in contrast, the fact that the reference to Christ is arthrous, together with the placement of ζημίαν last in the sentence (see n. 19), is consistent with 'loss' being salient in this verse and the reference to Christ being of a supportive nature.

In 2.19-24 the anarthrous reference to Christ Jesus (v. 21) is also consistent with principle 5. Unfortunately, though, no further evidence for the validity or otherwise of the principle can be adduced from this short passage.

In part A of Philippians, the examples cited earlier of 'given' elements have been arthrous (4.14, 16). However, there appear to be no unambiguous references to known and particular referents which are anarthrous; although both ἐν κυρίῳ (4.10) and ἐν Χριστῷ Ἰησοῦ (4.19) are anarthrous, they are normally so, and may well be set expressions. Furthermore, all references to God are arthrous, including those that would appear to be salient (e.g. 4.18). Equally noteworthy is the fact that every phrase of 4.20 is arthrous (contrast Rom. 16.27, the first

37. Phil. 1.27, as punctuated here, provides another example of chiasmus involving salient elements; see the discussion of 3.3b in §2.

phrase of which is anarthrous). It is therefore quite possible that principle 5 does not apply to 4.10-20.[38]

In conclusion, this essay has sought to show that specific functional principles underlie the order of constituents in Philippians. Recognition of them, together with the significance of arthrous versus anarthrous references to known, particular entities, enables distinctions to be made between: (1) elements which begin sentences to provide a new point of departure for what follows versus those that are genuinely 'emphatic' or 'marked as salient'; (2) constituents in the rest of the sentence that also are salient versus those that are supportive. This, in turn, assists in choosing between conflicting interpretations of individual clauses and sentences.

The fact that the principles which do not apply to Koine Greek in general apply to both part B (including 2.19-24) and part C tends to confirm Garland's conclusion 'that 1.27–4.3 is a literary unit'.[39] In turn, the apparent failure of principle 5 (though not principle 3!) to apply to 4.10-20 sets it apart from the rest of the book and requires an explanation, whether in terms of a separate letter or in terms of Paul, rather than his amanuensis, being the author.

38. Phil. 4.21-23 provides no evidence to show whether principle 5 applies to the final verses of the book or not.

39. Garland, 'Composition and Unity of Philippians', p. 172.

IDENTIFYING THEME IN THE NEW TESTAMENT: INSIGHTS FROM DISCOURSE ANALYSIS

Jeffrey T. Reed

Introduction

Although it is fair to say that discourse analysis[1] is here to stay in the linguistic world, its fate in New Testament biblical scholarship is less certain. It faces a two-fold difficulty—the need to demonstrate its relevance for biblical studies without being too novel and without being too familiar. This study attempts to avoid such difficulty by introducing a concept from discourse analysis that is relatively new to the field of biblical scholarship but by treating it in terms of the more mundane concepts of theme and emphasis. Furthermore, it treats the concept of prominence in terms of New Testament discourse (and Hellenistic Greek discourse), applying the theory to an actual text and leaving it open to the critical review of others.

The Theory of Prominence in Discourse Analysis

One way to build thematic structure in discourse is by creating *prominence* (also known as emphasis, grounding, relevance, salience), i.e. by drawing the listener/reader's attention to topics and motifs which are important to the speaker/author and by supporting those topics with other less significant material. This is not entirely new to New Testament

1. At its broadest level, 'discourse analysis' (or textlinguistics) refers to the study of both the spoken and the written communication of humans; cf. M. Stubbs, *Discourse Analysis: The Sociolinguistic Analysis of Natural Language* (Language in Society, 4; Oxford: Basil Blackwell, 1983), pp. 1, 9-10. More specifically, studies in discourse analysis emphasize (a) the dynamic between intended meanings of speakers and variant responses of hearers, (b) the grammar of language beyond the level of the sentence, (c) the social and pragmatic functions of language, and (d) the ways in which language is used to create cohesiveness in discourse.

studies. Scholars frequently claim that certain language in the New Testament is 'emphatic'. By this they generally mean some linguistic element (either a word or clause) is being emphasized by the author. This is often discussed in terms of word order. For example, if a prepositional phrase is placed at the front of a clause (a supposedly marked word order), the author is said to be trying to emphasize that item. Although this type of interpretation is not inherently flawed, there are problems with it. First, the term 'emphasis' is rarely defined. Secondly, it is not treated in a semantic network, leaving us to wonder what a non-emphatic sentence is. Lastly, one author's study of word order in the book of Acts reveals that emphasis plays only an infrequent role in the understanding of the text. When the subject of a clause precedes its verb (a supposedly untypical word order) 'emphasis accounts for little more than 10% of the examples'.[2] How does one, therefore, explain other variant word order patterns?

The study of prominence by discourse analysts provides a more linguistic, methodologically rigorous approach to questions of theme and emphasis. Prominence is defined here as those *semantic and grammatical elements of discourse that serve to set aside certain subjects, ideas or motifs of the author as more or less semantically and pragmatically significant than others.*[3] Without prominence discourse would be dull, flat and, to a certain degree, incoherent. As Robert Longacre humorously comments,

2. S.H. Levinsohn, *Textual Connections in Acts* (Atlanta: Scholars Press, 1987), p. xv.

3. Other approaches to the concept of prominence have been carried out under the auspices of theories such as macrostructure or proposition-based analysis (T. van Dijk, *Macrostructures: An Interdisciplinary Study of Global Structures in Discourse, Interaction, and Cognition* [Hillsdale, NJ: Lawrence Erlbaum, 1980]), story-grammars (F.R. Yekovich and P.W. Thorndyke, 'An Evaluation of Alternative Functional Models of Narrative Schemata', *Journal of Verbal Learning and Verbal Behavior* 20 [1981], pp. 454-69), text networks (R. de Beaugrande, *Text, Discourse and Process* [London: Longman, 1980]), and staging (J.E. Grimes, *The Thread of Discourse* [The Hague: Mouton, 1975]). Especially relevant for this study is T. Givón's 'topicality hierarchy' ('Topic, Pronoun, and Grammatical Agreement', in C.N. Li [ed.], *Subject and Topic* [New York: Academic Press, 1976], pp. 149-88).

> If all parts of a discourse are equally prominent, total unintelligibility results. The result is like being presented with a piece of black paper and being told, 'This is a picture of black camels crossing black sands at midnight.'[4]

Levels of Prominence

Rather than speak in terms of emphatic and non-emphatic features of texts (as most New Testament grammarians do), most discourse analysts suggest at least three, sometimes more, levels of prominence. With regards to New Testament discourse I propose three levels: background, theme and focus.[5]

BACKGROUND refers to those linguistic elements in the discourse which, in the case of narrative, serve to carry the story forward supporting the main plot with secondary participants and events (e.g. scenery) and, in the case of non-narrative, serve to support the main argument providing ancillary comments, explanations, conclusions and summaries. Background elements can often be eliminated without drastically obscuring the main message. This does not mean that background material is unimportant, but that it is less important to the message than other discourse material.

THEME, on the other hand, is information central to the author's message.[6] In narrative, thematic elements consist of major participants and events often occurring along some chronological line [+sequential]. In non-narrative [–sequential], the chronological element is usually absent, as in an argument (e.g. lawyer's cross-examination), an exhortation (e.g. eulogy) or an explanation (e.g. recipe). Thematic elements are

4. R.E. Longacre, 'Sentence Structure as a Statement Calculus', *Lang* 46 (1970), p. 10; cf. *idem*, 'Discourse Peak as Zone of Turbulence', in J.R. Wirth (ed.), *Beyond the Sentence: Discourse and Sentential Form* (Ann Arbor: Karoma, 1985), p. 83.

5. K. Callow (*Discourse Considerations in Translating the Word of God* [Grand Rapids: Zondervan, 1974], pp. 63-65) adds emphasis, which I believe is similar enough to focus to be combined into one category.

6. K. Callow ('Patterns of Thematic Development in 1 Corinthians 5:1-13', in D.A. Black *et al.* [eds.], *Linguistics and New Testament Interpretation: Essays on Discourse Analysis* [Nashville: Broadman, 1992], p. 195) identifies theme with the purpose of the author. She maintains that 'material at the factual end of the purposive chain is considered to be less prominent than material at the activity end; there is a graded increase in prominence as we move away from fact towards volition' (p. 197). Consequently, certain grammatical forms (e.g. imperative mood) are more prominent because of their pragmatic effect.

unique types of prominence in that after first appearing in the discourse, they are expected to appear again. For example, if an author states the theme and purpose of an essay by means of an introductory sentence, the reader expects the rest of the discourse to be about that theme. Consequently, subsequent appearances of thematic elements are often *reduced* to unmarked forms such as pronouns.

M.A.K. Halliday's discussion of THEMATIZATION and INFORMATION STRUCTURE—influenced partly by the Prague School linguists—has had notable influence on modern linguistics.[7] Its significance for the concept of prominence (especially theme) is worth mentioning here.[8] According to Halliday, *theme* is that element which states what is being talked about in the clause. The *rheme* is that element which contributes what is being said about the theme. The theme comes first in a clause—it sets the stage for what follows. The remainder of the clause is the rheme. In English the unmarked thematization is subject-predicate in a declarative clause, the predicator in a polar question, and the 'wh'-word in a 'wh'-question. Marked thematization (i.e. sentences which do not follow this pattern)[9] indicates focal material. Choosing between theme and rheme concerns informational *thematization*. Choosing between given and new information is another means of *information structuring*. *New* information is that which 'the speaker presents...as not being

7. M.A.K. Halliday, 'Notes on Transitivity and Theme in English', *Journal of Linguistics* 3 (1967), pp. 37-81, pp. 199-244; 4 (1968), pp. 179-215. In Prague School terms, the theme is that element in a clause which contributes least to the furthering of the communicative process; the rheme, conversely, contributes the most.

8. Thematization has been treated by linguists in primarily three ways: (a) as surface structure reorderings for the sake of style/rhetoric (N. Chomsky, *Aspects of the Theory of Syntax* [Cambridge, MA: MIT Press, 1965]; J. Katz, *Semantic Theory* [New York: Harper & Row, 1972]); (b) as reorderings for the sake of pragmatic effect (W.L. Chafe, 'Givenness, Contrastiveness, Definiteness, Subjects, Topics and Point of View', in Li [ed.], *Subject and Topic*, pp. 25-55.; R. Quirk *et al.*, *A Grammar of Contemporary English* [London: Longman, 1972]); and (c) as reorderings that affect the semantics of the sentence (J. Firbas, 'On Defining the Theme in Functional Sentence Analysis', *Travaux Linguistiques de Prague* 1 [1964], pp. 267-80; M.A.K. Halliday, 'Notes on Transitivity', pp. 199-244; *idem*, *Introduction to Functional Grammar* [London: Edward Arnold, 1985]); for a brief survey and critique of these, see D. Kies, 'Marked Themes with and without Pronominal Reinforcement: Their Meaning and Distribution in Discourse', in E.H. Steiner and R. Veltman (eds.), *Pragmatics, Discourse and Text* (London: Pinter, 1988), pp. 49-56.

9. E.g. contrast and movement (P. Werth, *Focus, Coherence and Emphasis* [London: Croom Helm, 1984]).

recoverable from the preceding discourse'.[10] *Given* information is that which is presented as recoverable from the previous discourse.[11] Unmarked information, according to Halliday, occurs when the tonic (accent) is on the last syllable. When information is marked, the tonic falls on any element except for the final syllable. That upon which it falls represents new information; everything else is given. The following examples from Halliday illustrate the principle.[12]

> // ^I'm /looking for the /caretaker who /looks after / this *block*//
> (unmarked)
> // *John* painted the shed yesterday// ('John' is new information)
> // John *painted* the shed yesterday// ('painted' is new information)

Since Halliday's discussion of given–new information treats spoken language, it is less helpful than theme–rheme for a discourse analysis of New Testament texts, where phonological units cannot be identified. Perhaps other grammatical devices signal given–new information in New Testament discourse; however, as of yet no convincing research has been proposed which applies to large selections of Koine Greek discourse.[13] Most importantly, one must recognize that theme–rheme and

10. Halliday, 'Notes on Transitivity', p. 204.

11. The concepts of given and new are described by functional sentence linguists in terms of communicative dynamism (CD). Given elements contribute least to the 'development of communication' (CD); new elements contribute most (M.P. Williams, 'Functional Sentence Perspective in the Context of Systemic Functional Grammar', in Steiner and Veltman (eds.), *Pragmatics, Discourse and Text*, pp. 77-78). Some main differences between a functional sentence perspective and systemic functional approaches are: (a) the former divides the rheme into transition (verb) and rheme (complement, adjunct) and (b) the former distinguishes between diathemes (non-proper themes such as the temporal clause 'When they arrived at the temple...') and proper themes.

12. Halliday, 'Notes on Transitivity', p. 207.

13. S.H. Levinsohn ('Phrase Order and the Article in Galatians: A Functional Sentence Perspective Approach', *OPTaT* 3 [1989], pp. 44-64) is perhaps the most noteworthy attempt. Although I am in general agreement with Levinsohn's approach his study does not account for (a) subjects that are not known, (b) the variant position of the verb with respect to subject and objects, (c) the role of the verb (it likely plays some role relative to the prominence of the larger discourse), (d) complements that split the verb or subject, (e) modifiers of substantives that are major participants (e.g. genitives), (f) new (non-given) information is frequently introduced as sentence-initial and, (g) after new information is introduced it is often grammaticalized in verbal inflections leaving given (non-new) information at the front of the sentence.

given–new represent different types of informational choices. It is important to emphasize that theme and given, rheme and new, do not always correspond (see the second example above). To conflate the two ways of information structuring is to err in the same way the Prague School linguists did.[14]

Whereas thematic prominence is not necessarily unexpected at the clausal level (i.e. it is often unmarked), FOCUS refers to those linguistic elements that stand out somewhat unexpectedly. Such elements may not carry much semantic weight (e.g. ἰδού); instead, they serve a more pragmatic function such as drawing the listener/reader back into the communicative process. After an extended discussion of a thematic element, which usually has been reduced to pronominal forms or zero-anaphora, the speaker/author may need to ensure the reader's interpretation by employing a focal element. In sum, when a thematic element is first introduced, it is in focus. Once it has been introduced, the thematic element is in the foreground of the reader's mind and thus not in focus. At times it is necessary for an author to reintroduce a thematic element, that is focus on it, to ensure that it is at the foreground of the reader's mind. In addition, focal elements often express feelings or arouse emotions. K. Callow uses the analogy of a stage. Focal prominence is likened to a spotlight highlighting particular key characters in a stage play. The reader cannot help but be drawn to focal elements. It is as if the speaker/author is slapping the listener/reader across the face and saying, 'Pay attention. This is important.'

Identifying Prominence in Discourse

The first factor to consider when analysing prominence is *what type (or genre) of discourse is under study*. One must differentiate, for example, between prominence in narrative and in non-narrative (e.g. exposition), despite their many similarities. What is true of prominence in narrative may not be true of prominence in non-narrative. Both types of discourse will have prominent persons (participants) and events, but the similarities sometimes end there. Whereas narrative develops along a chronological line, exposition develops along a theme line as in argumentative, hortatory or explanatory discourse.

Another factor to consider when analysing prominence is *the domain or extent to which a linguistic element has prominence in the discourse*.

14. For a critique of given-new theory, see Kies, 'Marked Themes', pp. 53-54.

Most linguistic elements move along a cline of prominence as they appear throughout the discourse. What was thematic in the previous paragraph may only be background in the next. For this reason, one must speak of the DOMAIN OF PROMINENCE, that is the extent to which a linguistic element maintains its degree of prominence. The domain of prominence may or may not extend throughout the whole discourse, but it will certainly extend somewhere. Determining the domain of an element's prominence is vital if one is to understand its relative importance for the discourse. The domain of prominence in New Testament discourse may involve the phrase (e.g. headword of a prepositional phrase), clause (e.g. rheme), paragraph (e.g. verbal aspect) or the entire discourse (e.g. epistolary formulas). Thus it is possible to speak of the *background* of phrases, clauses, paragraphs and discourses, the *theme* of phrases, clauses, paragraphs and discourses, and the *focus* of phrases, clauses, paragraphs and discourses. Koine Greek possesses certain grammatical features that are particular to one level and not to another, and some which are found at all levels.

Background elements have no limits as to their domain, since they coincide with a theme (which has no limit to its domain). Wherever a thematic unit is located (whether at the discourse, paragraph or clause level), one will likely find an associated background. Thus, backgrounds may be relegated to the phrase, clause, paragraph or discourse. Backgrounds may even be embedded within other backgrounds. For example, in Matthew 13 the author's narrative moves from one background to another (both in the same locale). In the first scene (Mt. 13.1-35) Jesus is speaking in parables while sitting in a boat along the shore of a lake surrounded by a crowd of people. In the second scene (Mt. 13.36-52) he has entered a house near the lake and is speaking in parables to his disciples. In each scene Jesus tells three parables, each with its own unique background, theme and focus. Each background must be distinguished as to its domain of prominence.

Thematic prominence occurs at all levels of discourse: phrase, clause, paragraph/section (and paragraphs within paragraphs) and discourse. On the one hand, an entire discourse may have a single theme that runs throughout (i.e. global theme). Within this theme other self-contained thematic units may have their own prominence. The theme of one domain should not be confused with that of another. Boundary markers (*Grenzsignale*) often signal the beginning and end of a thematic unit.

They mark topic-shifts.[15] An entire discourse, on the other hand, may not have just one theme. This is often true of New Testament discourses, especially those written in the epistolary genre.[16] Authors of ancient letters often develop several topics of discussion, not being confined to one, as Cicero notes: 'I have begun to write to you something or other without any definite subject, so that I may have a sort of talk with you'.[17] Distinguishing domains of prominence is necessary to account for the complexity of prominence in discourse. At the level of clause, what is thematic in the discourse is often background in the clause, and, consequently, what is thematic in the clause (the rheme) is background in the discourse. Furthermore, an item may be focal in the clause but thematic in the discourse.[18]

Focal prominence is typically relegated to the clause and occasionally to the paragraph. A particular participant may be focally prominent within a paragraph and then fall out of prominence in the next. The domain of focal elements is typically less than that of theme, since an element with a larger domain tends to become thematic, that is it becomes expected in the discourse. A focally prominent element with a larger domain will, of course, be more significant than one with a smaller domain. These essentially correspond to what Robert E. Longacre refers to as 'discourse peaks'.[19] They often occur at the end of a paragraph or discourse, bringing the author's immediate theme to its peak.

The final factor for identifying background, theme and focus is *knowing how the linguistic code of a given discourse is used to produce prominence*. Here one is concerned with the SIGNALLING DEVICES of prominence used in the language. Recent research suggests three basic forms of prominence: phonetic (obviously difficult for New Testament

15. On the term 'topic-shift', see especially D.W. Maynard, 'Placement of Topic Changes in Conversation', *Semiotica* 30 (1980), pp. 263-90, and R.C. Schank, 'Rules and Topics in Conversation', *Cognitive Science* 1 (1977), pp. 421-42.

16. Cf. D. Hellholm, *Das Visionenbuch des Hermas als Apokalypse: Formgeschichtliche und texttheoretische Studien zu einer literarischen Gattung*. I. *Methodologische Vorüberlegungen und makrostrukturelle Textanalyse* (ConBNT, 13; Lund: Gleerup, 1980), p. 45, who speaks of 'eine Hierarchie von Haupt- und Nebenstrategien'.

17. Cicero, *Epistulae ad Atticum* 9.10.1.

18. This frequently happens when an earlier topic is reintroduced into the discussion by means of a marked surface structure (e.g. vocative).

19. See esp. Longacre, 'Discourse Peak', pp. 81-98.

studies), syntactic and semantic.[20] Knowledge of these signalling devices is, of course, a preliminary requirement for analysing prominence and requires much more research with respect to New Testament Greek. To make matters worse, some signalling devices are dependent upon the genre of the discourse. An ancient letter may have different signalling devices than a biography. Furthermore, prominence is rarely signalled by one grammatical device, but more commonly is the result of a combination of grammatical categories. The analyst should not depend on the presence of one grammatical category to determine prominence, but an analysis of all signalling devices. By relying on several categories one will not be confused by apparent exceptions to the rule. For example, it appears that when the semantic function of verbal aspect conflicts with a verb's level of prominence, the semantic function prevails. In this case, other categories may combine to indicate prominence. The following list suggests some of the signalling devices used in New Testament discourse. As more Greek discourse is analysed, more devices will certainly be determined.

Semantic Fields. A semantic analysis of the discourse is an important part of determining prominence. Certain words are more prominent than others. For example, words of thinking, feeling, perceiving (mental processess) often signal upcoming, thematically prominent material (e.g. 'I beseech you...'). In addition, repeated use of words in the same semantic field also contribute to the prominence of discourse.

Research in both linguistics and psychology (originating from the Gestalt psychologists of the early twentieth century) suggests that certain semantic fields tend to appear in background and thematic material. These are typically discussed in terms of figure (theme) and ground (background), or 'more salient' and 'less salient' items.[21] Such theories start with the assumption that people are more interested in some things than others, and that they process information based on those interests. Wallace sets forth the major components of this theory. (1) People are more interested in other human beings (or at least in animate entities); (2) people tend to place themselves at the centre of attention; (3) individuated—especially concrete, definite, singular, countable—

20. Werth, *Focus*, p. 98.

21. See esp. S. Wallace, 'Figure and Ground: The Interrelationships of Linguistic Categories', in P.J. Hopper (ed.), *Tense-Aspect: Between Semantics and Pragmatics* (Amsterdam: Benjamins, 1982), pp. 211-18.

entities are more apt to attract interest than their opposites; (4) the real, the certain, the positive, the immediate, the bounded, the completed and the dynamic are more effective in moving a discourse forward, to constitute the foregrounded portion of a text, than their respective contrasting properties, which form the supportive background. The following table of semantic categories is useful for the analysis of prominence in New Testament discourse.[22] 'More salient' items are thematic; 'less salient' are background.

MORE SALIENT	LESS SALIENT
human	nonhuman
animate	inanimate
concrete	abstract
thing-like, solid, discrete	unformed, diffuse, shapeless, unbroken
well-defined, tightly organized	less definite, unstructured, loosely organized
contoured, surrounded, bounded, enclosed	boundless
localized	unlocalized
with distinguishable parts	without distinguishable parts
near	far
above, in front	below, behind
greater contrast	lesser contrast
stable	unstable
symmetric	irregular

Verbal Aspect. One function of verbal aspect is to indicate the prominence of clauses in relationship to the larger paragraph or discourse.[23] Background prominence is often signalled by clauses using the aorist tense (perfective aspect). Thematic prominence may be signalled by the present and imperfect tenses (imperfective aspect), as well as sometimes the future tense.[24] The three forms are probably needed to differentiate

22. Adapted from Wallace, 'Figure and Ground', pp. 212, 214.

23. See P. Hopper, 'Aspect between Discourse and Grammar: An Introductory Essay for the Volume', in *Tense-Aspect*, p. 5, who highlights the discourse function of aspect: 'The fundamental notion of aspect is not a local-semantic one but is discourse-pragmatic'.

24. Cf. S.E. Porter, *Idioms of the Greek New Testament* (Sheffield: JSOT Press, 1992), p. 23, who speaks in terms of background, foreground and frontground. Koine Greek is notably unique with respect to studies of universal grammar,

time in discourse, an important component of theme. However, each form has the same function with respect to prominence. Focal prominence is signalled by the perfect and pluperfect tenses (stative aspect). The two are used for temporal distinctions, but both serve the same function with respect to prominence. (The verb εἰμί does not indicate prominence, since it lacks a full aspectual system.) Despite its role as a marker of prominence, verbal aspect as a grammatical category primarily serves the function of indicating the author's viewpoint on the nature of a verbal event. The semantics of the aspectual categories lend themselves to discourse prominence. The perfective aspect lends itself to general descriptions of an event, whereas the imperfective aspect suggests that the author is focusing on the particulars of an event. The stative aspect is even more accented, since the attention is laid upon an event that has resulted from other circumstances (i.e. a stative event stands at the centre of activity). However, in the event that the aspectual function conflicts with its value of prominence, verbal aspect takes precedence. This may explain some apparent exceptions.

Verbal Voice. The active voice is predominant in the New Testament, with the middle voice being, by a small margin, the least used of the three voices in the Greek New Testament: active (approximately 20,697), middle (3500), passive (3930). The passive voice is often used to move an agent into the background of the discourse (but often the theme of the clause because it is the rheme), leaving some other

since the imperfective aspect plays a thematic role and the perfective aspect plays a background role (cf. Wallace, 'Figure and Ground', pp. 208-209). Note, however, that S.H. Levinsohn (*Discourse Features of New Testament Greek: A Coursebook* [Dallas: Summer Institute of Linguistics, 1992], pp. 164-66) argues for the aorist (imperfective) as the thematic marker and the imperfect tense-form (imperfective aspect) as the background marker. His analysis, most notably, does not take into account the other tense-forms and is apparently based on insights from universal grammarians rather than analysis of New Testament texts. He makes no mention of any of Porter's work on verbal aspect. W. Diver ('The System of Relevance of the Homeric Verb', *Acta Linguistica Hafniensia* 12 [1969], pp. 60-61) speaks of the central (aorist tense and active voice) and peripheral (imperfect tense and middle voice) relevance (= prominence) of the Homeric verb. He unfortunately treats relevance in terms of binary opposition (based on the root) and thus does not treat all of the tense forms. In addition, it is unclear in his scheme if voice alone (viz. active and middle) or tense alone (aorist or imperfect) signals relevance or if the two must be used together.

grammatical subject to take its place. Some research suggests that the active voice in English texts prefers animate objects (which tend to have thematic prominence) and passive clauses prefer inanimate ones.[25] In addition, passives have modal auxiliaries (e.g. 'can', 'could', 'would') more often than actives. Initial research in Greek also suggests that passives occur when the logical object (grammatical subject) is anaphoric and the logical subject (grammatical agent) is not (esp. if it is a weak impersonal). The passive enables the surface structure to follow the anaphoric/non-anaphoric pattern (see below on word order). The middle voice, a continuing enigma for Greek grammarians, is typically used with thematic material and often focally thematic items. It enables the author to grammaticalize actor involvement in the subject position as well as highlight the particular involvement of the actor in the action.

Verbal Mood. Modality plays a role in distinguishing between background and thematic prominence. Under normal circumstances one would expect an audience to be more interested in what is asserted as real or factual (indicative mood). What someone asserts as actually happening is likely to be the centre of attention in discourse as opposed to what is merely projected or purported to happen (i.e. what might, may, could occur). Accordingly, the indicative mood tends to grammaticalize thematic material. The subjunctive and the optative, because their function is essentially that of 'non-assertion' or 'projection', are used with background material.[26] This partly explains their frequent use in subordinate clauses (e.g. purpose clauses) which typically play a rhetorically supportive role. The imperative mood, however, regularly plays a thematic role, probably because of its forceful pragmatic function.

Noun–Verb Relations. The use of nouns and verbs in combination is an important signal of prominence. First and second person combinations typically signal thematic prominence; third person signals background prominence. Singular verbs generally signal thematic prominence; plural verbs (if they are of a generic type) signal background prominence. These are all with respect to the domain of the paragraph or discourse; they are regularly thematic at the level of clause. The nominative case generally signals a thematic element (either of the clause, paragraph or

25. J. Svartvik, *On Voice in the English Verb* (The Hague: Mouton, 1966), pp. 49-50.

26. Cf. Grimes, *The Thread of Discourse*, p. 65.

discourse). The vocative case is also a good signal of thematic material at the level of discourse and focal material at the level of clause.[27] A study of Philippians suggests that the basic word order is V (Verb) and VO (verb – object): this is the unmarked grammatical construction. If a subject is added to this basic word order, the clause has marked word order; therefore, the subject is probably thematic or focal either with respect to the clause or the larger discourse. Once a thematic participant has been introduced by the nominative case, continued reference to it will be made by use of pronouns or verbal suffixes. It is usually only reintroduced in full form (e.g. in the nominative case) for the sake of focus or to prevent ambiguity.

Word Order. Word order (especially when subjects and verbs are both grammaticalized) is another signalling device of prominence.[28] Various

27. See C. Poynton, 'Forms and Functions: Names as Vocatives', *Nottingham Linguistic Circular* 13 (1984), pp. 1-34.

28. Levinsohn ('Phrase Order', p. 51) claims that in Galatians arthrous predicates (or pronominal elements) 'occur immediately after the verb if they present "known" [thematic] information' and that anarthrous predicates ('unknown' or 'new' information) typically occur between the subject (if present) and the verb. This implies that the use of the article (arthrous = known; anarthrous = new) and word order indicate prominence. (Levinsohn allows for explainable exceptions, viz. if a known element is anarthrous then it is more prominent [salient] or if an unknown element is arthrous it is being downplayed. These are difficult to substantiate or even debate since it is a quite subjective decision to make about clausal saliency.) In contrast, an analysis of two intermediate participants (God and Christ) in Philippians suggests that the article is not useful for determining relative prominence in non-narrative discourse. Both θεός and κύριος 'Ιησοῦς Χριστός first appear without the article (as the rule states). The second occurrence of θεός is articular (as projected), but the second occurrence of Χριστὸς 'Ιησοῦς is not. The rest of the occurrences (like the second occurrence of Χριστός) do not appear to follow the supposed rule, even when allowing for the exceptions. For example, of the twenty-three occurrences of all forms of θεός, thirteen are arthrous and ten are anarthrous. All but one subject (out of eight) has the article (2.13 may be a case where the articular participle is the actual subject), leaving six instances of a non-subject with the article and nine instances of a non-subject without the article. Clearly this does not follow the rule, even considering Levinsohn's exceptions. For example, in 4.20 the phrase τῷ θεῷ is at the beginning of the doxology, being both focal, thematic and known (cf. 4.19), and yet at the same time arthrous. Of course, one could say that this is because it is sentence-initial; but that does not explain the marked use of the article. Aside from the use of the article with subjects, it is difficult to see how Levinsohn's theory satisfactorily handles the majority of instances.

word order constructions are motivated by informational requirements of the discourse and they should not be understood simply as stylistic variants.[29] Since word order in Greek is somewhat flexible, the use of prominence may help to explain apparently random variations of word order, which many have dismissed as an insignificant feature of an inflected language.[30] Here, for example, one asks: Why does one sentence have SVO word order and another VSO word order?[31] The answer is apparently related to the relative prominence of the linguistic components in clauses, that is, their informational structure. Most New Testament clauses have V, VO (verb – object), OV word order. This is the unmarked pattern, that is, it does not indicate prominence because the subject is not grammaticalized (probably because it is already known). When a subject is grammaticalized, the unmarked word order is SO, with the verb falling before or after the object (SVO, SOV, SO).[32] Alterations to this pattern (OSV, OVS, VOS, OS) will be marked and thus prominent in some way.[33] A general rule to follow is that the more to the right an item occurs in the clause, the more prominent it is in the clause.[34] The more to the left an item occurs in the clause, the more prominent it is in the paragraph (or discourse). The following chart summarizes the effect of word order on prominence at the level of clause and discourse. (Note: given/anaphoric and new/non-anaphoric

29. Werth, *Focus*, p. 12.

30. See similar criticisms by R. Radney, 'Some Factors that Influence Fronting in Koine Greek' (MA Thesis, University of Texas at Arlington, 1982).

31. The letter 'O' signifies various types of sentence completives, including dative and genitive direct objects, rank-shifted infinitival and participial clauses, and indirect objects.

32. J.A. Hawkins ('Implicational Universals as Predicators of Word Order Change', *Lang* 45 [1969], p. 630) argues that Classical Greek has a basic SOV clause structure. J.H. Greenberg (*Some Universals of Grammar with Particular Reference to the Order of Meaningful Elements* [Cambridge, MA: MIT Press, 1963], p. 107) maintains that Modern Greek has SVO word order.

33. The major difference is that the object (complement) precedes the subject. Levinsohn (*Discourse Features*, pp. 22-23) argues that verbs occur first in sentences where there is continuity with the previous discourse. However, in Phil. 1.3, 12; 2.19; 4.21—examples of epistolary forms that clearly signal discontinuity—the verbs occur sentence-initial.

34. Cf. I. Larsen, 'Word Order and Relative Prominence in New Testament Greek', *Notes on Translation* 5 (1991), pp. 29-34.

information tends to be static, i.e. it recurrently falls in the same slots of the sentence.)

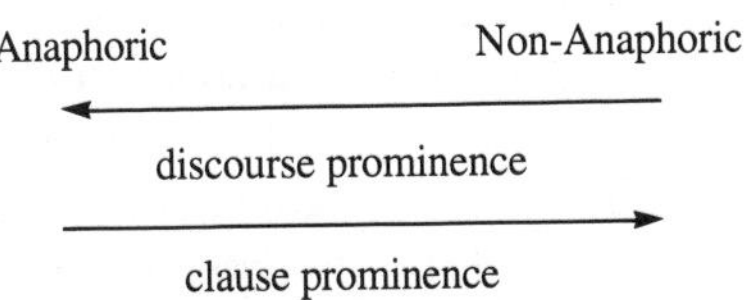

Rather than the terms 'given' and 'new' I prefer the terms 'anaphoric' and 'non-anaphoric'. Semantic material is distributed in the sentence so as to respect the order of anaphoric and non-anaphoric,[35] although syntactic elements may be moved for the sake of focus (e.g. contrast).

Boundary Markers. An important part of any language's code concerns words that have minimal semantic content, but serve to connect the various thematic units of a discourse together. These are termed here 'boundary markers' and generally consist of particles and conjunctions, but may include larger units. They connect paragraphs with paragraphs, and clauses with clauses. For example, clauses lacking connecting particles (asyndeton) are unmarked, that is they neither mark prominence nor do they not mark prominence. καί, used as a clausal connector, indicates co-ordinated sameness[36] not prominence; as an adverb, it often indicates focal prominence.[37] Levinsohn argues that in the book of Acts δέ is used to signal development units (DU) that reflect the author's purpose and to introduce new units into the discourse. As Callow remarks,

> The speaker uses δέ as a signal, saying, 'This is the next step.' It may be a little step or a big one, it may be a step forwards, or sideways, or even backward-looking, but it is always the next step, and with it the speaker or writer is progressing one thought at a time along a purposeful line of development.[38]

35. This point is based on the rigorous study by Werth, *Focus* (see esp. p. 220).

36. See R. Buth, 'Οὖν, Δέ, Καί, and Asyndeton in John's Gospel', in Black *et al.* (eds.), *Linguistics and New Testament Interpretation*, pp. 152-54.

37. See K. Titrud, 'The Function of καί in the Greek New Testament and an Application to 2 Peter', in Black *et al.* (eds.), *Linguistics and New Testament Interpretation*, pp. 240-70.

38. K. Callow, 'The Disappearing Δέ in 1 Corinthians', in Black *et al.* (eds.), *Linguistics and New Testament Interpretation*, p. 192.

It often functions to mark what follows as new. The use of καί and τε indicates relationships between sentences in the development unit (DU).[39] Certain particles indicate thematic prominence: οὖν, διὰ τοῦτο, ὅθεν, ἄρα, δίο, δέ (when not used in a contrastive sense), νῦν (when not used temporally meaning 'now'). For example, in Rom. 12.1 the combination of οὖν, the verb of beseeching, several present-tense forms, and imperatives signal a thematically prominent section of Paul's discourse. Several other particles in Greek indicate thematic (and usually focal) prominence. These include μέν, γέ, δή (then, indeed), δήπου (surely, indeed), εἰ μήν, μενοῦν (surely, certainly), μήτιγε (how much more), πάντως (indeed, certainly, in any event), ἀλλά (certainly, emphatically), adverbial καί (indeed), ἰδού, ἴδε,[40] ἄγε (look, listen, pay attention), ὦ (Oh!).

Formal Features of Genre. One of the best ways for determining prominence at the discourse level (i.e. determining thematic units of discourse) is to analyse the genre of that discourse. 'Once upon a time' and 'They lived happily ever after' are well known generic features that mark off the boundaries of a text. 'Have you heard the one about...' is another example of a marker of prominence originating from a genre of discourse. The epistolary formula 'I wish for you to know...' (Phil. 1.12), for example, signals the beginning of a thematic unit. One must first establish the relative genre of a New Testament discourse and then analyse other works of the same genre for formulaic elements and their functions.

The above signals of prominence must be treated in terms of the entire system of Greek grammar. No single category signals prominence on its own, but must be studied with respect to the surrounding discourse.

Theme in Paul's Letter to the Philippians

I have entitled this section 'Theme in...Philippians', rather than 'The Theme of Philippians', purposefully to avoid the misnomer that a New Testament text contains a single theme, often encapsulated in one key

39. Levinsohn, *Textual Connections*, pp. xv-xvi.

40. See R. Van Otterloo, 'Towards an Understanding of "Lo" and "Behold": Functions of ἰδού and ἴδε in the Greek New Testament', *OPTaT* 2 (1988), pp. 34-64.

passage (e.g. Rom. 1.16-17). I have also used the term 'theme' because of its relevance for a long-standing debate whether Philippians is composed of one, two or three separate letters (perhaps with even other interpolations). Those contesting the unity of the letter have had to bear the burden of proof, while those maintaining its unity have taken a more reactionary stance. However, recent advocates for its unity are more proactive, arguing that the *thematic structure* of Philippians suggests that it represents one letter, not a combination of several.[41] Little has been mentioned, however, about a linguistic methodology for determining thematic structure—Watson (and Bloomquist) uses rhetoric, Alexander uses epistolary studies, and Garland uses literary approaches (with little definition of what that entails). It is my contention that thematic structure in Philippians, or any New Testament text, should in part be understood in terms of linguistic prominence—background, theme and focus. To isolate the study of theme from a text's background and focal elements (as discussed above) misrepresents how actual texts are constructed. The above theory of prominence is now applied to the text of Philippians, with interspersed remarks on its relevance for the question of unity. (I am less concerned about the question of integrity, however, than I am about analysing the final form of the text.) Prominence is analysed primarily at the level of discourse and paragraph (and paragraph clusters), with occasional comments on prominence at the level of clause.

At the top of the hierarchy of discourse is the genre or register of the text. The genre determines the structure of the discourse. Furthermore, it represents the controlling factor of the text's prominence. The genre of Philippians is undoubtedly that of an ancient epistle. The epistolary genre served to bridge the spatial separation between communicants.[42] This need gave rise to obligatory linguistic formulas which are found in

41. Most notably, D.E. Garland, 'The Composition and Unity of Philippians: Some Neglected Literary Factors', *NovT* 27 (1985), pp. 141-73; D.F. Watson, 'A Rhetorical Analysis of Philippians and its Implications for the Unity Question', *NovT* 30 (1988), pp. 57-88; L. Alexander, 'Hellenistic Letter-Forms and the Structure of Philippians', *JSNT* 37 (1989), pp. 87-101; and L.G. Bloomquist, *The Function of Suffering in Philippians* (JSNTSup, 78; Sheffield: JSOT Press, 1993).

42. Cf. the epistolary definitions of G.J. Bahr, 'The Subscriptions in the Pauline Letters', *JBL* 87 (1968), p. 27; J.L. White, 'The Ancient Epistolography Group in Retrospect', *Semeia* 22 (1981), p. 91; and W.G. Doty, 'The Classification of Epistolary Literature', *CBQ* 31 (1969), p. 193.

the three slots of the letter: opening, body, closing. The fact that spatial and temporal distance separated the author and recipient demanded the need for an opening that identified the participants. The body of the letter accounted for the specific communicative needs of the author. The closing of the letter seems to have developed as a conventional means to wrap up the communicative process—to bring closure and secure the continuing relationship between the participants. Similarly, White delineates three primary functions of the epistolary genre: 'the maintenance of contact, the communication of information, and the statement of request or command'.[43] The interpersonal function of maintaining contact is expressed in the opening and closing. Or, as White notes, 'The writer's presence and disposition in writing is conveyed to the recipient(s)' in the opening and closing.[44]

The following analysis of prominence in the letter to the Philippians is guided by the epistolary framework and its distinct units. Once the epistolary elements are delimited, the following indicators of prominence are analysed: boundary markers (organic ties), discourse participants/events (cohesive ties), word order, and verbal aspect. Each of these will be treated according to their domain (phrase, clause, paragraph, discourse) and level of prominence (background, theme, focus).

Epistolary Opening (1.1-11)

The epistolary opening set the social and interpersonal context of the entire discourse. Elements commonly found in this section are the superscription (sender), adscription (addressee), salutation/greeting and thanksgiving. These served as boundary markers of the epistolary discourse, setting the stage for the body of the letter.

Prescript (1.1-2). The epistolary prescript typically took the form of: A (nominative) to B (dative), greetings (e.g. χαίρειν), or B (dative) from A (nominative) without the greeting. This, of course, was necessary due to the spatial distance between the individuals. The superscription and adscription were often expanded through the addition of epithets, titles, terms of relationship (A to his mother B) and endearment (A to my most beloved friend B), and geographical location. These optional

43. J.L. White, *Light from Ancient Letters* (Philadelphia: Fortress Press, 1986), pp. 218-19.

44. White, *Light*, p. 219.

additions set the stage for the audience's reception of the rest of the discourse.

Phil. 1.1-2, despite its brevity, is a thematic statement of the entire discourse. It identifies the thematic participants (Παῦλος, Τιμόθεος, and τοῖς οὖσιν ἐν Φιλίπποις[45]) and the nature of the ensuing communication. Although these participants are thematic at the level of discourse, they may or may not be thematic at the level of paragraph or clause. They are mentioned in 1.1 with full noun phrases, and later with first (e.g. 1.2 ἡμῶν) and second (e.g. 1.2 ὑμῖν) person pronouns or verbal inflections (unless being brought into focus with a full noun phrase). The use of the first person plural pronoun ἡμῶν describes the interpersonal relationships between the major participants. They all share the same religious tradition. Minor participants are also introduced in this unit (Θεοῦ πατρός and κυρίου Ἰησοῦ). The epistolary opening also plays the role of a boundary marker.

Thanksgiving (1.3-11). Prayer and thanks to the gods concerning the recipient's wellbeing appear in several ancient epistolary openings. Paul also mentions the combined act of prayer and thanksgiving in Phil. 1.3-11. More importantly, he modifies it in such a way that sets the stage for the rest of his discourse.

The thematic unit in 1.3-11 concerns Paul's thankfulness for the involvement of the Philippians in the ministry of the gospel. The epistolary thanksgiving formula serves as a boundary marker, setting the unit apart from the next thematic unit beginning in 1.12. Paul gives thanks (εὐχαριστῶ) to God (τῷ Θεῷ) concerning the Philippians in view of their participation in the work of the gospel. Similar to many letters, Paul's thanksgiving precedes the body of his letter.[46] However, his is unique in two respects. First, Paul thanks one god whereas most letter writers thank a plurality of gods, or at least a god different from that of Paul (e.g. Serapis). This is easily accounted for by the differing religious traditions, but, nonetheless, would have been salient to Christians at

45. Certain leaders (σὺν ἐπισκόποις καὶ διακόνοις) are singled out as participants of the letter.

46. White ('Epistolary Formulas', p. 297) remarks that epistolary thanksgivings customarily appear 'in or near the opening'. See H.G. Meecham, *Light from Ancient Letters* (New York: Macmillan, 1923), p. 113; and with reference to the Pauline letter, W.G. Doty, *Letters in Primitive Christianity* (Philadelphia: Fortress Press, 1973), p. 27.

Philippi who received many letters in which thanks was given to the gods (plural) or a god of a different religious tradition. Secondly, whereas most letters express thanks for the wellbeing of the recipient or for the sender's own wellbeing, Paul thanks God for the spiritual wellbeing of the Philippians.

Several scholars argue that the epistolary thanksgiving introduces or summarizes the general theme of the letter.[47] The following analysis of the body of Philippians suggests otherwise. For example, Paul's role in the thanksgiving is unlike the role he plays in 1.12-25. The Philippians' role in the thanksgiving is at times so generic that using it to point to themes in the discourse provides little, if any, insight into the structure of the letter. More importantly, this study maintains that there is no one theme in the body of the letter and thus there can be no one thematic indicator in the thanksgiving. Similarities in language should not be confused with thematic foreshadowing.

Paul and the Philippians are the thematic participants of this paragraph, being expressed with pronouns and verbal inflections (as is expected with thematic, non-focal, elements). Background participants include God and Christ Jesus, being expressed with nominal phrases. Other potential topic entities exist in this unit (e.g. prayer, heart, gospel, love) but their role is to describe the actions of the main participants. Consequently, they serve at the clausal level as comments upon the thematic participants. That is, their thematic domain is limited to the clause, but they are background at the level of the section/paragraph. It is worth repeating here that the value of prominence of a participant or event is relative to a domain. This paragraph concerns Paul's prayer and thanksgiving for the Philippians. The events/actions in which he participates involve words and phrases from these semantic fields. Paul gives thanks (1.3), petitions (1.4), is confident of (1.6), esteems (1.7), holds them in his heart (1.7), desires them (1.8), and prays for them (1.9). The Philippians are the objects of Paul's actions. They also participate in a recognizable event structure. They share in the task of the gospel (1.5) and are partakers in grace (1.7). They are also described in terms of future roles: completing a good work (1.6), abounding in love that is full of knowledge and perception (1.9), discerning (1.10), sincere and

47. E.g. D.E. Aune, *The New Testament in its Literary Environment* (Philadelphia: Westminster Press, 1987), p. 186; Doty, *Letters*, p. 33; and R. Jewett, 'The Epistolary Thanksgiving and the Integrity of Philippians', *NovT* 12 (1970), p. 53.

without offence (1.10), and fulfilling the work of righteousness (1.11).

The use of word order further illustrates the use of prominence in this unit. The basic word order is VO, which is typical of New Testament discourse. In only three cases is the word order OV: 1.4 τὴν δέησιν ποιούμενος, 1.7 τοῦτο φρονεῖν and 1.9 τοῦτο προσεύχομαι. In 1.4 δέησιν is initial because it is both theme/topic and anaphoric information. In 1.7 τοῦτο is initial because it too is anaphoric information, referring back to the preceding clause (cf. 1.6 πεποιθὼς αὐτὸ τοῦτο). Phil. 1.9 is similar to 1.7—τοῦτο refers back to his desire for them (i.e. his desire to be with them).[48] When a subject is present the word order is SVO or SV. Paul and the Philippians are the subjects in all but two cases: 1.6 ὁ ἐναρξάμενος ἔργον ἀγαθὸν ἐπιτελέσει and 1.8 μάρτυς...μου ὁ Θεός.[49] Both refer to God (the first implicitly, the second explicitly). Notably, the second example is the only case of VS word order, probably because the testimony of God (not the person of God) is focal.

The use of verbal aspect also reflects the thematic structure of the thanksgiving. The present tense is used the majority of times (9×), with the aorist used only once and the perfect twice. Most of the paragraph is thematic, that is, it contributes to the function of the thanksgiving. The one time a background element is used as a subject (SOV word order), Paul uses the aorist tense (background aspect) with a participle. The two uses of the perfect tense (frontground aspect) indicate focal prominence. The first (1.6 πεποιθώς)[50] introduces Paul's affirmation of the worth

48. Against P.T. O'Brien, *Philippians* (Grand Rapids: Eerdmans, 1991), p. 73, who takes it with the following ἵνα clause. Verses 8-9 are reminiscent of Paul's 'apostolic parousia' expression. For example, in Rom. 1.8-12 (also an epistolary thanksgiving) Paul speaks of his desire to visit the Roman Christians so as to minister among them. The language is similar to that of Philippians: appeal to God as a witness to his desire to visit (Rom. 1.9; Phil. 1.8); use of the term 'desire' ἐπιποθῶ (Rom. 1.11; Phil. 1.8); the use of a ἵνα clause to indicate the purpose for coming, viz. to minister in some way (Rom. 1.11; Phil. 1.9); and the mention of prayer for all of this to happen (ἐπὶ τῶν προσευχῶν, Rom. 1.10; προσεύχομαι, Phil. 1.9). The parallels, both in terms of genre and language, suggest that τοῦτο refers to the desire to visit—his ability to minister there is dependent upon his ability to visit them.

49. In 1.9 the grammatical subject is ἡ ἀγάπη, but the modifying genitive ὑμῶν indicates that it is the Philippians' love that is in view. Nevertheless, that Paul grammaticalizes 'love' as the subject suggests that it becomes a thematic element for this clausal unit.

50. Expressions of confidence such as this are found elsewhere in the papyri;

and continuing growth of the Philippians (1.6-11)—this would be expected with a verb indicating 'confidence' (i.e. one who is persuaded) rather than mere 'belief'. It is dependent upon the thanksgiving formula, providing extra information about the author's view of his audience. It is introduced with the perfect tense (frontground aspect) so as to focus the audience's attention on the ensuing statements. It says, 'Take note of what I'm going to say next'. In 1.11 Paul concludes the thanksgiving formula with a participial clause using the perfect tense. The clause ('fulfilling the fruit of righteousness') is not only significant theologically for Paul, it seems to indicate what will happen if the Philippians carry out his preceding exhortations (1.9-10). 'Pay attention', so indicates the perfect tense, since how you Philippians live will result in the fulfilment of the fruit of righteousness.

Epistolary Body (1.12–4.20)

The epistle's body typically contained the information of the letter—the *what* of the communicative event. Thus the form and function of the body varied: contract, travel plans, philosophical treatise, list of purchases, and so on. But it is still necessary that letters have some type of body. Besides the core function of the epistolary genre—communication between spatially separated individuals—the function(s) of the body corresponds to the main theme(s) of the discourse. They are, therefore, what most scholars are interested in when analysing Paul's writings.

Paul's Status (1.12-26). The disclosure formula in 1.12 (γινώσκειν...βούλομαι), a common epistolary formula used at the beginning of the body, signals a new thematic unit. In addition, δέ in 1.12 marks a new development in the discourse. First person is predominant throughout, since Paul is revealing 'things regarding himself that have come about for the advance of the gospel'. Besides himself other unspecified participants play a major role in this section, viz. the ones proclaiming the gospel. Verbal aspect is a key indicator of prominence in this section. The aorist appears three times, once in 1.13 where Paul makes a background statement about the result of his apparent imprisonment (set against the present tense in 1.14 which is thematic and thus further developed) and twice in 1.21, 23 where Paul debates between dying and being with Christ or remaining alive and ministering to the

e.g. P. Mert. 1.12.9 (58 CE) using the present tense.

Philippians. The former statements (dying and being with Christ) use the aorist, probably because they represent the choice that he believed would not be fulfilled—thus background information. The perfect tense (stative aspect) is used frequently (1.12, 14, 16, 19, 25 [2×]), typically with verbs of saying or confidence. They serve to draw attention to particularly important statements of the author. The present tense (thematic aspect) is used 18 times, primarily with statements regarding two topics: (1) the expansion of the gospel albeit through good and bad motives and (2) Paul's probable release from prison and visit to Philippi.

Be Worthy of the Gospel (1.27-30). The imperative mood is used for the first time here, signalling a new thematic development (albeit with ties to the preceding one). The particle μόνον and the shift to second person also signals this development. The Philippians are now the theme of the discourse. Only the aorist and present tenses are used in this section. The ten uses of the present occur in thematic material (see especially the initial 1.27 followed by the present στήκετε and two present participles). The aorist occurs in background material. For example, the aorist passive ἐχαρίσθη is not thematic, but is followed by thematic material.

Promote Unity (2.1-18). The second use of an imperative begins this section, which is part of a conditional clause set off from the preceding discourse by the particle οὖν. Here, however, it is in the aorist (background) tense. This is not because it is not thematic, but because it is set in contrast to the ensuing clauses (using present tense forms) which best capture the theme of this section, viz. unity and self-sacrificing love. This is a typical pattern, in which a more generic verb using the aorist tense is followed (or, more rarely, preceded) by more specific verbs using the present. After the initial aorist imperative, the present tense is used until 2.5. At that point the supposed christological hymn provides an example of what it means to care for the needs of others rather than oneself. Especially significant is that the hymn uses the aorist throughout, not because it is a past-time event (note the future events in 2.10, 11) but because it plays a background or supportive role to the theme of this section. The so-called 'kenosis of Christ' is not the high-point of this section, but supportive to the theme of 'unity'. In 2.12 Paul continues with an aorist imperative and the particle ὥστε (frequently used with imperatives at the close of sections in Paul's writings), which serves as a general command that is followed by two more specific (thematic) commands (κατεργάζεσθε and ποιεῖτε). Another interesting feature of prominence in this section is the use of OV (Object/Complement–Verb) word order in 2.2-5, where the complement occurs first in view of its thematic importance (viz. they all deal with the idea of unity or oneness).

Commendation of Timothy (2.19-24). In this and the next section new participants enter into view: Timothy and Epaphroditus. This section is introduced with the indicative (in contrast to the preceding imperatives) as well as the connective δέ (used to mark a new development). In addition, a common epistolary formula used in letters of commendation occurs in 2.19, marking this section off as a thematic unit. However, in this epistolary commendation and the next (2.25-30) the aorist predominates and the present is infrequent. This is especially strange in 2.19, 23, 25, 28, where the verb for 'send' is in the aorist although it represents the apparent theme of the section. There are several possible explanations. First, the use of the aorist could indicate that these sections are of less importance with respect to the rest of the letter. Secondly, in the commendation of Timothy the present tense forms (thematic aspect) and the one perfect tense form are often used in expressions that convey Paul's feelings or attitudes. This is especially obvious in 2.24 where Paul emphasizes that he also (καί) will be coming to see them. It is almost as if Paul is more concerned with what he is to gain from the sending of Timothy than with the commendation of Timothy itself. Thirdly, the aorist is not indicating prominence.

Commendation of Epaphroditus (2.25-30). This section is set apart by the initial thematic marker δέ and the epistolary formula (note also the continued use of the indicative mood). Whereas in the commendation of Timothy the focus is more on Paul, here the attention is directed towards the relationship between Epaphroditus and the Philippians. This is most clearly indicated by the only use of the present tense forms (thematic aspect) in 2.26 (the longing of Epaphroditus for the Philippians) and 2.29 (their need to receive him and honour those like him). The fact that Epaphroditus almost died plays only a background role in this section (aorists are used throughout). It provides the reason for which they should receive him in the Lord with all joy, i.e. it supports the theme (viz. their acceptance of him).

Confidence in the Flesh versus Confidence in Christ (3.1–4.1). From this point forward, the analysis of prominence becomes more difficult in view of the disjointed exhortations and lack of clear transitions. Nevertheless, on the whole the use of indicators of prominence resembles those found in chs. 1 and 2. Phil. 3.1 is a conundrum, and due to limitations of space will be left unanalysed except for mention of the vocative ἀδελφοί as marker of thematic focus and λοιπόν as boundary marker, but not necessarily a marker of the 'final' section. It surely plays a transitionary role, but what type of role is unclear. Phil. 3.2 most noticeably begins with three imperatives (all clause-initial), redirecting the focus upon the Philippians. The verb probably precedes the complement because the idea of 'caution' is the theme, not necessarily the objects of that caution (who are notably unidentified and perhaps fictitious). Although the Philippians are major participants in the section, Paul in his typical fashion follows his imperative with lengthy supportive statements that have little or nothing to do with his audience. Not until 3.17 with the use of ἀδελφοί do the Philippians come back into view. Like elsewhere, the present tense predominates, most of the material being on the theme line. The perfect tense, in addition, is used frequently here with verbs of volition or will. Two special occurrences (not with verbs of volition) are in 3.12, 13 where Paul draws special attention to the fact that he is not 'perfect'. Such focal prominence is especially evident in v. 13 where a combination of focal indicators is used (ἀδελφοί, ἐγὼ ἐμαυτόν, perfect tense). This section also provides a good example of the use of word order to indicate prominence. Phil. 3.15 (τοῦτο ὁ Θεὸς ὑμῖν ἀποκαλύψει) has marked word order (OSV). The complement precedes the verb, functioning as the topic/theme in light of its reference to the preceding clause. In other words, the sentence begins where the preceding clause left off.

Various Instructions (4.2-9). This section is set apart from the preceding by a device often found in ancient letters, viz. the παρακαλῶ formula. Such a common formula may explain the lack of a connective. In addition, the various units seem disjointed, appearing one after the other with few or no connectives. Nevertheless, there is some macrostructure as is seen by the use of λοιπόν in 4.8 which probably signals that this is the last of Paul's exhortations. The use of imperatives and present tense forms suggests that most of this section is thematic, each unit playing its own part in the exhortation. The aorists in 4.9 are easily explained in the light of their background role in relation to the present imperative πράσσετε. The sole use of the aorist tense with an imperative in 4.5, however, is more problematic. It may be that (1) the aorist passive is used because the verb 'make known' is really non-thematic or (2) this clause is subordinate to the following statement ὁ κύριος ἐγγύς, that is, 'the Lord is near, therefore make your kindness known to all humanity'. Finally, 4.2 and 4.8, 9 are good examples where OV word order is used to indicate thematic prominence at the level of the paragraph.

Thanks for the Philippians' Assistance (4.10-20). Besides δέ this section is set apart by the use of the indicative mood and change of person. This section deals with a topic that is found in several ancient letters: mention of and thanks for items received from the recipient(s). However, as many have noted, Paul's thankfulness is obscured here in the light of his repeated mention that he can live without assistance from the churches. It is for this very reason that Paul apparently uses the present tense forms when discussing his ability to live in all circumstances and the aorist tense forms when mentioning the gift from the Philippians. In other words, the fact that Paul can do without is more prominent in this section than the fact that the Philippians have sent him assistance.

Epistolary Closing (4.21-23)

Just as most dialogue requires some sort of close to the communicative event, letters also developed forms that finalize the discourse. In Paul's closing he not only gives greetings (4.21-22) but also a farewell (4.23). Together they frame the most prominent part of the letter, the body. The greetings all begin with the verb, all being the thematic focus of that section. However, the first form is in the aorist, the other two in the present. This perhaps indicates that the greetings directed towards the Philippians are more prominent than the greetings that the Philippians are to give to every saint. In other words, the author–recipient relationship is more important than the author–peripheral recipient relationship.

Conclusion

One of the central tasks of discourse analysis is the study of textual cohesiveness, that is, how the linguistic units of the text cohere (or do not cohere) into a unified whole. The study of prominence is one aspect of this type of analysis. Prominence refers to those semantic and grammatical elements of discourse that serve to set aside certain subjects, ideas or motifs of the author as more or less semantically and pragmatically significant than others. Prominent elements in discourse consist of background, theme and focus, which are best understood in terms of a cline. The above study suggests eight aspects of Greek grammar and discourse that may signal prominence: semantic relations, verbal aspect, verbal voice, verbal mood, noun–verb relations, word order, boundary markers, and formulas of genre. These are surely not the only devices, but they are some of the more obvious; hopefully, they will encourage further research in this largely unstudied area of New Testament Greek grammar.

A study of discourse prominence in Philippians reveals that there is no one theme in the letter. There is a bipartite structure alternating throughout—Pauline matters and Philippians matters: surrounded by the epistolary framework. According to some scholars, if there were one theme it would support the single-letter theory. This approach to the problem of the letter's integrity begs the question: does a letter need only one theme to be considered a single letter? More useful than seeking after a single theme is the analysis of grammatical and semantic devices that reveal the linear and hierarchical structure of the discourse. In Philippians the devices used to signal prominence (be it background, thematic or focal) are used in a consistent manner throughout. Such evidence should be part of any investigation of the literary integrity of the canonical letter of Paul to the Philippians. More importantly, they represent an important part of the literary analysis of the final form of the text, whether it be a redactor's later compilation or Paul's unitary composition.

In conclusion, although the studies in this volume on discourse analysis disagree at significant points, they are similar in their general application of discourse analysis and the view that this field of modern linguistics has much to offer New Testament studies. Hopefully, they have demonstrated successfully its worth while recognizing the need for continued research and critique.

DISCOURSE ANALYSIS AND PHILIPPIANS

Moisés Silva

Since I welcome every available opportunity to pontificate on subjects that I know nothing about, a colloquium on discourse analysis provides a singularly apt occasion to display this rare skill. My ignorance of the discipline is cleverly disguised (I am sure no one noticed the ruse) in a commentary I wrote a few years back. Using a scholarly footnote, I noted that discourse analysis

> still lacks a standardized terminology and has not been fully integrated into the more traditional approaches... I have not considered it advisable to attempt a full-scale analysis of Philippians along these lines, since a considerable amount of space would be taken up defining specialized terms and explaining the method.[1]

I was trying to communicate to the unwary reader that my knowledge of the subject was so immense that I saw no way in which I could explain it concisely.

If truth be told, there has been a growing confusion on my part about the character of the discipline. Indeed, the more I read the more lost I feel. Every researcher seems to be following his or her own agenda—usually quite an expansive agenda. Certain that the problem was not the early onset of senility, I picked up the recent and fine collection of papers edited by David Black,[2] with the hopes of clarifying matters once and for all. My anxiety, however, was only aggravated to realize in a fresh way that discourse analysis is about...*everything*! It is grammar and syntax, pragmatics and lexicology, exegesis and literary criticism. In short, fertile ground for undisciplined minds.

1. M. Silva, *Philippians* (Wycliffe Exegetical Commentary; Chicago: Moody, 1988; repr. Baker Exegetical New Testament Commentary; Grand Rapids: Baker, 1992), p. 13 n. 13.

2. D.A. Black *et al.* (eds.), *Linguistics and New Testament Interpretation: Essays on Discourse Analysis* (Nashville: Broadman, 1992).

Do not misunderstand me. I do *not* consider everyone involved in discourse analysis—or for that matter, even a large proportion of those working in this discipline—to be guilty of sloppiness. That is not my point. My concern is rather with the character of the discipline itself, which has the potential for encouraging loose thinking and for preventing some scholars from doing their best work. It is not totally unfair, I hope, to say that much of what goes under the rubric of discourse analysis involves one or more of the following: (a) restating the obvious using unnecessarily forbidding terminology; (b) giving expression to exceedingly general and vague ideas, the significance of which escapes at least this reader; (c) attempting to support particular interpretations with arguments that have no probative value whatever.

The comments that follow are restricted to the one feature of discourse analysis that I can understand, namely, the attempt to give a systematic explanation for the way in which units of text larger than the sentence function within the structure of the discourse as a whole. I consider that goal worthwhile and important. Anyone who helps me perceive the flow of an argument or narrative deserves my deepest thanks.

I hasten to add, to be sure, that a J.B. Lightfoot—not well known as a discourse analyst—often helps me in this endeavor a good bit more than some of the publications in so-called text linguistics. But, of course, this is not significantly different from what happens in linguistics more generally. I myself have paid much attention to, and have learned a great deal from, modern research into lexical structure,[3] but I hardly think that exegetes who lived before this era had no understanding of words. There is need for some balance here: it would be foolish to be content with Lightfoot if we wish to develop a consistent and self-conscious approach to the vocabulary. Similarly, it is quite appropriate, and even necessary, to formulate principles of discourse structure that go beyond the intuitive insights of our better exegetes.

But let us not fool ourselves into thinking that a well-designed approach to the functions of paragraphs will in itself solve exegetical problems. Like everything else, it will 'merely' provide a broader base for our interpretive task. It is only seldom that a careful word-study or syntactical analysis leads us directly to an exegetical conclusion. That kind of research, to be sure, helps us eliminate options (a most valuable function); moreover, it furnishes the exegete with patterns of linguistic

3. M. Silva, *Biblical Words and their Meaning: An Introduction to Lexical Semantics* (Grand Rapids: Zondervan, rev. edn 1994 [1983]).

use that facilitate responsible interpretation. But there is not normally a one-to-one correspondence between such research and exegetical conclusions. Likewise, a self-conscious and formal analysis of the way paragraphs are linked is simply one more aspect of the whole process. Researchers in this field should not feel pressured to demonstrate that their conclusions have a direct exegetical pay-off. When they attempt to do that, more often than not it weakens the research.

I will not try to say anything profound about the general theoretical frameworks worked out by Reed and Guthrie. Even if there were space to do that, I really would not be able to contribute much. Focusing then on the analysis of the text itself provided by our three contributors, I am most sympathetic to Guthrie's, but (given the character of this colloquium) perhaps for the wrong reason, namely, it is more traditional in approach than that of either Reed or Levinsohn. In spite of some of his charts, the actual discussion of the text exemplifies responsible but generally accepted exegetical argumentation. If his theoretical framework has helped him treat the text more clearly or consistently, so much the better. However, one suspects that he could have given the same analysis without that framework or even without the methodological reflections that precede the analysis. In other words, additional effort is needed if theory and practice are to be properly integrated.

Reed and Levinsohn are more venturesome, and I am sincerely grateful that they have been willing to take the risk. Precisely because their papers are more provocative, of course, it is easier to identify potential problems. One of them is a certain vagueness about the implications of their work. I am not sure what to do, for example, with Levinsohn's comparisons between parts of Philippians on the one hand and the Koine as a whole on the other, or between two different parts of Philippians, or between Philippians and Galatians. For example, if Levinsohn's fourth principle applies to Philippians but neither to Koine as a whole nor even to Galatians (p. 69 and n. 27), does not that very fact suggest that the principle in question is ineffective in discriminating between similar texts? Similarly, while reading Reed's analysis I sometimes felt I could not clearly identify the issue at hand or the purpose of the argument.

In addition, I found myself disagreeing with a variety of issues. Reed's decision to focus on the subject of prominence in Philippians seems to me totally legitimate; I think it has the potential to advance our understanding of Paul's discourse structure. Nevertheless, the implementation of the principle raised too many questions. Part of the reason is Reed's heavy dependence on Paul's choice of verbal aspect. Undoubtedly, one of the functions of verbal aspect is to reflect discourse shifts, but I doubt whether it is its primary function—and I am sure it is not its only function. Reed in practice assumes, apparently, that aspectual choice is regularly a sure indication of prominence or lack of it.

Moreover, one must question what appears to be an indiscriminate use of aspects, in particular, the mixing of indicative and non-indicative forms in the presentation of the evidence. (It is not clear whether this trait reflects a denial or a downplaying of temporal reference in indicative forms. Regardless of one's theoretical approach to this issue, however, it is indisputable that, in fact, temporal reference is at least associated with the indicative forms in the overwhelming majority of cases, and it makes no sense whatever to ignore that element when analyzing the text.) Thus, the use of the aorist indicative rather than the present when Paul describes Epaphroditus's being in danger of dying is no evidence that this topic plays only a background role. The use of the present was not an option for Paul here. On the other hand, the use of the present in v. 26 is readily accounted for by the simple fact that Epaphroditus's longing for the Philippians is not merely a past event but is true at the time of writing. But, of course, there is an even more fundamental question here. The view that the aorist functions as background while the imperfective indicates prominence is merely assumed by Reed, presumably on the basis of Porter's important but controversial work. The very fact that Levinsohn (in line with the more common understanding of aspect) exactly reverses those functions should at least give us pause about the validity of the method.

I wish I had the time and the ability to evaluate Levinsohn's claims adequately. My knee-jerk reaction to his analysis is that it is overly subtle. Certainly on the basis of this paper alone I would have to say that the thesis is unproven. One of my difficulties, which I have faced with other comparable studies, is that the linking of a particular form with a particular semantic content is seldom demonstrated case by case (e.g., the claim that an element at the beginning of the sentence indicates topicality). The researcher perhaps intuitively comes to that conclusion or thinks that it should be obvious to everyone. The total effect is that perhaps circular reasoning is playing a more substantive role than it ought to.

For example, on p. 68 Levinsohn tells us that the phrases in Phil. 1.4

and 1.7 ‘should both be interpreted as topicalized elements providing the point of departure for what follows. This is because, in both cases, a “given” constituent of the predicate precedes the verb.’ At this point, however, the very principle which I think needs to be demonstrated (that when a given constituent precedes the verb, that position indicates topicalization) is *assumed* as the explanation. I was particularly puzzled by the way the presence of the article was interpreted. Specifically, on 2.13 (p. 72), I do not think that the textual variation at all affects the NIV translation, ‘it is God who works in you’: that sense, I think, is conveyed by the entire construction θεὸς...ἐστιν ὁ ἐνεργῶν.

I hope that my criticisms are not construed as lack of appreciation for the work presented here. To the extent that I am not persuaded by these papers, the reason may well be that those of us who come with a more traditional orientation need to be taught with greater simplicity and patience. Indeed, my comments are not intended to discourage this type of research, but to encourage these obviously competent scholars to work a little harder at helping us see the significance of their contribution.

How Can Biblical Discourse be Analyzed?: A Response to Several Attempts

Stanley E. Porter

A salient thematic statement that brings coherence to these three essays on discourse analysis is the prominent refrain (paraphrased from the book of Judges), 'there was no agreed upon method of discourse analysis, and everyone did what was right in his own eyes'. For the book of Judges this is an implicit commentary on the need for monarchy; for New Testament scholars it is a welcome and much overdue yet equally necessary occasion to attempt to discover or prescribe some common features of discourse analysis that will aid in the interpretative task.

It is not necessary for me to summarize these essays being assessed, except to restate the obvious. Reed's essay provides the kind of overview that is so necessary for a collection such as this, one which begins from the broad assumptions that biblical scholars will tend to hold in common and proceeds to application to a specific text or to specific texts. Guthrie's essay assumes many of the fundamentals articulated in Reed's essay but develops them along more specialized lines. Levinsohn's essay is the most specific, dealing almost exclusively with one particular feature of the Philippian discourse, constituent order and the article. In fact, it may be so specific that it distinguishes the style of the writer of this book from that of other books traditionally within the same Pauline corpus, such as Galatians!

I

Discourse analysis is a discipline, like many in linguistic circles, that has been and continues to be developed primarily in terms of oral texts and modern language users. Being able to say anything useful about ancient written texts means that many of the criteria of discourse analysis must at the least be significantly adapted, if not created *ex nihilo*.

Methodological and definitional questions are, therefore, all the more important. It is for this reason that Levinsohn's essay, at least in this context, is the least satisfactory. He assumes a model that has become quite widespread in some circles (e.g. for Bible translation by those in the Summer Institute of Linguistics) but is not particularly well known outside of these circles. The tendency of much SIL work is to function in a vacuum, without suitable reference to work done outside their limited sphere of influence. More to the point, however, I have some question about what it means that this essay is an exercise in discourse analysis as opposed to a study in sentence grammar or syntax, since he essentially confines himself to the level of the clause or sentence. Other very important topics in discourse analysis are not considered, such as discourse boundaries, prominence, and coherence and cohesion.

There are more specific questions raised in Levinsohn's treatment that I think need to be addressed, however. One, and the one I wish to concentrate on, is the problem of adequately defining topicality and focality, especially in terms of (a) whether these elements are grammatically equated with particular word classes, such as topicality with nouns, and focality with verbs, (b) whether these are grammatically or semantically based criteria, and (c) whether topicality or focality is something predetermined by the interpreter and then seen to be realized syntactically or whether it actually emerges from the syntax. The danger of circular reasoning is a very real one here. Note Levinsohn's statement that 'to give special treatment of a topical element, Greek topicalizes it' (p. 60). Does this mean that the element is already topicalized or that syntax makes it so?

As an example, let me examine briefly his first principle. Levinsohn states (note the prescriptive not descriptive tone) this principle as follows: 'To provide a new point of departure for what follows, place the element which expresses that point of departure at the beginning of the clause or sentence concerned' (p. 61). The section attempts to distinguish among topical elements and those that are given special treatment by their being topicalized, and the reasons for this. Regarding Phil. 2.22, Levinsohn notes that τὴν δοκιμὴν αὐτοῦ is placed first and provides the point of departure. But note further that in 2.23 τοῦτον is placed first even though Timothy has already been introduced in v. 19, where his initial reference is not fronted. Perhaps the argument would be that in 2.23 Timothy becomes the point of departure, even though introduced earlier, but this simply illustrates the need for a more sophisticated criterion than simply equating new points of departure with placement at the beginning of a clause. Furthermore, Levinsohn sees 'his character' (v. 22) in contrast with the 'all' of v. 21. It is not clear how this is established, since οἱ πάντες is in its usual word order in the main Pauline letters (see 1 Cor. 10.17; 2 Cor. 5.14), that is, not given special treatment (but cf. Eph. 4.13; Tit. 3.15), although it is the only appearance of this construction in Philippians. The contrast of οἱ πάντες, as Levinsohn asserts, may be with the 'I' of vv. 19-20, although again the pattern is that 'I' is introduced by the verb form alone in v. 19a and the pronoun is not introduced until v. 19b.

With regard to the overall domain for the entire book of Philippians, Levinsohn states that on the one hand it is established by the author(s) and addressees. But what does that mean for Philippians? (In one sense virtually all letters have the same domain, 'I/we' and 'you', but Levinsohn surely must mean more than this.) The letter claims Paul and Timothy as the authors (1.1-2), while the letter continues in v. 3 in the singular, which Levinsohn recognizes. But his explanations are inadequate. First, he simply states that 'Paul and Timothy' becomes 'I', yet the overall domain remains the same. Secondly, he cites Greenlee's recognition that most commenators agree that Paul is the letter's author (n. 12). This however is a historical-critical judgment, not a linguistic one. It has not explained the number shift in terms of overall domain, especially since the singular reference is maintained throughout the rest of the letter. Although recognizing that topicalization with ἐγώ has occurred at 1.3 in some manuscripts (D F G), Levinsohn rightly rejects this, but uses it to claim that the overall domain is assumed throughout, even though this domain becomes 'I'.

More important still, however, is the introduction of the topic of thanksgiving, reflected in most outlines of the letter (1.3-11). Levinsohn says that it is possible to change subject without topicalization, but most commentators would not agree with his minimization of the thanksgiving here. The verb εὐχαριστῶ, it might be argued, is topicalized syntactically by its initial placement and conceptually by its introduction of a new topic. This has direct implications for the unity question, since a similar structure is found at 3.2 with βλέπετε, at 4.10 with ἐχάρην, and at 4.21 with ἀσπάσασθε, all places suggested as marking boundaries of the individual letter units. This would also be consistent with 1.1-2 having been added to the unified letter as a common introduction.

There is the further problem of Levinsohn's characterization of the overall domain as 'I' and 'you' when he discusses 1.9a, 9b, 10a. He claims that v. 10a shows how the domain reverts to 'you', with the post-verbal use of ὑμᾶς. But why has not the topic shifted to 'testing', since the infinitive is placed first? Levinsohn's tool does not seem to be sufficiently refined to differentiate these movements.

The same kind of analytical procedure could be done with the subsequent four principles, each one being subject to some confusion. I have much sympathy for Levinsohn's attempt to solve the dilemma of the Greek article, but I think that there is more going on than the issue of saliency. This is again an instance where a vicious circular reasoning has been created. That there is something more going on is indicated by several examples. For example, if we accept Levinsohn's analysis of the use of the article with Χριστόν in 1.17 in contrast to its anarthrous usage in 1.18, why does Χριστόν appear with the article in 1.16—supposedly to supply again 'given' information? I would contend that there are some instances where the article is required, not to mark given information but to help disambiguate syntax. For example, in 1.27 the article probably appears with Χριστόν to avoid its being taken as appositional with εὐαγγελίου, something that is desirous in 2.11 both with the nominative of Ἰησοῦς Χριστός in relation to κύριος and πατρός with θεοῦ. The same can probably be seen in 3.18, 20 and 4.23 (but cf. 3.8).

Let us imagine that, with appropriate refinement, Levinsohn could demonstrate his results. He claims to have defined at least two criteria that are not found in extra-New Testament Greek but are found in Philippians (this raises serious questions in its own right regarding the validity and applicability of his results to 'discourse' in any larger sense), thus warranting in his mind the conclusion that 1.27–4.3 (why not 4.9?) forms a literary unit. He assumes that this means that the entire segment came from Paul's hand at one time, since he posits various alternatives regarding a separate letter or Pauline involvement for the section that does not cohere with his criteria (4.10-20). But his criteria cannot be extended so far. Since his establishment of what constitutes topicality or salience is determined within the individual sub-units of the letter, his criteria will establish only that 1.27–4.3 came from the same author, but they say nothing of when, so the unity question is essentially unanswered.

II

Guthrie and Reed address the question of unity at the very points where Levinsohn fails by placing their comments within the larger context of a theory of discourse analysis and arguing that there are extra-segmental unifying factors that illustrate textual unity. Guthrie has outlined a several step procedure that begins with grammatical analysis but that almost immediately moves to semantic analysis at his second stage. The use of the concept of 'constituent' as synonymous with 'semantic' will be unfamiliar to many linguists, who are used to more formally based criteria. But this raises in my mind the major issue in Guthrie's approach, and that is how one establishes and pursues criteria for determining significant textual features. Guthrie recognizes that there may be a tension between constituents that are grammatically and semantically on different levels. He chooses to pursue the semantic criteria. I think that in some ways this is unfortunate, because it leaves a whole range of grammatical phenomena unexplored, such as verbal aspect, pronominal forms, word order and so on. As his schema regarding semantic or constituent analysis indicates, semantic components are discussed without adequate definition or consideration of their relations to grammatical phenomena, and thus eliminating what I consider to be the necessary starting point for discourse analysis, that is, the grammatical and lexical phenomena in the text itself. This is also seen when Guthrie discusses unit boundaries in terms of cohesion, focusing upon conceptual unity as established by such techniques as inclusio (although his use of such devices as hook words is potentially quite useful, but see below), and interrelatedness of units in the discourse, concentrating upon logical progressions. There are many useful insights in Guthrie's program, and I believe that many of them ultimately will be seen to be valuable and quantifiable, but at this stage they are, to my mind, inadequately substantiated on the basis of the phenomena of the language itself.

The results of Guthrie's kind of analysis can be seen in his analysis of Philippians. Much of what he has found is, I believe, valid, and this because it can be substantiated. For example, he claims to have found unit breaks on the basis of use of forms of χαίρω at 1.18, 2.17-18, 3.1, 4.4 and 4.10. In fact, apart from 2.28, which I believe warrants discussion, these are the only uses of this verb and its derived cognate forms in the book. Not only that, but in all of the instances but 4.10 it is not only a single use but an accumulation of uses that marks the transition. Not all of the analysis is this convincing, however. For example, Guthrie cites reference to Christ in 1.13 and 18 as marking 1.12-18 as a unit, use of οἶδα and τοῦτο in 1.19 and 25-26 as marking 1.19-26 as a unit, and the use of ἀλλὰ καί in 1.18 and 2.17 as marking a new unit. There are thirty-five instances of the use of Χριστός in Philippians, with significant uses in 1.15 and 17 as well. οἶδα appears in 1.16 and 4.12 and 15 as well. And ἀλλὰ καί is also used in 1.29, 2.27 and probably 2.4. In fact, it does not actually appear in 2.17; instead ἀλλὰ εἰ καί is used, a slightly different transition marker. I am not saying that the phenomena Guthrie cites are not significant but that further argumentation is needed to substantiate this. One would have to calculate how much these contradictory considerations mitigate Guthrie's findings to know, for example, whether he is convincing when he says that τὸ λοιπόν is used at 3.1 and 4.8 to sum up a brief series of exhortations. Note further that 3.1 and 4.8 not only begin with τὸ λοιπόν, but have a plural nominative of direct address ἀδελφοί following, and then an imperative.

A last example to illustrate my claim that reference to specific quantifiable criteria is a necessary starting point is found in Guthrie's attempt to extend Garland's argument for the unity of 1.27–4.3. Guthrie argues that 4.4-9 should be included in this section, because of parallels with 1.27-30. He cites reference to anxiety and God's provision as two of his three criteria. However, the word for 'anxiety' in 4.6, μεριμνάω, does not appear in 1.28, only at 2.20. No significant vocabulary, apart from θεός, is shared in 4.7 and 1.28. Thus this inclusio must be reconsidered. Guthrie also offers several negative arguments for unity, including, for example, reference to the pronouns of 3.1 not having identifiable referents if this passage were not part of the original composition. As I understand the unity issue, one could well argue that all of the material is authentically Pauline and was sent to the Philippian church, and therefore referring to specific people known to that Christian community, even though not all of it was part of a single composition. Thus there could be unity of verb, actor and subject between the various sub-units on the basis of Paul being the writer to the Philippian church even if he did not write all of it at the same time. Thus cohesive criteria such as topic, actor or subject, etc., could cohere even if the book does not.

III

Reed sees discourse analysis as part of a larger project of New Testament hermeneutics. I am very sympathetic to this gestalt, having tried in my work on verbal aspect to see Greek grammar as a hermeneutical stance.[1] His discussion of the relationship between biblical studies and linguistics as brought to bear in discourse analysis helps to place our discussion within a larger interpretative framework, one that could help to overcome many of the barriers that apparently hinder modern methodologies from moving into the mainstream of biblical exegesis. Reed usefully notes several fundamental principles that will enable discourse analysis to communicate meaningfully with other areas of biblical exegesis, including his concern for determining authorial meaning by means of the phenomena of the text, his delimitation of discussion of texts larger than the sentence, his recognition of the social function of language and discourse, and his application of these criteria to coherent discourse. My approach to discourse analysis is similar, as summarized in my *Idioms of the Greek New Testament*.[2]

Although I recognize that informational structure could well be traced as well in the analysis of discourse, as Guthrie does, I believe that significant conclusions will only be found when analysis works with the basic phenomena as well as the larger conceptual categories. These micro- and macro-structures can be seen in terms of the analogy of a pyramid. The pyramid is composed of various layers, including word (or morpheme), phrase (or group), sentence (or clause), pericope (or paragraph) and discourse. The pinnacle of the pyramid represents the entire discourse, since it is at this level that singular topics or thematic structures can be stated and analysed. The discourse is then broken down into an increasingly larger number of smaller units, its constituent units. At the base of the pyramid are the formal units of language which comprise the larger structural and conceptual units. In discourse analysis one can begin at the top (the pinnacle of the pyramid), or the bottom (the base), but one must work through all of the stages, from both directions, to provide a full analysis. This is something that Reed attempts. The

1. S.E. Porter, *Verbal Aspect in the Greek of the New Testament, with Reference to Tense and Mood* (SBG, 1; New York: Peter Lang, 1989, 1993), pp. 1-16.

2. S.E. Porter, *Idioms of the Greek New Testament* (Biblical Languages: Greek, 2; Sheffield: JSOT Press, 1992), pp. 298-307.

three major components of discourse analysis, it seems to me, are discourse boundaries, directly relevant to this discussion, since the topic is that of asking whether discourse analysis can say anything useful to the question of what the discourse boundaries are of the book of Philippians, that is, whether it is one single bounded discourse or whether it contains a number of smaller bounded units; prominence, the topic that Reed emphasizes; and coherence, the topic that Guthrie stresses.

When he applies his method, Reed focuses upon the concept of prominence, creating what is to my mind the fullest and most complete description of the various features of discourse analysis. Inevitably any scheme related to language must be somewhat reductionistic, but Reed's program is more inclusive, more formally based and less reductionistic than most. Such categories as background, theme and focus are important for capturing the relationship between narrative and exposition. Each has a function and a domain of prominence that moves from broader to more highly articulated categories. These are reflected in various signaling devices. It is here that such important categories as semantic or cohesive ties, verbal aspect, verbal voice, verbal mood or attitude, person and number (what Reed calls noun–verb relations), word order and boundary markers play a vital role. Along the way, Reed points out where there has been confusion or simply, for example regarding definitions of verbal aspect, and estimations of word order, areas where discourse analysts are dependent upon fundamental research. There has been a significant amount of work done in some of these areas, but unfortunately a good portion of what has been published is still unknown to not only traditional exegetes but many discourse analysts as well.

It is inevitable that such a comprehensive program for interpretation can only be selectively applied in an essay such as this. Reed's beginning with the genre of the text, the ancient epistle, is a necessary corrective to studies that appear simply to be imposing modern categories on ancient texts without consideration of the features of the texts as the ancients themselves would have viewed them. I wonder, however, whether this does not predispose discourse analysts in their estimation of textual unity, since the epistolary genre itself imposes a number of restrictions on how to interpret the textual phenomena, including reference to various communicants, the necessity and type of disjunctions to be expected, and so on. It also helps to avoid isolationist exegesis, in which matters of historical background are considered irrelevant in the light of the 'literary' structure of the text. Features unique to the individual author or book, including the Pauline prescript, or the thanks offered to a single God for spiritual wellbeing, can be appreciated. This approach to discourse analysis helps to correct several interpretative mistakes as well, including illustrating that the thanksgiving (and I would say, *contra* some recent work, the closing) does not encapsulate or summarize the general theme (or themes) of the letter. In the final analysis, however, this generic approach might mandate finding a unity to this epistle, effectively bracketing out the question of whether it is a composite of several different epistles redacted by the early church.

So far as treating individual linguistic phenomena, Reed, although not as systematically rigorous here as Levinsohn (although perhaps not with Levinsohn's consequent problems as well), does show the relationship between these phenomena and how to view the discourse as a whole. For example, his consideration of word order and verbal aspect in the thanksgiving begins with observation of the phenomena. After observing that the word order is standard apart from three examples of altered structure, Reed then proceeds to an explanation, rather than positing an explanation and then finding commensurate phenomena. He rightly begins with Verb – Object (VO) as the standard order, recognizing that grammaticalization of the subject is often redundant or not required, and hence merits special consideration. Even more interesting, to my mind, is his discussion of the use of verbal aspect, in particular the use of the perfect tense in 1.6, πεποιθώς. Reed says that this verb

> introduces Paul's affirmation of the worth and continuing growth of the Philippians (1.6-11)—this would be expected with a verb indicating 'confidence' (i.e. one who is persuaded) rather than mere 'belief'. It is dependent upon the thanksgiving formula, providing extra information about the author's view of his audience. It is introduced with the perfect tense (frontground aspect) so as to focus the audience's attention on the ensuing statements. It says, 'Take note of what I'm going to say next' (pp. 95-96).

Confirmatory of Reed's analysis here is the fact that, of the seventeen perfect tense verbs used in Philippians, six of them are perfect forms of πείθω (1.6, 14, 25; 2.24; 3.3, 4). This verb is only used 23 times in the perfect tense in the New Testament, and fully one quarter of them in this book (the next closest is Romans with four). Reed could stress even more than he does the tone of conviction demonstrated by Paul in this letter, and found in two of the sections often posited as forming individual letters. Reed's conclusion is that his analysis provides for no single theme in the letter. Of course, for those who posit establishment of a single theme as the criterion for textual unity this conclusion will prove disappointing, since he is more concerned with tracing the structure of discourse, which, he maintains, is consistently maintained throughout this epistle. I am not sure whether this means that the letter should be seen as a unity or whether it implies that there was a redactor or that all of the sub-units originated with the same author, although possibly on different occasions.

IV

In conclusion, discourse analysis is probably much further along in establishing itself as a productive exegetical procedure than many have realized, although it still leaves a number of questions unasked and unanswered. It is not a magic wand that can be waved over significant exegetical issues to make all of their problems disappear or come clear. But any exegetical procedure that results in closer attention to the text itself, in particular to its grammatical phenomena, is to be welcomed.

Part II
OTHER TOPICS

ON THE OTHER TOPICS

D.A. Carson

In a book entitled *Discourse Analysis and Other Topics in Biblical Greek*, someone must introduce the other topics, and I have been elected. But before doing so it may be useful to sketch the shape not only of contemporary discussion on linguistics, but also of one of its stepchildren.

I

The Biblical Greek Language and Linguistics unit of the Society of Biblical Literature has had as its primary aim during its short life the fostering of competent linguistic study of the Greek Bible. But just as the field of biblical studies has exploded into a swarm of subdisciplines, so linguistics in its own right has spawned so many subdivisions that it is difficult if not impossible to keep up with them all, let alone master them. Moreover, because linguistics has often bred its own specialist terminology, breaking into the discipline can seem at least as daunting to biblical specialists as breaking into, say, sociological approaches to the New Testament, or the intricacies of the New Criticism and the subsequent reactions to it.

Fortunately, there are now several surveys that are eminently useful. For an introduction to linguistics characterized by brevity and accessibility, an article in the *Expository Times* is hard to beat.[1]

More generally, it is quite clear that developments in the study of literature have been mirrored, sometimes earlier and sometimes later, in biblical studies. A focus on the meaning the writer imposes on the text (tradition and redaction criticism) gave way to a focus on the text itself, in large measure divorced from the writer (some branches of linguistics, stylistics, structuralism). Gradually the hearer/reader was given more

1. S.E. Porter, 'Keeping up with Recent Studies: 17. Greek Language and Linguistics', *ExpTim* 103 (1992), pp. 202-208.

place (New Criticism, rhetorical analysis, some early forms of reader-response criticism). Today many scholars argue that one cannot usefully speak of meaning in texts at all (or, alternatively, one may speak of an excess of meaning in texts): readers are the ones who impose meaning on texts (post-structuralism, deconstruction).

Writing of linguistics as applied to the Hebrew Bible, van Wolde has recently summarized linguistic developments as no less revolutionary than (and sometimes as a contribution to) those that have taken place in the study of literature and in biblical studies. What she writes with reference to the Hebrew Bible is no less applicable to the relevance of linguistics for the Greek Bible:

> Two major shifts have taken place within three fields of linguistics—syntax, semantics, and pragmatics—which are reflected in linguistic Bible studies. Traditionally, the longest unit to be studied in linguistics was the sentence. In the past decades, however, certain branches of linguistics have begun to study the hierarchical relationships between sentences in a text. Thus, besides sentence syntax we now have text syntax; besides word semantics we now have text semantics; and besides the pragmatics of a sentence we now have the pragmatics of the text as a whole. The second shift that has taken place in linguistics is closely related to this: the relationship between elements of meaning is no longer studied independent of the language user: After all, linguistic conventions do not merely act as suppliers of elements to be selected. The language user makes concrete combinations in discourses and thus creates new relationships and meanings. The study of linguistics can no longer be restricted to linguistic conventions but will have to include actual realizations.[2]

My purpose in this short note, however, is to point out that some of the developments that have taken place are mutually contradictory—or, more precisely, that some of the more recent developments contradict the linguistic heritage from which they originally sprang.

I shall choose an example from Jacques Derrida, sometimes called the father of deconstruction. Toward the beginning of this century de Saussure, the father of modern linguistics, had argued that words, as linguistic signs, whether oral or written, are arbitrary. There is nothing that necessarily connects 'tree' in English or 'arbre' in French with any particular tree, or with the concept of treeness.[3] In his usage, *signifier*

2. E. van Wolde, 'A Text-Semantic Study of the Hebrew Bible, Illustrated with Noah and Job', *JBL* 113 (1994), pp. 19-20.

3. F. de Saussure, *Course in General Linguistics* (trans. R. Harris; LaSalle, IL: Open Court, 1986), pp. 65-68.

referred to the sound pattern or written form of the word, *signified* referred to the concept itself, and *sign* to the combination of the two. The signifier, then, is arbitrary. What ensures that it has meaning are the *differences* between any one signifier and all other signifiers. For a competent English speaker, what gives 'tree' its meaning is nothing intrinsic to the word itself, but precisely what it is not, that is how it differs from all other words ('tea', 'three', 'thee', 'these', and so forth). In other words, 'two signs *a* and *b* are never grasped as such by our linguistic consciousness, but only the difference between *a* and *b*'.[4] This perspective generated his much-quoted claim,

> *In the language itself, there are only differences.* Even more important than that is the fact that, although in general a difference presupposes positive terms between which the difference holds, in a language there are only differences, *and no positive terms*.[5]

Part of this can be challenged, and de Saussure himself backs down a little. But Jacques Derrida begins at this point, and develops it in ways never foreseen by de Saussure. Derrida says that the rigid maintenance of the distinction between the signifier and the signified gives the impression that there exist signifieds quite apart from signifiers.[6] Such a concept Derrida calls a 'transcendental signified'. Western philosophy, he contends, has been shot through with the assumption that these transcendental signifieds—God, consciousness, truth, intentionality, meaning, self, being and so forth—have some genuine reassuring existence apart from signifiers, and are actually present with us.[7] In reality, there is no escape from language. And each word is able to signify only because of the differences it sustains with all other words. Each signifier functions only because of its relationships with what it is not, with that from which it is distinct. 'Nothing, neither among the elements nor within the system, is anywhere ever simply present or absent. There are only, everywhere, differences and traces of traces.'[8] So tightly bound is everything and every concept to language that Derrida recognizes that his implicit overthrow of Western metaphysics is forced to use the

4. De Saussure, *Course*, p. 116.

5. De Saussure, *Course*, p. 118 (emphasis his).

6. J. Derrida, *Positions* (trans. A. Bass; Chicago: University of Chicago Press, 1981), p. 19.

7. This theme constantly recurs in Derrida. See, for example, *Of Grammatology* (Chicago: University of Chicago Press, 1976), p. 49.

8. Derrida, *Positions*, p. 26.

categories of metaphysics, since we have inherited no other. Moreover, if de Saussure could say that difference is what enables signifiers to have meaning, Derrida goes further and insists that meaning is present only as an effect of linguistic difference.

Indeed, he invents a new word at this juncture, the French neologism *différance*, that is *différence* spelled with an *a*. What Derrida means by this is complicated,[9] but nicely laid out by Moore, who comments that *différance* is 'Saussurean *différence* writ large'.[10] It is not a thing, a being, but is everything that makes concepts possible in linguistic expression. The play of differences means that no single element can be simply present or absent itself, for any element achieves meaning by playing off all the things it is not.

At this juncture Derrida takes two crucial steps. First, he elevates the written word above the oral word. Most of us accept that oral speech is in some respects prior to writing. This is so not least in Christianity. Before there is the Bible, God speaks. God makes himself present through speech. Even the Son of God is called the Word (Jn 1.1). This idea, which links speech and presence, Derrida labels 'logocentrism' and condemns it as 'an ethnocentric metaphysics. It is related to the history of the West.'[11] If I understand him correctly, Derrida labels the hurly-burly of linguistic elements playing off one another to achieve meaning *writing*, and insists that this writing is necessarily antecedent to speech. Such writing is thus not the fossilization of speech, or a container for speech; rather, it is the necessary presupposition of speech. And secondly, Derrida (and some other deconstructionists, for that matter) thinks that all language refers only to other language; it is incapable of referring to entities other than language.

Such is one small part of the complex thought of the thinker who is usually thought of as the world's leading deconstructionist. My purpose in setting out these elements of his thinking is simply to provide an example of development that completely overturns the heritage of thought from which in part it has sprung.

Let us begin with the claim that texts can only refer to other texts. Even R. Rorty, who by analogy with the ancient cosmology of elephants

9. J. Derrida, 'Difference', in *Margins of Philosophy* (trans. A. Bass; Chicago: University of Chicago Press, 1982), pp. 1-27.

10. S.D. Moore, *Poststructuralism and the New Testament: Derrida and Foucault at the Foot of the Cross* (Minneapolis: Fortress Press, 1994), pp. 21-25, esp. p. 21.

11. Derrida, *Of Grammatology*, p. 20.

'all the way down' has concluded, in a much-quoted saying, 'It's all words, all the way down',[12] offers these trenchant comments:

> As usual with pithy little formulae, the Derridean claim that 'There is nothing outside the text' is right about what it implicitly denies and wrong about what it explicitly asserts. The *only* force of saying that texts do not refer to nontexts is just the old pragmatist chestnut that any specification of a referent is going to be in some vocabulary. Thus one is really comparing two descriptions of a thing rather than a description with the thing-in-itself...
>
> There are, alas, people nowadays who owlishly inform us 'philosophy has *proved*' that language does not refer to anything nonlinguistic, and thus that everything one can talk about is a text. This claim is on a par with the claim that Kant proved that we cannot know about things-in-themselves. Both claims rest on a phoney contrast between some sort of nondiscursive unmediated vision of the real and the way we actually talk and think. Both falsely infer from 'We can't think without concepts, or talk without words' to 'We can't think or talk except about what has been created by our thought and talk'.

A further connection is then often made, especially in American scholarship. From the assumption that texts cannot talk about 'reality', it soon begins to appear that the only thing they can talk about is 'their inability to do so'.[13] Rorty quotes Gerald Graff's remark that 'from the thesis that language cannot correspond to reality, it is a short step to the current revisionist mode of interpretation that specializes in reading all literary works as commentaries on their own epistemological problematics'. He then remarks,

> It is in fact a rather long step, and a step backward. The tendency Graff speaks of is real enough, but it is a tendency to think that literature can take the place of philosophy by *mimicking* philosophy—by being, of all things, *epistemological*. Epistemology still looks classy to weak textualists. They think that by viewing a poet as having an epistemology they are paying him a compliment. They even think that in criticizing his theory of knowledge they are being something more than a mere critic—being, in fact, a philosopher. Thus conquering warriors might mistakenly think to impress the populace by wrapping themselves in shabby togas stripped

12. R. Rorty, *Consequences of Pragmatism* (Minneapolis: University of Minnesota Press, 1982), p. xxxv.

13. To use the language of I. Wright, 'History, Hermeneutics, Deconstruction', in J. Hawthorn (ed.), *Criticism and Theory* (London: Edward Arnold, 1984), p. 90, whose essay led me to these particular remarks by Rorty.

> from the local senators. Graff and others who have pointed to the weirdly solemn pretentiousness of much recent textualist criticism are right, I think, in claiming that such critics want to have the supposed prestige of philosophy without the necessity of offering arguments.[14]

Probably no one has done a better job than John Ellis at pointing out the flaws in Derrida's argument.[15] Derrida's charge that the entire Western tradition, including de Saussure, is guilty of ethnocentrism in promoting speech above writing, is a major historical misunderstanding. De Saussure openly opposed the ethnocentrism of Western linguists who had tended to elevate the written language above speech. They inevitably focused on cultures with a lengthy written tradition, and, focusing on written texts, developed their philology around written materials. De Saussure reversed this by demonstrating that the oral language is the driving agent of change in any language.[16]

As for arguing that writing is prior to speech, the countervailing evidence is abundant. To quote what Ellis marshals:

> 1. Speech quite clearly existed long before the invention of writing.
> 2. There still exist in the world languages that are spoken but not written, but none that are written without being spoken.
> 3. There are large numbers of individuals who speak without writing, but none who write without speaking (except when their physical capacity to produce speech is deficient).
> 4. There are many different forms of writing, but linguists of all persuasions agree that *no* form of writing in general use is adequate to record all that there is in language; intonation, stress, pitch, and other communicative features are not adequately dealt with even in the best writing systems. All writing systems are *in principle* only attempts to represent languages that *must* in varying degrees be incomplete.[17]

Derrida tries to cover himself without frankly admitting it:

> If 'writing' signifies inscription and especially the durable institution of a sign (and that is the only irreducible kernel of the concept of writing), writing in general covers the entire field of linguistic signs. In that field a certain sort of instituted signifiers may then appear, 'graphic' in the narrow and derivative sense of the word, ordered by a certain relationship

14. R. Rorty, 'Nineteenth-Century Idealism and Twentieth-Century Textualism', in his *Consequences of Pragmatism* (Brighton: Harvester, 1982), pp. 154-56.

15. J.M. Ellis, *Against Deconstruction* (Princeton: Princeton University Press, 1989), pp. 18-28.

16. Ellis, *Against Deconstruction*, pp. 19-20.

17. Ellis, *Against Deconstruction*, p. 21.

> with other instituted—hence 'written', even if they are 'phonic'—signifiers. The very idea of institution—hence of the arbitrariness of the sign—is unthinkable before the possibility of writing and outside its horizon.[18]

Ellis points out three holes in the argument. First, the idea that the institution of signs is unthinkable before the *possibility* of writing is useless. 'To assert that as soon as speech arises, writing it down is possible, might *at best* be to argue for the *equal* status of speech and writing.'[19] But that would not meet the exigencies of Derrida's insistence that writing is prior, and in any case the evidence is against it. Secondly, Derrida has warped the meaning of the word 'writing' by saying that the 'only irreducible kernel of the concept of writing' is the 'durable institution of signs'. That is not true. 'What is irreducibly essential to the idea of writing is the *visual* recoding of the sign.'[20] This key omission is what permits him to proceed to the next error, and it is the most important. Thirdly, he falls into a logical mistake. It is worth quoting Ellis at length:

> We begin with three terms: language, speech, and writing. The first contains the second and third. The question is now which of these last two has priority. Derrida is attempting to prove that the third has priority over the second, in the face of some obvious arguments to the contrary. To do so, he replaces the first triad of terms (language, speech, writing) with a different triad: writing, phonic, graphic. He substitutes the second triad for the first, and now writing has precedence over everything.
>
> It is not difficult to see what is wrong with this procedure. First of all, the nature of the phenomenon concerned has *not* been changed. If we decide arbitrarily to call language 'writing', speech 'phonic' and writing 'graphic', we have not changed the relation of the three entities: what we ordinarily call 'language' still stands in the same relationship to speech and writing whether we use these three names or the other three. Secondly, this procedure does, of course, involve a misuse of English. Language does *not* mean writing, and if we use 'writing' to substitute for 'language' we have misspoken.[21]

18. Derrida, *Of Grammatology*, p. 44.
19. Ellis, *Against Deconstruction*, p. 23.
20. Ellis, *Against Deconstruction*, p. 24.
21. Ellis, *Against Deconstruction*, p. 24. The same problems exist, of course, in French, the language in which Derrida writes. Ellis's argument is not weakened by his reference to 'misuse of English'.

Derrida's real concern, of course, is a kind of moralizing condemnation of speech, because it seems to some to be closer to tying language and presence together. So Derrida brands it 'logocentrism' and, in charged moralistic expressions, defends the priority of writing.[22]

It would not be hard to show that a great deal of Derrida's thought resorts to extreme and sometimes misleading antithesis. From de Saussure's insight that thought or concepts without words are impossible, and that formally words are arbitrary, and that (in a slightly exaggerated expression) the meanings of words turn on difference, what extreme and disputable inferences have been drawn! It is one thing to say, 'Man does not live in relation to being as such, but in relation to being as it is present to him, and that means in language'.[23] It is certainly appropriate to work through the difficulties language has in 'presenting' being. It is another to resort to what Decombes calls 'the grammatical reduction of ontological propositions'.[24]

Contrast, then, this line of thought, which has as its aim the establishment of the view that texts have an excess of meaning but no univocal or objective meaning, that all interpretation so imposes its own grid on the text that the responsible way forward is creatively to discover oppositions and contradictions 'in' the text and thus to deconstruct it by setting it against itself, contrast this, I say, with the concerns of de Saussure. Among the early working axioms that modern linguistics developed (still a working axiom among most contemporary linguists, provided they have not been overly influenced by deconstruction) is that anything that can be said in one language can be said in another. Of course, very often it will not be said in the same way. Never can everything that is said in one language be said as briefly in the receptor language. But in principle there is no semantic weight—denotation, connotation, emotional colouring or whatever—that cannot be got across in the receptor language.

Clearly these are two very different worlds. De Saussure's world entertains no doubt that texts have specific meaning that is in principle recoverable; Derrida denies both points.

22. For a detailed critique, see Ellis, *Against Deconstruction*, pp. 30-66.

23. R.W. Funk, *Language, Hermeneutic, and Word of God* (New York: Harper & Row, 1966), p. 51.

24. V. Descombes, *Objects of All Sorts: A Philosophical Grammar* (trans. S. Scott-Fox and J. Harding; Baltimore: The Johns Hopkins University Press, 1986), pp. 112-37.

My purpose here is not to mediate this particular dispute, though I have tried to do so elsewhere.[25] I am simply pointing out that linguistic and literary developments are taking place at such a pace that it is not always noticed that in some cases the offspring are eating their parents. Where that is the case one cannot responsibly treat parents and offspring as independent interpretative techniques or approaches, each of which brings a valuable slant to the text, to the interpretation of the text. Some of the (post)modern options are mutually destructive, and we are going to have to choose, and defend our choice.

II

I turn now to the essays that make up this section of the book. Each year at SBL we have held two sessions of the Biblical Greek Language and Linguistics unit. One has been devoted to a defined topic, and contributors have been invited; the other has been 'open', in order to spur as broad a diversity of contributions as possible. The essays in this section of *On Discourse and Other Topics* have been drawn from the second session in each of the last two years.

Of course, they might have dealt with an enormous breadth of issues, and deployed a remarkable range of subdisciplines. In fact, four of the five deal with the meaning of a single word or short expression, usually with respect to a particular context. Thus four of the five following essays serve incidentally to display the range of approaches that can be taken in what used to be called 'word studies'. Two of these are remarkably 'classical' in approach: anyone trained in biblical studies can readily follow the argument undaunted by new technical jargon. A third is essentially classical in approach, but sometimes uses a little of the terminology cherished by linguists since de Saussure. All three have one important feature in common: they resort to the IBYCUS system and Thesaurus Linguae Graecae to secure the data that are then examined. The fourth study in this group, however, approaches its target expression through 'text rhetoric'.

The only study of the five that does not focus on a single expression is as broad as the others are narrow. It attempts to survey some of the interpretative problems in Paul as they are cast in contemporary linguistics and translation theory. It may be useful to summarize the five papers.

25. D.A. Carson, *The Gagging of God* (Grand Rapids: Zondervan, forthcoming).

The general essay, 'Interpreting the Language of St Paul: Grammar, Modern Linguistics and Translation Theory' by Dennis L. Stamps, argues that in addition to the kind of interpretative theological pluralism widely shown today to belong to all interpretative endeavours, we are now faced with 'a pluralism in grammatical theory'. Contemporary linguistic theory has generated developments in lexical semantics that question the approach (or at least the popular utilization) of a standard tool like BAGD, while developments in syntax question the usefulness and accuracy of large parts of BDF. But while challenging the standard works, these linguistic developments are not built on a monolithic theoretical basis: Chomskian linguistics, text linguistics, systemic linguistics and other theories all jostle for a place at the table.

In addition, there are older problems on which there is still no universal agreement: for example, the precise nature of the Greek of the New Testament and its place in the Hellenistic world, and the impact of diverse translation theories. Turning to Paul, his long and complex sentences, difficult euphemisms, expressions with wide-ranging denotations and connotations (e.g. σάρξ), disputed structures with considerable exegetical significance (e.g. πίστις θεοῦ), peculiar style (and even what 'style' means!), forms of argumentation and rhetoric, all conspire, Stamps suggests, to leave more questions open-ended than we have been accustomed to in the past.

Of the four studies of words or short expressions, the first three utilize, in different ways, the IBYCUS system and the data collected by the Thesaurus Linguae Graecae project, and the first two are the most traditional in approach, but certainly not less interesting for that.

The first, 'On the Use of the Word παστός in Patristic Greek' by Eugene N. Lane, follows up an earlier article in which he argued that the word παστός in Greek of the Hellenistic and Roman periods always refers, 'in authors who are careful with its meaning', to a bridal cloth or a canopy of some sort, and then, especially in the epigrammatists, comes to be used 'as a sort of banal symbol of marriage or of sexual union'.[26] It does not refer to a bridal bed or a bridal chamber, despite the claims of modern dictionaries, and despite the misunderstanding even of some sources in late antiquity. The original article included a treatment of the occurrences of the word in the Septuagint, and noted the Vulgate's mistaken rendering *thalamus*. Lane's present article probes the occurrences in Patristic Greek.

26. E.N. Lane, 'ΠΑΣΤΟΣ', *Glotta* 66 (1988), pp. 100-23.

In a work remarkable for its informed and subtle reading, Lane in his present study argues that earlier usages continue, but with one or two remarkable developments. Some writers clearly understand the meaning of the word. In both pagan and Christian writings παστός is still used in a non-comprehending way 'as a banal symbol of marriage'. But many of the church fathers use it in such a way that the marriage itself is symbolic, not least when they are engaged in allegorical interpretations of Ps. 19.5 and Joel 2.15-16. Further, it is only in Christian authors that παστός becomes confused with παστάς, which is phonically similar but not etymologically related. This probably accounts for the translation error *thalamus* in the Vulgate and for the confusion in modern scholarship.

The essay by Andreas J. Köstenberger, 'Syntactical Background Studies to 1 Timothy 2.12 in the New Testament and Extrabiblical Greek Literature', like that of Lane, is far from deploying the tools and technical vocabulary of linguistics developed this side of de Saussure. In some respects it reflects a traditional approach to syntax. But it is innovative in its use of the IBYCUS system to define and resolve a well-known problem in 1 Tim. 2.12. The passage in question reads: διδάσκειν δὲ γυναικὶ οὐκ ἐπιτρέπω οὐδὲ αὐθεντεῖν ἀνδρός, ἀλλ' εἶναι ἐν ἡσυχίᾳ. Köstenberger views the meaning of αὐθεντεῖν, based on traditional word studies, an open matter: the evidence is not decisive. After surveying the more important literature on the force of οὐδέ in similar contexts, he sets himself the task of recovering every instance in the Greek New Testament, in the LXX, and in the relevant extrabiblical Greek literature of the construction: (1) negated finite verb[27] + (2) infinitive + (3) οὐδέ + infinitive, and, if available, + (4) ἀλλά + infinitive.

What he argues, in brief, is that without exception in the substantial number of examples, the two infinitives joined by οὐδέ in this construction are either both positive in connotation but their exercise is prohibited or their existence denied owing to circumstances or conditions adduced in the context, or both viewed negatively by the author, and consequently their exercise is prohibited or to be avoided or their existence is denied. In no case was one viewed positively and the

27. Strictly speaking, as his examples show, this element is restricted in the extrabiblical sources to negated finite verbs *in the indicative*, which is of course relevant to 1 Tim. 2.12, though of course it makes his conclusions a little less comprehensive.

other negatively. The results for contemporary exegesis of 1 Tim. 2.12 are significant.

The third study, by H. Alan Brehm, is titled 'The Meaning of Ἑλληνιστής in Acts in Light of a Diachronic Analysis of ἑλληνίζειν'. The well-known *crux interpretum* at Acts 6.1 cannot easily be resolved, owing primarily to the rarity of the noun in the New Testament and related Hellenistic materials, but also to the stark fact that the proposed solutions do not tie up the loose ends—for example, it is difficult to make any solution mesh easily with the other occurrences of Ἑλληνιστής in Acts (6.9; 9.29; 11.20) and with Paul's use of the parallel term Ἑβραῖοι in Phil. 3.5 and 2 Cor. 11.22. The dominant three solutions, of course, are (1) that 'Hebrews' and 'Hellenists' refer in both cases to Jews, but to distinctions in linguistic orientation: the first group spoke Aramaic, and the second Greek; (2) that the two terms refer to groups with different attitudes to the law and to temple ritual; (3) that the two terms refer to a geographic distinction, viz. Jews from Palestine and Jews from the Diaspora respectively (a solution that substantially overlaps, though not in connotation, with the first solution). There are of course many variations on these solutions.

What Brehm does is examine, with the help of IBYCUS and the TLG database, the use of the cognate verb in the relevant literature. In the first instance his approach is diachronic. This enables him to demonstrate that in the first century both the linguistic and the cultural usages occur. Synchronic, syntagmatic and paradigmatic examinations of the relevant expressions in the New Testament follow. Brehm concludes that Pauline usage must be judged different from that of Acts, and that in Acts 6.1 the best distinction is the linguistic one.

Micheal Palmer contributes the final essay: 'τί οὖν; The Inferential Question in Paul's Letter to the Romans with a Proposed Reading of Romans 4.1'. Influenced by the linguistic theory of Leech,[28] Palmer seeks to establish what kind of discourse marker τί οὖν; is in the letters of Paul, particularly in Romans. By 'discourse marker' he refers to a linguistic unit that signals 'a relationship between discourse units larger than individual sentences or utterances'. Palmer concludes that, with variations, τί οὖν; displays two major and quite different functions. The expression may introduce a question that is based on a false inference in order to eliminate a potentially distracting argument from the flow of the rhetoric; alternatively, introduced questions that carry no implied

28. G. Leech, *Principles of Pragmatics* (LLL; London: Longman, 1983).

false inference function so as to create pauses that focus on some crucial principle in the argument.

Palmer classifies every instance in Romans, drawing attention to subtle details as he proceeds. He finds the rhetorical structure at the beginning of ch. 4 sufficient warrant to support further the suggestion of R.B. Hays,[29] to the effect that Rom. 4.1 be punctuated, τί οὖν ἐροῦμεν; εὑρηκέναι Ἀβραὰμ τὸν προπάτορα ἡμῶν κατὰ σάρκα; ('What then shall we say? Have we found Abraham [to be] our forefather according to the flesh?').

29. 'Have we Found Abraham to be our Forefather according to the Flesh? A Reconsideration of Romans 4:1', *NovT* 27 (1985), pp. 76-98.

INTERPRETING THE LANGUAGE OF ST PAUL: GRAMMAR, MODERN LINGUISTICS AND TRANSLATION THEORY[1]

Dennis L. Stamps

Introduction

The discipline of biblical studies has always lived with the reality of theological pluralism, that is, it is readily acknowledged that differing theological perspectives determine or at least affect a critic's exegesis of a biblical text.[2] But in the recent upsurge of grammatical analyses of the New Testament or Hellenistic Greek based on modern linguistic theory, New Testament interpreters are faced with a pluralism in grammatical theory.[3]

Many New Testament specialists are trained in the theory of historical-critical or historical-grammatical exegesis.[4] The goal of this theory is

1. For a much expanded version of this paper with a much different emphasis, see D.L. Stamps, 'Interpreting the Language of St Paul', in D. Jasper (ed.), *Translating Religious Texts: Translation, Transgression and Interpretation* (New York: St Martin's, 1993), pp. 21-43.

2. The classic statement is still R. Bultmann, 'Is Exegesis without Presuppositions Possible?', in *New Testament and Mythology and Other Basic Writing* (trans. S.M. Ogden; London: SCM Press, 1984), pp. 145-53.

3. D.D. Schmidt, *Hellenistic Greek Grammar and Noam Chomsky* (SBLDS, 62; Chico: Scholars Press, 1981); J.P. Louw, *Semantics of New Testament Greek* (Philadelphia: Fortress Press, 1982); S.E. Porter, *Verbal Aspect in the Greek of the New Testament, with Reference to Tense and Mood* (SBG, 1; New York: Peter Lang, 1989), and *idem*, *Idioms of the Greek New Testament* (Biblical Languages: Greek, 2; Sheffield: JSOT Press, 1992); B.M. Fanning, *Verbal Aspect in New Testament Greek* (Oxford: Clarendon Press, 1990); P. Cotterell and M. Turner, *Linguistics and Biblical Interpretation* (London: SPCK, 1989).

4. E. Krentz, *The Historical-Critical Method* (Guides to Biblical Scholarship; Philadelphia: Fortress Press, 1975). Exegetical manuals include G. Fee, *New Testament Exegesis* (Philadelphia: Westminster Press, 1983); H. Conzelmann and A. Lindemann, *Interpreting the New Testament* (trans. S.S. Schatzmann; Peabody, MA: Hendrickson, 1988).

complicated, but can be essentially stated as twofold. First, critics seek to understand the text in its original language as the original author intended within the context of the original historical situation and audience. Secondly, critics seek to communicate this understanding in their own language or so that others can share the critics' professionally and 'scientifically' secured understanding of the original text. In effect, the exegetical interpretative process is a matter of grammar and translation.

The two main tools of exegesis which assist the critic in working towards an understanding of the original text remain, first, the lexicon (e.g. Liddell and Scott for classical Greek, and Bauer, Arndt, Gingrich and Danker for Hellenistic and especially New Testament Greek),[5] which is usually supplemented by Kittel's theological dictionary, and secondly, the reference grammar (e.g. Blass, Debrunner and Funk, or A.T. Robertson).[6] Modern linguistic theory regarding both lexical semantics and syntax has brought both tools under question.[7]

For instance, the meaning of words is shown to be dependent upon the theory of meaning one subscribes to, and there is no modern consensus for biblical scholars to anchor their lexical analysis upon. Theories of meaning include referential, ideational or mentalistic, meaning-is-use, and truth-conditional perspectives.[8] What Liddell and Scott, and Bauer *et al.* have done is to mask the theoretical issue.

The same situation applies to matters of grammar. For example, understanding verbs in the New Testament depends on the grammatical notion of time and aspect one adopts for the Greek verbal system.[9] Similarly, as one recent article has exposed, the standard exegetical resource grammar, 'BDF', is fatally flawed in terms of modern linguistic theory.[10] Not only is BDF dependent on an archaic notion of language, comparative philology, but it is also linguistically naive and downright

5. M. Silva, *Biblical Words and their Meaning: An Introduction to Lexical Semantics* (Grand Rapids: Zondervan, 1983), esp. pp. 18-32.

6. S.E. Porter and J.T. Reed, 'Greek Grammar since BDF: A Retrospective and Prospective Analysis', *FN* 4 (1991), pp. 143-64.

7. S.E. Porter, 'Keeping up with Recent Studies: 17. Greek Language and Linguistics', *ExpTim* 103 (1992), pp. 202-208.

8. Porter, 'Keeping up', pp. 202-203. See also Cotterell and Turner, *Linguistics*, pp. 77-105; Silva, *Biblical Words*, pp. 137-69.

9. Porter, 'Keeping up', pp. 203-206; Porter and Reed, 'Greek Grammar', pp. 149-56.

10. Porter and Reed, 'Greek Grammar', pp. 143-49.

sloppy when it comes to grammatical analysis of New Testament Greek on a structural level.[11]

So while grammatical studies of the New Testament utilizing modern linguistic insights are 'correcting' some of these faults, they are not presenting a single, conclusive grammatical approach to all aspects of Hellenistic Greek grammar. Some studies utilize Chomskian linguistics, others systemic linguistics.[12] The biblical critic needs to understand the options before using a 'look-up and footnote' approach to grammars when interpreting a text.

In the study which follows, a number of key interpretative problems associated with the writings of St Paul will be 're-exposed', especially as their interpretative dilemmas impinge on the analogous matter of translation. These interpretative problems are not only exacerbated because the traditional critical tools are themselves suspect, but because modern linguistics provides a smorgasbord of theoretical options. The primary question that emerges is whether, in light of this interpretative conundrum brought on by or at least latent in the recent application of modern linguistics to the study of New Testament Greek grammar, the exegetical goal needs redefining.

Interpretative Issues in the Language, Style and Rhetoric of St Paul's Writings

St Paul's writings have always posed distinct interpretative problems. Little has been written recently of a general or broad nature that addresses the issue of how Paul's language and style impinge upon the specific issues of linguistics, grammar and translation.[13] Most comments that relate to such issues are buried away in discussions of specific exegetical problems found in Paul's writings. Many earlier discussions of Paul's language and style occupy themselves with Paul's personality, that is, how does he come across in the way he writes? One well-known modern grammarian stated the situation this way: 'St Paul's Epistles

11. Porter and Reed, 'Greek Grammar', pp. 143-49.

12. Consider the various linguistic models used in the grammars noted in n. 3.

13. A.B. Spencer's *Paul's Literary Style* (Jackson, MS: Evangelical Theological Society, 1984) is an exception, but see the review by S.E. Porter, *JETS* 28 (1985), pp. 502-504. N. Turner, *A Grammar of the Greek New Testament.* IV. *Style* (Edinburgh: T. & T. Clark, 1976), has a chapter on the style of Paul, but mainly to prove Semitic influence.

surge along with the fervid heat of a very agile mind and a highly strung temperament, thinking and feeling as an Aramaean, but thoroughly familiar with the vocabulary of the Greek world'.[14]

A key problem with Paul's language and style is that his writings are composed in a 'dead' language: Hellenistic Greek.[15] Since there are no native speakers, the lexical, grammatical, and syntactical forms and structures are foreign and second-hand to any reader or critic. The full nuances of Paul's linguistic expressions remain locked away in a linguistic code to which no modern critic or translator has all the keys.

With the above in mind, it makes any assessment of Paul's language and style somewhat arbitrary. Nevertheless, something can be said about the kind of Greek found in Paul's letters, and about the lexical and syntactical peculiarities sometimes associated with interpreting and translating Paul's Greek.

First, a point needs to be made about Paul's linguistic code.[16] Scholars a long time ago thought the Greek of the New Testament was a 'Holy Ghost Greek'.[17] It was imagined that just as God had incarnated himself in a perfect man, Jesus, so God accommodated his revelation in a 'holy' language, New Testament Greek. After the papyri were unearthed, A. Deissmann and J.H. Moulton over-corrected all that by demonstrating that the words and grammar of the New Testament were aspects of the common everyday 'non-literary' language of the Mediterranean world.[18] Literary Greek was preserved in the upper social classes, in the court and among the philosophers and poets.

The debate regarding the nature of New Testament Greek persists, with some concluding that, in contrast to classical Greek writings

14. C.F.D. Moule, *An Idiom Book of New Testament Greek* (Cambridge: Cambridge University Press, 2nd edn, 1957), p. 3.

15. The best discussion 'defining' Hellenistic Greek in relation to the New Testament is S.E. Porter, *What is New Testament Greek?* (Sheffield: Sheffield Academic Press, forthcoming). See also S.E. Porter (ed.), *The Language of the New Testament: Classic Essays* (JSNTSup, 60; Sheffield: JSOT Press, 1991).

16. See Porter, *Verbal Aspect*, pp. 141-56.

17. See the discussion, S.E. Porter, 'Introduction: The Greek of the New Testament as a Disputed Area of Research', in *Language*, pp. 27-28.

18. A. Deissmann, *Light from the Ancient East* (trans. L.R.M. Strachan; London: Hodder & Stoughton, 1910), and *The Philology of the Greek Bible: Its Present and Future* (trans. L.R.M. Strachan; London: Hodder & Stoughton, 1908); J.H. Moulton, *A Grammar of New Testament Greek*. I. *Prolegomena* (Edinburgh: T. & T. Clark, 3rd edn, 1908).

and even literary writings contemporary with the New Testament, the language of the New Testament appears crude, a corrupted and diluted Greek spoiled by all the dialectical inbreeding from 'inferior' cultures.[19] Such conclusions are backed up by sociological analysis of the first Christians as emanating from the lower-class within the Hellenistic world.[20] But recent linguistic study of New Testament Greek and recent sociological studies of early Christians show that there was social diversity both in the language employed and in the people who wrote it.[21] Even within the spectrum of New Testament writings there exists what one might call a stylistic continuum which most likely existed throughout the Mediterranean world.[22] Regarding Paul's Greek, when one compares it with so-called vulgar Greek, when one considers that he wrote to a number of Greek speaking cities scattered throughout the Mediterranean world, and when one realizes that the patristic commentators on Paul's writings say virtually nothing about his Greek being inferior, all of this makes it likely that he was simply using the Hellenistic Greek common to his day.[23]

In sum, it appears that the source language of Paul's writings is of a quality associated with a fluent speaker of the primary language of his day. But a critic's decision about the quality and status of Paul's Greek in the context of the ancient world will affect interpretation of those Greek texts believed to have been composed by Paul.

Perhaps what Paul's Greek is best known for is its protracted and detoured sentences. N. Turner notes, 'Paul allows himself to be drawn along on the wings of his thought in sharp bursts, resulting in parentheses and discords, while particles and participles are brought in to weave over gaps in the diction'.[24] Two classic Pauline examples are Gal. 2.6 and 1 Tim. 1.3 where the relationship between clauses seems as complex

19. Compare the interesting remark by J. Lambrecht, 'Rhetorical Criticism and the New Testament', *Bijdragen* 50 (1989), p. 246, about the New Testament having 'sub-literary' texts.

20. Usually supported by reference to 1 Cor. 1.26.

21. A.J. Malherbe, *Social Aspects of Early Christianity* (Philadelphia: Fortress Press, 1983), pp. 29-59; G. Theissen, *The Social Setting of Pauline Christianity* (trans. J.H. Schütz; Edinburgh: T. & T. Clark, 1982), pp. 69-119; E.A. Judge, *The Social Patterns of Christian Groups in the First Century* (London: Tyndale Press, 1960), pp. 49-61.

22. Porter, *Verbal Aspect*, pp. 152-56.

23. Porter, *Verbal Aspect*, p. 156.

24. Turner, *Style*, p. 86.

as a spaghetti junction. Long sentences are not necessarily peculiar to Paul or to the Greek of his day, however. The problem with Paul, as noted above, is trying to determine the syntactical connections and relationships within a nexus of independent and subordinate clauses. Given the lack of punctuation in the original language, Paul's sentences lack rounding off or an obvious finish, especially Paul's harsh use of parentheses (Rom. 1.13; Eph. 2.5) and anacolutha (Rom. 9.22, 23; 2 Cor. 12.17). Quite simply the problem is that many of the syntactical relationships that are problematic in these sentences become accentuated in a receptor language like English. These complex sentences are not necessarily concrete instances of bad Greek, but grammatical expressions of ambiguous and complex thought relationships which a critic and translator must decide to keep ambiguous or interpret and translate unambiguously.

More specific than Paul's Greek writing style is the problem of the lexical distance between ancient Greek and any modern receptor language. For example, there are euphemisms. Does γυναικὸς μὴ ἅπτεσθαι (1 Cor. 7.1) mean, 'not to marry' as in the TEV, or more basically and literally, as in the AV, 'not to touch a woman'? More Pauline is the repetitious and polyvalent use of σάρξ, literally 'flesh', which the NIV translates variously as 'the body' (Col. 1.22), or 'sinful nature' (Rom. 13.14), or 'human nature' (Rom. 1.3), or 'from a worldly point of view' (2 Cor. 5.16), or even 'by human standards' (1 Cor. 1.26), but which the AV leaves in almost all cases as 'the flesh'.[25] Is Paul's use of the word σάρξ euphemistic so that translating according to its different connotations correctly captures the sense of the word in each context, or is Paul's use of the word stylistic thereby possibly justifying a literal translation in most cases? Modern linguistic theories of meaning do not solve the matter, but open up the options. The challenge is for critics to know why they interpret/translate a word the way they do.

More problematic in Paul's Greek lexicography and semantics is the use of the Greek genitive case. This presents real theological problems for interpreters and translators. For example, there is fierce debate over

25. For examples of studies which address this specific issue, see A.C. Thiselton, 'The Meaning of *Sarx* in 1 Cor. 5.5: A Fresh Approach in the Light of Logical and Semantic Factors', *SJT* 26 (1973), pp. 204-28; R. Jewett, *Paul's Anthropological Terms: A Study of their Use in Conflict Settings* (Leiden: Brill, 1971).

πίστις Χριστοῦ as either an objective genitive, 'faith in Christ', or a subjective genitive, 'Christ's faithfulness'.[26] Equally ambiguous is the often used phrase, ἡ ἀγάπη τοῦ θεοῦ. Translators of Paul must also wrestle with key concepts like 'righteousness' and 'reconciliation', with expressions like 'justification by faith' and 'in Christ', with the Pauline antitheses, death/life, sin/righteousness, flesh/spirit, law/grace, works/faith, slave/free, old/new man. Rendering all these into a receptor language entails another decision between leaving the translation as ambiguously literal, if not opaque, or as an unambiguous transparent interpretation.[27] And is that unambiguous interpretation always decided on the basis of merely the literary context, or is there theological motivation? Or can a critic-cum-translator even hope to distance him- or herself from any 'ideological/theological' bias?

An even more ambiguous and often overlooked matter with respect to Paul's style and linguistic self-presentation is his rhetoric. Scholars debate how much Paul's writings show evidence of a deliberate use of the ancient art of classical rhetoric.[28] But few interpreters of Paul are unimpressed by the rhetoric of argumentation in evidence in his writings whatever the degree of classical influence.

For instance, there is Paul's rhetoric of argumentation in which one encounters the rhetoric of religious assertion versus philosophical demonstration, what G.A. Kennedy has called 'radical Christian rhetoric'.[29] One critic of Paul's rhetoric, D. Jasper, has noted the appearance of argumentation in Rom. 5.18-21 in which the discourse proceeds with logical connectives: ἄρα οὖν, 'it follows, therefore', v. 18; ὥσπερ γάρ, 'for as', οὕτως καί, 'thus also', v. 19; ἵνα ὥσπερ, 'so that just as'

26. For arguments for the subjective and objective positions respectively, see M.D. Hooker, 'ΠΙΣΤΙΣ ΧΡΙΣΤΟΥ', *NTS* 35 (1989), pp. 321-42; J.D.G. Dunn, *Romans 1–8* (WBC, 38a; Dallas: Word Books, 1988), pp. 166-67.

27. On transparent versus opaque, see S. Prickett, *Words and 'The Word'* (Cambridge: Cambridge University Press, 1986), pp. 35-36.

28. See the discussions, S.E. Porter, 'The Theoretical Justification for Application of Rhetorical Categories to Pauline Epistolary Literature', in S.E. Porter and T.H. Olbricht (eds.), *Rhetoric and the New Testament* (JSNTSup, 90; Sheffield: JSOT Press, 1993), pp. 100-22; but compare H.D. Betz, 'The Problem of Rhetoric and Theology according to the Apostle Paul', in A. Vanhoye (ed.), *L'Apôtre Paul: Personnalité, style et conception du ministère* (BETL; Leuven: Leuven University Press, 1986), pp. 16-48.

29. G. A. Kennedy, *New Testament Interpretation through Rhetorical Criticism* (Chapel Hill: University of North Carolina Press, 1984), p. 7.

...οὕτως καί, 'thus also', v. 21—but is actually a series of assertions and antitheses strung together by some 'hidden' logic.[30] One New Testament critic sanctifies this authoritative rhetoric, calling it 'the rhetoric of faith argumentation'.[31] Interpreting Paul's rhetoric presents a serious problem for the interpreter or translator: how to convey this manner of argumentation in the translation or commentary.

In this brief discussion, the matters and problems of translating Paul's language, style, vocabulary, rhetoric, and so forth, can only be hinted at. When interpreting the writings of Paul, one also confronts the issues of what Paul did or did not write even though his name is attached to a given text as the author (or at least as the sender),[32] of the text's historical texture which recreates a historical distance between the modern reader and the ancient text, and of the text's literary structure as a personal letter following ancient epistolary form.[33]

Conclusion

Paul's language, style and rhetoric pose interpretative problems. Many of those problems relate to matters of word meaning and grammatical analysis. The standard lexicons do not establish meaning for the critic/translator, but present a classification of meanings in a receptor language. The critic has the responsibility for deciding which classification, if any, applies to the word under scrutiny. Yet, as modern linguistics has made clear, that decision is subject to the implications of the models of linguistic meaning the critic is working with.

At this point something needs to be said about the allusions to translation sprinkled throughout this study. In many senses, what seminary and university students, and often their teachers, are after in their exegesis is an understanding of the Greek text by means of English or another

30. D. Jasper, *Rhetoric, Power and Community* (London: Macmillan, 1992).

31. W. Wuellner, 'Paul's Rhetoric of Argumentation in Romans', *CBQ* 38 (1976), p. 351.

32. Cf. G.J. Bahr, 'Paul and Letter Writing in the First Century', *CBQ* 28 (1966), pp. 465-77, who sees the amanuensis as having a large role in the writing of the text; and E.R. Richards, *The Secretary in the Letters of Paul* (WUNT, 2/42; Tübingen: Mohr, 1991), who gives extensive details about the epistolographers in the ancient world, but few hints about the role of the secretary in the Pauline epistles.

33. On this, see D.L. Stamps, *The Rhetorical Use of the Epistolary Form in 1 Corinthians: The Rhetoric of Power* (JSNTSup; Sheffield: Sheffield Academic Press, forthcoming).

receptor language. In many cases the driving force in exegesis is this second-language interpretation. But the Greek of the New Testament is structurally different from English and other modern Indo-European languages. So any explanation of New Testament Greek with reference to English grammar falls into a 'translation' gap.[34]

Does not this situation of a plurality of linguistic theories for meaning and grammar, this situation of explaining Greek texts in a secondary language, pose a hermeneutical dilemma? Should critics not abandon the goal of finding the meaning of a text and surrender to the reality that critics only offer readings of a text and that every text has many readings? Such readings are affected not only by the theological system a critic subscribes to, but also by the linguistic theory a critic subscribes to.

34. S. Bassnett-McGuire, *Translations Studies* (New Accents; London: Routledge, 1980), pp. 15-38; B. Hatim and I. Mason, *Discourse and the Translator* (Language in Social Life Series; London: Longman, 1990), pp. 55-75; G. Steiner, *After Babel: Aspects of Language and Translation* (Oxford: Oxford University Press, 1975), pp. 1-109.

ON THE USE OF THE WORD παστός IN PATRISTIC GREEK

Eugene N. Lane

In an earlier article[1] I investigated the use of the word παστός in Greek of the Hellenistic and Roman periods. I was able to show that in authors who are careful with its meaning, the word always refers to a bridal canopy or cloth of some sort, similar in use to the Jewish *chuppa*, not to a bridal bed or chamber, as present-day dictionaries have it, and as it was sometimes misunderstood even in late antiquity. In this sense it still survives in some parts of Cyprus, where the word is used to designate the cloth which covers the chest on which bride and groom sit to receive their guests. I was also able to show that the Vulgate mistranslates the word as *thalamus* in the various places in which it occurs in the Septuagint (where it represents Hebrew *chuppa*), something which has caused widespread mistranslation in modern languages. But most commonly the word comes to be used, particularly in the epigrammatists and in Nonnus's *Dionysiaca*, as a sort of banal symbol of marriage or of sexual union. One very widespread commonplace uses the word in epitaphs for both men and women who die young, as a symbol of the marriage which they did not achieve.

In that article I did not pursue the use of the word very far into Patristic Greek, except to cite one usage each from Cyril of Alexandria and from pseudo-John Chrysostom and two from Clement of Alexandria, all of which I will repeat below. The acquisition by the University of Missouri Classics Department of an IBYCUS scholarly computer and the Thesaurus Linguae Graecae CD ROM has enabled me to extend my search further. In the following article I will pass in review all the passages which I found in this fashion, as well as those cited in G.W.H. Lampe's *Patristic Greek Lexicon*[2] and a few additional

1. 'ΠΑΣΤΟΣ', *Glotta* 66 (1988), pp. 100-23.

2. Oxford: Clarendon Press, 1961. I have omitted only Lampe's citation from Alexander Salaminius, as there seems to be no recent or accessible edition of the text in question.

examples which have come to my attention by chance. There can be no doubt but that other instances of the word are lurking in unindexed works, but those that I have collected suffice to show that ecclesiastical authors who use the word are very heavily indebted to the two passages in the canonical Old Testament where it is used, Ps. 19.5 and Joel 2.15-16. This fact results in another symbolic usage of the word, by authors who, like Nonnus and the epigrammatists, had little idea of what it actually meant, but this time not as a symbol of a physical marriage, but in an entirely new spiritualized sense. The two Old Testament passages, which the reader will need for reference, follow:

> Ps. 19.5: καὶ αὐτὸς (sc. ἥλιος) ὡς νυμφίος ἐκπορευόμενος ἐκ παστοῦ αὐτοῦ ἀγαλλιάσεται ὡς γίγας δραμεῖν ὁδὸν αὐτοῦ.
> And he (the sun) proceeding like a bridegroom from his παστός will rejoice like a giant to run his course.

> Joel 2.15-16: σαλπίσατε σάλπιγγι ἐν Σίων, ἁγιάσατε νηστείαν, κηρύξατε θεραπείαν, συναγάγετε λαόν, ἁγιάσατε ἐκκλησίαν, ἐκδέξασθε πρεσβυτέρους, συναγάγετε νήπια θηλάζοντα μαστούς, ἐξελθάτω νυμφίος ἐκ τοῦ κοιτῶνος αὐτοῦ, καὶ νύμφη ἐκ τοῦ παστοῦ αὐτῆς.
> Sound the trumpet in Sion, make holy a fast, announce a service, bring together the people, make holy an assembly, receive the elders, bring together the babes suckling the breasts, let the bridegroom come out from his bed, and the bride from her παστός.

But before I start listing the instances of the word in ecclesiastical Greek, let me cite two previously undiscussed uses in pagan literature. Both of these, however, simply use the word as a banal symbol of marriage, like the instances gathered from epigraphy, the Greek Anthology, and so on, in my earlier article.

1. Pseudo-Bion, *Epithalamium Achillis et Deidamiae* 8-9:

> ᾇδες...χὤπως ἐν κόραις Λυκομηδίσιν...ἠείδη κατὰ παστὸν Ἀχιλλέα Δηιδάμεια.
> You sang...and how among the daughters of Lycomedes...Deidameia knew Achilles in the παστός.

It is interesting that this poem, which has attracted virtually no scholarly attention, uses a word otherwise unknown in the bucolic tradition, but at home among the epigrammatists. This may provide some clue as to its actual authorship.

2. 'Musaeus', *Hero and Leander* 280-81:

> Σιγὴ παστὸν ἔπηξεν, ἐνυμφοκόμησε δ' Ὀμίχλη,
> καὶ γάμος ἦν ἀπάνευθεν ἀειδομένων ὑμεναίων.
> Silence set up the παστός, Fog adorned the bride,
> and the marriage was without sung wedding-hymns.

This passage is informative only in that it recognizes that the παστός is something (e.g., a shelter) that needs to be set up.[3]

Let me turn now to the passages in Christian authors. As might be expected, most of them are either banal wedding imagery (as in the pagan authors, but with a Christian twist) or quotations of or references to the two Old Testament usages of the word, in Psalms and Joel, with various Christianizing interpretations of wedding imagery.[4]

I will list the citations, starting with those most stylized, but not necessarily least informative, and leading up to those which actually show some knowledge of the nature of a παστός as a physical object. They will be listed alphabetically by author's name, rather than chronologically. Some passages which merely repeat the scriptural verses will be relegated to footnotes. I of course take my conclusion, established in the earlier article, that a παστός, provided the author knows what real object the word refers to, is always a cloth such as a canopy, as my basis for passing judgment on the reliability of these newly considered passages.

3. I cite here some passages from the grammarians, which shed almost no light on the situation. (For that reason they were generally left out of consideration in the earlier article.)

Herodian Grammaticus (2nd cent.; *De Prosodia Catholica* 3.1.217.4 in A. Lentz [ed.], *Grammatici Graeci* [repr. Hildesheim: Olms, 1965]) cites παστός among words (e.g., μαστός) ending in -στος that are accented on the ultima.

Pseudo-Herodian (of late but uncertain date) in his *Partitiones* three times cites the word: (a) 93.15, as a definition for νυμφεῖος, which he cites among a list of words beginning in νυ-, and (b) and (c) 173.12 and 263.11, likewise as a definition for νυμφεῖος, which he is distinguishing from νυμφίος (= γαμβρός).

This at least dates pseudo-Herodian to a time when iotacism had led to such confusion that it needed to be set straight. It is also unclear what noun the author understands with the adjective νυμφεῖος in order to be able to gloss it with παστός. At all events, the author is aware that the word is somehow connected with marriage.

4. Such as we have seen in the Christian inscription of Rome, discussed on p. 110 of my earlier article. Significantly, the first editor of this inscription thought it was an epithalamium, rather than a Christian hymn.

3. First on our list is a passage in the *Acta Thomae* (124.23, ed. M. Bonnet, in *Acta Apostolorum Apocrypha* II, 2 [Leipzig: Mendelssohn, 1903]) contrasting an earthly with a heavenly marriage:

> ἐκεῖνος ὁ γάμος ἐπὶ γῆς ἵστησιν φιλανθρωπίαν δροσίζων, ἐκεῖνος ὁ παστὸς λύεται πάλιν, οὗτος δὲ διὰ παντὸς μένει.
> That marriage, refreshing, establishes affection on earth; that παστός is dissolved again, but this one remains forever.

This is Christianized wedding imagery, but without reference to the scriptural passages.[5]

4. Athanasius[6] uses the word three times in his works, the first (*Sermo de Patientia*, *PG* XXVI, 1308.38) being a simple quotation of the passage from Joel. The second (*Expositio in Psalmos*, *PG* XXVII, 124.43), however, is an explication of the psalm passage. First Athanasius defines the σκήνωμα (tabernacle) as οἶκος (house), and then says, τοῦτον τὸν οἶκον καὶ παστὸν ὠνόμασεν, 'He (the Lord) also called this house παστός'. Thus the tabernacle in which the sun is said to dwell is equated with the παστός out of which he is said to come through their both being a house. This exegesis shows no real knowledge of the word's meaning. In the third passage (*Vita Sanctae Syncleticae*, *PG* XXVIII, 1489.42) the subject of the biography is being compared with Thekla. For both of them, their union with Christ is being compared with a marriage and the church is said to be their παστός. The reference to Psalms or Joel is missing, but we have mere banal wedding imagery, Christianized.

5. The word is to be found three times in the writings of Clement of Alexandria. The first citation (*Eclogae Propheticae* 56.1.4) merely quotes the psalm passage given above. The second time, *Protrepticus* 2.15.3.4 (ed. Mondésert, Paris: Cerf, 1949), Clement gives the alleged formula of the Attis mysteries:

5. In the sixteenth homily on Psalm 5, a spurious work attributed to Asterius Amasenus (*PG* XL, 404 C), we find a slight variant on our psalm passage:

> καὶ ὁ ἥλιος ὡς νυμφίος ἐκ τοῦ παστοῦ τῆς ἀνατολῆς προέρχεται.
> And the sun like a bridegroom comes forth from the παστός of the East.

6. See also under Origen, below, where there is mention of a gloss attributed to Athanasius.

> ἐκ τυμπάνου ἔφαγον, ἐκ κυμβάλου ἔπιον, ἐκερνοφόρησα, ὑπὸ τὸν παστὸν ὑπέδυν.
> I ate from the drum, I drank from the cymbal, I carried the kernos, I got under the παστός.

This passage is atypical for the use of the word among Christian authors, as it cites what purports to be a pagan formula. Certainly Clement, knowing the scriptural passages, must have known that a παστός was an accoutrement of marriage, and he seems to be using the word to hint vaguely at lascivious goings-on in the cult of Attis. In this he is followed by Eusebius (see below). In a second passage from the same work (4.54.6.7) Clement is referring to the behavior of Demetrius Poliorcetes in Athens:

> Λαμίαν δὲ τὴν ἑταίραν ἔχων εἰς ἀκρόπολιν ἀνῄει, καὶ τῷ τῆς Ἀθηνᾶς ἐνεφυρᾶτο παστῷ, τῇ παλαιᾷ παρθένῳ τὰ τῆς νέας ἐπιδεικνὺς ἑταίρας σχήματα.
> He went up onto the Acropolis with the prostitute Lamia and had sex with her [or so the euphemism seems to mean] in Athena's παστός, showing off the wiggling of the young prostitute to the old virgin.

Provided Clement knows of the actual existence of some object referred to as a παστός on the Athenian Acropolis, it would seem to be some sort of fabric structure for ritual use, but probably unconnected with marriage, given Athena's reputation as a virgin. The associations of the word, however, allow Clement to switch easily to lascivious implications.

6. Cyril of Alexandria uses the word twice. In his *Commentary on Joel 7* (*PG* LXXI, 341B) he says,

> πλὴν οὐ τεθρήνηκεν ἡ τῶν Ἰουδαίων συναγωγὴ τὸν ἐξ οὐρανοῦ νυμφίον, τοῦτ' ἔστι Χριστόν. αὕτη γὰρ ἀπέκτεινεν καὶ πεπαρῴνηκεν εἰς αὐτόν. τοιγάρτοι τῶν θείων εἴργεται παστῶν, ἔξω τε τῶν ἱερῶν ἐστι γάμων, καὶ τῆς ἑορτῆς ἀμέτοχος παντελῶς.
> Except that the Jewish synagogue has not mourned over the heavenly bridegroom, that is, Christ. For she [the synagogue] killed him and behaved drunkenly towards him. Therefore she has been excluded from the heavenly παστοί, and is outside the holy marriage, and has absolutely no part in the festival.

Here the use of our word has clearly passed over into the realm of Christ-as-bridegroom imagery.

And in *Commentary on John's Gospel 2* (*PG* LXXIII, 232 D), taking as his starting point the wedding at Cana, and expanding the lesson from the inhabitants of Galilee to all the heathen, Cyril says that Jesus εἰς τὸν οὐράνιον εἰσάξει παστόν, εἰς τὴν τῶν πρωτοτόκων Ἐκκλησίαν δηλαδή, 'will lead [them] into the heavenly παστός, that is, into the Church of the first-born'. The use of a word full of wedding imagery was probably suggested by the wedding at Cana, which is, after all, what Cyril was commenting on.

7. In two passages of pseudo-Epiphanius (*Homilia in Laudes Mariae Deiparae*, *PG* XLIII, 489.23, and *Testimonia ex divis et sacris scripturis* 5.44.3) we have quotations of the psalm passage, in the first of which the sun coming out of his παστός is clearly taken as a metaphor for Christ. A few lines before the quotation, the author, writing in his own words, uses the term παστάς, obviously the same for him as παστός. These two words, superficially similar, actually refer to quite different objects—παστάς is a side-room or women's chamber—and although both can refer obliquely to sexual activity, there is no etymological relationship. So we can conclude that the word had no real meaning for him.[7]

8. In one of the Sermons of Eusebius of Alexandria (*PG* LXXXVI/1, 432D) we read, in reference to the parable of the wise and foolish virgins:

> αἱ πέντε φρόνιμοι παρθένοι...οὐχ ὕπνωσαν, ἀλλὰ τοῦ νυμφῶνος ἀνοιγέντος εἰσῆλθον μὴ παρεμποδιζόμεναι εἰς τὸν βασιλικὸν παστόν.
> The five wise virgins...did not sleep, but when the bridal chamber was opened they entered unhindered into the royal παστός.

Once again we are in the realm of spiritualized wedding imagery.

9. Eusebius of Caesarea uses the word three times: once (*Praep. Evang.* 2.3.18.4) he quotes the so-called Attis-formula, which we already know from Clement of Alexandria, who may be supposed to be Eusebius's source.

7. For confusion caused by the superficial similarity of the etymologically unconnected words παστός and παστάς, see the discussion in my earlier article, pp. 107-108. Can it be concluded from this that pseudo-Epiphanius had no knowledge of Cypriot usage, something that his namesake must have acquired as Bishop of Constantia? The Cypriots are the only people to have retained παστός in their vocabulary.

Twice (*Generalis Elementaria Introductio* 82.6 and *Commentaria in Psalmos*, *PG* XXIII, 192.11) he quotes the psalm passage. It is hard to see how Eusebius, familiar with this passage, could have avoided connecting the usage here with that of the 'Attis-formula'. Thus he too, like Clement, must have assumed some sexually lascivious goings-on in the Cybele and Attis cult—the word here would have retained for him its sexual meaning only, without the benefit of spiritual allegory. Thus it is impossible to justify the meaning 'cave' suggested by some modern authorities.[8]

10. Hesychius of Jerusalem quotes the psalm passage twice (*In Sanctum Lazarum* 11.8.9; 10.10, ed. Aubineau, *Subsidia Hagiographica* 59, 1978) and thus shows no independent knowledge of the word. It is clear, however, from the second passage, in which the author goes ahead to paraphrase παστοῦ with παστάδος, that confusion between the two terms was already complete.

11. Hippolytus uses the word once, *In Proverbia* (*PG* X, 617A), speaking of virtues which elevate one's knowledge of God:

> ἃς (sc. ἀρετὰς) ὁ τηρῶν τὴν σοφίαν τιμᾷ· μισθὸς δέ, τὸ μετεωρισθῆναι καὶ περιληφθῆναι ὑπ' αὐτῆς ἐν τῷ ὑπερκοσμίῳ παστῷ.
>
> The person who observes these [virtues] honors wisdom. And the reward is to be lifted up towards her and included by her in the supramundane παστός.

Here we have a sort of spiritualized marriage with divine wisdom.

12. John Chrysostom, or an author or authors writing under his name, also provide us with several passages.

In two places (*De Virginitate* 30.26 and *Ad Populum Antiochenum*, *PG* XLIX, 52.50) the genuine John Chrysostom simply cites the passage from Joel to bolster the argument he is making. Five others (*Ad Populum Antiochenum*, *PG* XLIX, 116.24, *Ad eos qui scandalizati sunt* 7.15.8, *In Genesim*, *PG* LIII, 57.64, *In Ioannem*, *PG* LIX, 153.37, and *In Epistulam ad Ephesios*, *PG* LXII, 67.60) are citations of the psalm passage. In one of them (that to the people of Antioch) John Chrysostom shows that he, like pseudo-Epiphanius, confuses παστός

8. E.g., M.J. Vermaseren, *Cybele and Attis* (London: Thames & Hudson, 1977), p. 117 (discussed in my previous article, p. 119).

and παστάς, for he paraphrases the psalm with the words καθάπερ... ἐκ παστάδος τινὸς νυμφίος φανείς.

The next passages, not directly quoting either the psalm or Joel, are all from works falsely attributed to John Chrysostom, and show considerable imagination in using a word whose meaning is obviously not understood.

In *In Sanctum Pascha* 45.3.6 pseudo-John Chrysostom is apparently describing how God made himself in Jesus a proper receptacle (δοχεῖον) for the Holy Spirit. There is a series of aorist active participles describing how God separated out what was bad in human nature, and then how he purified that which was clean and transparent (καθαρὸν καὶ διαυγές). One of these participles is the remarkable and, so far as I know, unique formation παστώσας. Clearly, therefore, a παστός was something pure and admirable in pseudo-John Chrysostom's mind. Its association with the participle παρθενεύσας ('virginizing') shows for sure that our author does not know what the word means—wedding imagery has been stood on its head!

Secondly, in *De Paenitentia* (*PG* LX, 687.5) pseudo-John Chrysostom is enumerating the various punishments meted out to evil-doers. He says,

> εἰς τὰς αἰωνίους μονὰς ἀπηνεῖς κληρονομίαν οὐκ ἔχουσιν, εἰς τὸ ἐμὸν παλάτιον ἄσπλαγχνος οὐκ εἰσέρχεται, εἰς τὸν οὐράνιον παστὸν ἀνελεήμων οὐκ ἀξιοῦται, εἰς τὰς ἄνω μονὰς ἀμετάδοτος οὐ κατοικεῖ...
> Harsh people do not have inheritance in the eternal dwellings, an unfeeling person does not enter my palace, an unmerciful person is not judged worthy of the heavenly παστός, an uncommunicate person does not live in the dwellings above...

Again, a παστός is obviously good, a reward denied the evil, but there is no hint of genuine knowledge.

And in *In Illud, Pater Si Possibile Est* (*PG* LXI, 754.66) pseudo-John Chrysostom, apparently putting words into Jesus' mouth, refers to Judas. Talking about people falling into their own traps, he says,

> οὐκ οἶδεν ὅτι ὃν μέλλει ἱστᾶν σταυρὸν ἐμοὶ μέν ἐστι παστός, ἐκείνῳ δὲ σταυρός· ἐμοὶ μέν ἐστι θάλαμος, ἐκείνῳ δὲ θάνατος.
> He does not know that the cross which he is going to set up is a παστός for me, but a cross for him; it is a [bridal] chamber for me, but death for him.

The conjunction of the word θάλαμος—the word which, Latinized, mistranslates παστός in the Vulgate[9]—although used for its similarity in sound to θάνατος ('death'), at least shows us that pseudo-John Chrysostom, in this passage, remains in the mainstream of Christianized wedding imagery.

Next, in a passage (*In Adorationem Venerandae Crucis*, *PG* LXII, 752.43) describing how the heavens became dark at the Crucifixion, pseudo-John Chrysostom describes the sky *inter alia* as

> τὸν κυανοβαφῆ θάλαμον, τὸν πυρσοφόρον παστόν, ἐν ᾧ ἥλιος καὶ σελήνη, ὡς νυμφίος καὶ νύμφη, προκάθηνται.
> The blue-dyed chamber, the torch-bearing παστός, in which Sun and Moon, like groom and bride, sit publicly.

Banal wedding imagery abounds, but no real knowledge is shown of a παστός, in spite of the fact that the term is now used in Cyprus for something on which a newly married couple sits. Only by a violent figure could a παστός be called 'torch-bearing', as it might catch fire from the torches! The only hint of our author's having some inkling of the real meaning of the word is if one thinks he may have been referring to a baldachin of some sort.

Finally, in *Contra Theatra* (*PG* LVI, 551.31), speaking of Abraham's planned sacrifice of Isaac, the author contrasts Isaac with a bridegroom:

> ἀντὶ στεφάνων δεσμά, ἀντὶ γυναικὸς μάχαιρα...παρίσταται δὲ καὶ ὁ νέος, οὐ παστοῖς ἐστεφανωμένος, ἀλλὰ βωμῷ δεδεμένος, καὶ φορῶν οὐκ ἐσθῆτα γαμήλιον, ἀλλὰ σχῆμα θανάσιμον.
> Instead of wreaths, fetters; instead of a woman, a knife...The young man is also present, not crowned with παστοί, but tied to an altar, and wearing not wedding attire, but a death-costume.

In this passage it becomes fairly evident that the author had no exact idea what a παστός was, except that it was connected with marriage. However, if one could be crowned with one, then in this author's conception it certainly is not a chamber or a bed, and is likely to be a cloth object. We may, however, have helped establish that all these works by pseudo-John Chrysostom are by the same hand, if they all show the same kind of fondness for the extravagant use of a misunderstood word.[10]

9. See the discussion in my earlier article pp. 107-108, 119.

10. Another John, the lesser-known John Philoponus, simply cites the Psalm passage, *De Opificio Mundi* 142.16.16. Likewise, in contrast to the ebullient and

13. 'Macarius'—that is to say, the name to which much Egyptian ascetic literature is ascribed—uses the word somewhat imaginatively again, in both cases in a context of Christianized wedding imagery. The first time (*Sermones 64* 2.12.16.7) he is re-telling the story of Moses:

> ἡ γὰρ ῥάβδος καὶ ἡ πέτρα μεγάλην ἑορτὴν τοῖς Ἰσραηλίταις παρεῖχε καὶ ὥσπερ εἰς παστόν τινα καὶ νυμφῶνα ἔθαλπον αὐτούς.
> The staff and the stone provided the Israelites a great feast and, so to speak, cared for them in a kind of παστός and a bridal chamber.

And in a listing of various paradoxical attributes of Christ (*Homiliae 7* 52.7.12), he says,

> αὐτός ἐστιν ὁ νυμφίος, καὶ αὐτός ἐστιν ἡ νύμφη· αὐτός ἐστιν ὁ νυμφών, καὶ αὐτός ἐστιν ὁ παστός.
> He is the groom, and he is the bride; he is the bridal chamber, and he is the παστός.

The association both times with the word νυμφών ('bridal chamber'), to say nothing of the further wedding associations in the second passage, show the context in which Macarius knew the word. But there is nothing to indicate that he had any idea of what the object was, besides the little that can be derived from Psalms and Joel.

14. We turn now to Nonnus of Panopolis, whom we have already observed to be, in his pagan epic, the *Dionysiaca*, one of the most prolific users of the word παστός,[11] even if he is one of those most guilty of using it with meaningless vagueness. When Nonnus writes a Christian work, his verse paraphrase of St John's Gospel, he also uses the word three times (2.2.5, 14, and 55). It should come as no surprise that all three uses are apropos of the wedding at Cana. But, as such, they show a continuation of the pagan use of the word in regard to actual human weddings, not a metaphorical, Christianized use of the word. The vocabulary of the passages also continues to reek of contrived, late

imaginative use by pseudo-John Chrysostom of a word whose meaning he did not know, it is sobering to turn to the two uses of the word by the admittedly much earlier Justin Martyr (*Apologia* 40.4.2 and *Dialogus cum Tryphone* 64.8.8). Both are extensive quotations from Ps. 19, used as part of Justin's argumentation.

11. See my earlier article, p. 101. In his pagan epic, Nonnus uses the term as a vague symbol of marriage or sexual union no fewer than 43 times. Strangely enough, ten of these instances take place under water, something which may be indicative of a peculiar obsession on Nonnus's part.

pagan poetic diction, rather than the typical (and simpler) usages of the Church Fathers. One example suffices (2.2.14):

> οἴνου δ᾽ ἡδυπότοιο θυώδεες ἀμφιφορῆες
> πάντες ἐγυμνώθησαν ἐπασσυτέροισι κυπέλλοις
> πινομένου, στυγνοὶ δὲ φιλακρήτῳ παρὰ παστῷ
> οἰνοχόοι δρηστῆρες ἀβαχεύτοιο τραπέζης
> ἀβρέκτοις παλαμῆσι μάτην ἥπτοντο κυπέλλων.
>
> The sweet-smelling amphoras were all denuded of wine, sweet to drink, since it was being drunk with ever swifter cups, and the glum wine-stewards by the παστός fond of unmixed wine, culprits of the un-Bacchussed table, vainly touched the cups with unmoistened palms.

In this curious, barely Christianized work, παστός is used as if a synonym for a wedding or a wedding-feast. Except for its Christian content, this passage could have been classed with those of Pseudo-Bion and Musaeus. We may, however, with our observation, have helped lay to rest any lingering suspicion about the attribution of this work to Nonnus.

15. The word παστός is three times to be found in the corpus of Origen. All instances are quotations from or indebted to Psalm 19. In *Selecta in Psalmos* (*PG* XII, 1244.13)—a dubious work—there is a quotation from the psalm followed by the explanation that the bridegroom is Christ. In *Scholia in Canticum Canticorum* (*PG* XVII, 277.54), Origen uses an allusion to the psalm to say that Christ came from the heavenly παστός. The most interesting, however, is *Fragmenta in Psalmos* 18.6.3-5—a dubious work—not because of anything Origen says, but because of an attached gloss attributed to Athanasius:

> Παστὸν τὴν Παρθένον ἐκάλεσεν, ἐξ ἧς ὁ νυμφίος Χριστὸς ἐπορεύετο, παντὸς ῥύπου καθαρός, ἀπὸ καθαρᾶς παστάδος προερχόμενος.
>
> He called the Virgin a παστός, from which the bridegroom Christ proceeded, clean from all filth, coming forth from a clean παστάς.

This odd interpretation of course shows the lack of comprehension which Athanasius had of a παστός, but also displays the confusion with παστάς, which I have already had occasion to mention in the case of pseudo-Epiphanius and John Chrysostom.[12]

12. Finally among the Christian authors who show no real understanding of the word is Theophilus of Antioch. In his *Ad Autolycum* 3.12.23 he simply includes a quotation of the passage in Joel.

Let us turn now to those Christian authors who seem to betray some knowledge of what a παστός really is.

16. Hesitantly here I include Amphilochius. In *De recens Baptizatis* 90 and 91, he uses the word παστός twice in rapid succession, in speaking of Christ's crucifixion and resurrection:

> σταυρὸς ἔστη καὶ Χριστὸς ἐφηπλώφη καὶ θάνατος ἄδικος ἦν τὸ φαινόμενον, καὶ θάλαμος ἅγιος ἦν τὸ γινόμενον· σταυρὸς ἦν τὸ φαινόμενον, καὶ παστὸς ἦν τὸ τελούμενον· χθὲς ἀνέστη παστὸς καὶ σήμερον ἐτέχθη λαός.
>
> A cross was set up and Christ was spread out on it and an unjust death was the appearance and a holy bride-chamber was the happening; a cross was the appearance and a παστός was the event. Yesterday a παστός was set up and today a people was born.

This passage, with its contrast of παστός and σταυρός, θάνατος and θάλαμος, is quite reminiscent of one of the passages from pseudo-John Chrysostom. Nonetheless, I have chosen to include it here because (a) like the banal pagan use of παστός, it seems to have a firm grasp of the use of a παστός in a real marriage, which leads to childbirth, but primarily because (b) the use of the verb ἀνέστη ('was set up') indicates, however faintly, that Amphilochius may have had an actual canopy-like structure in mind. The word also, of course, serves as a pun on Christ's ἀνάστασις or resurrection. Note also the play on τελούμενον and τελετή ('ceremony').

17. An author or authors posing as St Basil also use the word, three times. One (*De Jejunio*, *PG* XXXI, 1508.30) is a mere quotation of Joel in a context in which pseudo-Basil is discussing fasting, a topic also discussed by Joel.

But the other two are of greater interest—one showing some knowledge of what a παστός is, but the other using such a violent mixed metaphor as to make one think that pseudo-Basil did not know the nature of the object. In *Homilia de Virginitate* 78.79.5, discussing the parable of the wise and foolish virgins, pseudo-Basil says,

> καὶ διὰ τοῦτο νύμφαι οὐκ ἤκουσαν, καὶ εἰς ἄφθαρτον νυμφῶνα οὐκ ἔφθασαν, καὶ παστὸν αὐτῶν οὐκ ἐξέτειναν, καὶ διὰ τοῦτο βασιλείας οὐρανῶν στέφανον οὐκ ἐδέξαντο, καὶ τῷ ἀθανάτῳ νυμφίῳ οὐκ ὡμίλησαν.

> And on this account the maidens [or 'brides'] did not hear, and did not arrive at the incorruptible marriage-chamber, and did not stretch out their παστός, and on this account they did not receive the crown of the kingdom of heaven, and did not converse with the heavenly bridegroom.

There is, remarkably, no reference to Psalms or Joel, and, although the context—as indeed the parable being glossed—uses a wedding in a figurative sense, one gets the impression that pseudo-Basil has the details of a real wedding before his eyes. The παστός is to be stretched out, and the specifically Christian use of crowns or wreaths in the marriage ceremony is also alluded to.

What a change, therefore, in an earlier passage of the same work (1.44.6) and in reference to the same parable, when pseudo-Basil tells his addressee,

> στέφανον καθαρὸν λόγοις ἁγνείας συμπλέκων προστίθει, ἵνα ἐκεῖνα ποθοῦσα (sc., the addressee's daughter) προθύμως ἐπιβαίνῃ εἰς τὸν ἄχραντον τοῦ Χριστοῦ νυμφῶνα, ταῖς φρονίμοις παρφένοις συντρέχουσα, ὅπως καὶ σὺ ὁ γεννήσας παστὸν βασιλείας τρυγήσῃς, καὶ αὐτὴ ἀφθαρσίας στέφανον δέξηται.
> Weaving a clean crown [wreath] with words of holiness, add it to her, so that desiring those things she may eagerly go up to the unsullied bridal-chamber of Christ, concurring with the wise virgins, that you her father may press out the vintage of the παστός of the kingdom and she may receive the crown of incorruptibility.

To make a παστός the object of a grape-harvest is so exuberant (and untranslatable) a conceit that, here, at least, pseudo-Basil cannot have had any specific object in mind.[13]

18. Eustathius was Bishop of Thessalonike, but his principal writings are a commentary on Homer, and thus concerned with grammar, not theology. I might therefore have been justified in classing him with Herodian and pseudo-Herodian, rather than here. But his better knowledge of the word deserves separate treatment. At all events, in both passages where he uses the word παστός he is discussing the use of the verb πάσσειν in Homer, from which he, probably correctly, derives the noun παστός.

In *Commentary on the Iliad* 4.119.2, after mentioning παστός the salt meat, he says,

13. The confused usage by pseudo-Basil reminds me of the confused imagery by Harriet Beecher Stowe in the well-known *Battle Hymn of the Republic*: 'He is trampling out the vintage where the grapes of wrath are stored'.

> μεταφορικῶς δὲ καὶ παστὸς ὁ νυμφικός, ὁ ἔχων πέπλους οἷς ἐμπάσσονται τρόπον τινὰ τὰ ἐπιπολῆς δαίδαλα ποικίλματα, κατὰ τὸ 'πολέας δ' ἐνέπασσεν ἀέθλους'.[14]
>
> Metaphorically there is also the bridal παστός, which has hangings into which are worked (ἐμπάσσονται) in a certain way the superficial elaborate decorations, as in the passage, 'she worked in (ἐνέπασσεν) many feats'.

Likewise, in 4.254.25 of the same work, he says,

> τὸ δὲ ῥηθὲν 'πάσσειν' Κυπρίων, φασί, λέξις, ὅθεν καὶ 'παστός'.
>
> The πάσσειν we are talking about is, they say, a Cypriot word, whence is derived παστός.

Eustathius clearly knows, then, what a παστός really is. The latter passage, indeed, is extremely tantalizing, as it possibly indicates that Eustathius knew of the survival of the word παστός in Cyprus in his own day, the twelfth century CE.

16. Penultimately, Palladius, *Historia Lausiaca* 82.5 and 7, speaking of a certain Amoun, one of the saints of Egypt, compelled by his uncle reluctantly to marry:

> καὶ μὴ δυνηθεὶς ἀντισχεῖν τῇ τοῦ θείου ἀνάγκῃ, ἔδοξε καὶ στεφανοῦσθαι καὶ καθέζεσθαι ἐν παστῷ, καὶ πάντα ὑπομεμενηκέναι τὰ κατὰ τὸν γάμον. μετὰ δὲ τὸ ἐξελθεῖν πάντας κοιμήσαντες αὐτοὺς ἐν τῷ παστῷ καὶ τῇ κλίνῃ, ἀναστὰς ὁ 'Αμοῦν ἀποκλείει τὴν θύραν, καὶ καθίσας προσκαλεῖται τὴν μακαρίαν αὐτοῦ σύμβιον καὶ λέγει αὐτῇ...
>
> And not being able to withstand his uncle's compulsion, he decided to be crowned [in marriage] and to sit in the παστός and to have endured everything connected with marriage. After everyone had gone out, when they were supposed to sleep [?—the Greek is so ungrammatical as to defy translation] in the παστός and the bed, Amoun, getting up, locked the door, and, sitting, he summoned his blessed spouse and said to her [that they will henceforward sleep separately and keep their virginity intact].

Whatever may be made of the grammar, Palladius clearly has a real wedding in mind, as did Nonnus in his description of the wedding at Cana, and furthermore has a specific object in mind, on or under which the bride and groom first sat and which later was expected to cover the

14. This is the passage from *Iliad* 3.126, also cited by the Augustan-period grammarian Apollonius Sophista, who appears to know both the literal meaning and the correct etymology of παστός. See my earlier article, p. 111.

nuptial bed. Palladius thus goes one better than Nonnus, and is probably the most reliable of the Christian authors for the actual meaning of the word.

20. The last passage I wish to cite is from a dubious work of Anastasius Sinaita, *Stories Useful and Supportive to the Soul*, ed. F. Nau, *Oriens Christianus* 3 (1903), p. 74, line 28:

> καθεζομένου ἐμοῦ καὶ τοῦ Φιλίππου ἐν τῷ παστῷ τῷ νεοφωτιστικῷ, ἰδοῦ εἰσέρχεται ὁ προειρημένος ὅσιος ἐπίσκοπος εἰς ἐπίσκεψιν τοῦ Φιλίππου.
>
> While I and Philip were sitting in the παστός of the newly enlightened [i.e., newly baptized], behold, in comes the aforesaid holy bishop to visit Philip.

This unparalleled use of the word, in a vernacular document to be dated c. 700 CE, is taken by Lampe to refer to a baptistry. Since, however, the baptism had taken place some days before, we may imagine that the newly baptized Philip was assigned a place to sit under a special kind of canopy, just as we see elsewhere in this account (p. 75, lines 5-6) that he had a special garment to wear for some time after his baptism. In this case baptism may be viewed as a sort of marriage into the church. The passage certainly seems to think of the παστός as a specific object; it neither uses the term symbolically, nor is it indebted to Scripture.

Conclusion

Although I have ended with a few Christian authors who seem clearly to have known what a παστός was, they are greatly in the minority. The most significant thing, I think, which this collection of attestations has shown is a further development in the use of a non-understood word.

In my earlier article I showed not only what παστός really means, but also that the word was frequently used in a non-comprehending way as a banal symbol of marriage. I have now adduced further examples of this kind of usage from pseudo-Bion, Musaeus and Nonnus (in a Christian writing).

With all these people, although the παστός may be meaningless symbolism, at least the marriage is real enough. The majority of the Church Fathers, however, take matters one step farther. For them the marriage is itself symbolic. This fact, combined with allegorical interpretations of Psalm 19 and of Joel, allows the παστός to become something magnificently vague—indeed, the vaguer the more magnificent. This finds its culmination in some of the usages by pseudo-John Chrysostom, for whom one can be crowned with a παστός, for whom a παστός is the opposite of a cross, and for whom a παστός, through a derived verb, can end up being the equivalent of virginity! The word is thus totally stood on its head.

It is probably also significant that it is only in Christian authors (John Chrysostom, pseudo-Epiphanius, Hesychius of Jerusalem, and Athanasius glossing Origen) that we have found overt confusion between παστός and παστάς. In my earlier work on the word[15] I discussed the fact that these two etymologically unrelated, but similar-sounding words become confused in antiquity at least in the Vulgate and in the Hesychius glosses, and certainly become confused in modern scholarship. We are now able to see that this confusion, among Greek authors, occurs only in Christian writings. Since these are probably the Greek authors whom St Jerome most frequently read, we can now all the more easily see how he was misled into his translation of παστός as 'thalamus', something which continues to plague translations of the Bible into modern languages.

15. See my earlier article, pp. 107-108. I communicated my conclusions regarding the word παστός to the committee editing the NRSV of the Bible, and this resulted in the word 'canopy' rather than'chamber' being used in both Old Testament passages.

Syntactical Background Studies to 1 Timothy 2.12 in the New Testament and Extrabiblical Greek Literature

Andreas J. Köstenberger

Introduction

The statement in 1 Tim. 2.12, 'I do not permit a woman to teach or to exercise authority over a man', occupies a central position in the contemporary debate on the role of women in the church. To this day, no agreement has been reached regarding the proper rendering of this passage. While exegetical and hermeneutical issues cannot be dealt with here, this study will seek to establish an accurate translation of the text.[1] A new methodological approach will be taken, utilizing the IBYCUS system. A search of extrabiblical Greek literature in the relevant time period will provide a significantly enlarged database that will aid in the study of one syntactical construction found in 1 Tim. 2.12. It is hoped that the clarified translation of this text will advance its proper interpretation.

The Recent Debate

The most disputed translational matter in 1 Tim. 2.12 is the meaning of αὐθεντεῖν. Since this is the only instance in the entire New Testament and since the expression is also very rare in extrabiblical literature, certainty regarding its meaning remains elusive. Should αὐθεντεῖν be rendered 'to have or exercise authority' (NIV, NRSV and NASB) or 'to domineer or usurp authority' (NEB and AV; cf. TEV)? If the former, this passage could be seen as supporting the claim that women should not be

1. For a treatment that incorporates the findings of this study into a comprehensive interpretation of 1 Tim. 2.12, see H.S. Baldwin, A.J. Köstenberger and T.R. Schreiner (eds.), *Women in the Church: A Fresh Analysis of 1 Timothy 2:11-15* (Grand Rapids: Baker, forthcoming).

permitted to exercise authoritative teaching functions over men in the church. If the latter, 1 Tim. 2.12 would only prohibit women from teaching men 'in a domineering way'.

Word Studies

The primary approach taken to resolve this issue has been that of word studies.[2] The most recent study by Baldwin, using the IBYCUS system, concludes that 'to assume authority over' and 'to rule' are the only meanings for αὐθεντεῖν that are unambiguously attested for the period surrounding the New Testament. However, owing to the following factors word studies of αὐθεντεῖν need to be complemented by another approach.

First of all, the number of occurrences of αὐθεντεῖν in literature roughly contemporary with the New Testament is very small. Baldwin gives only three references from the first century BCE to the second century CE where the verb αὐθεντεῖν occurs: Philodemus's *Rhetorica* (first century BCE), Ptolemy's *Tetrabiblos* (second century CE) and a non-literary papyrus dated 27 BCE (BGU 1208). The scarcity of data should keep one from claiming certainty regarding the meaning of αὐθεντεῖν based on word studies alone.

Also, word studies are not the hard science they are sometimes made out to be. They can help establish the lexical core of a given term, but they should not be used to exclude the possibility that a word can take on a certain connotation, in the case of αὐθεντεῖν a negative one, as some have sought to argue.[3]

Finally, modern linguistics cautions against absolutizing any one lexical equivalent for a given term. It is agreed that, ultimately, a word's context is determinative for its meaning. Since word studies deal with a finite number of contexts, they should not be expected to settle with certainty the meaning of a word in any possible context. Owing to the

2. Cf. C.D. Osburn, '*Authenteo* (1 Timothy 2:12)', *ResQ* 25 (1982), pp. 1-12; G.W. Knight, 'Αὐθεντέω in Reference to Women in 1 Timothy 2.12', *NTS* 30 (1984), pp. 143-57; L.E. Wilshire, 'The TLG Computer and Further Research into Αὐθεντέω in 1 Timothy 2.12', *NTS* 34 (1988), pp. 120-34; *idem*, '1 Timothy 2:12 Revisited: A Reply to Paul W. Barnett and Timothy J. Harris', *EvQ* 65 (1993), pp. 43-55; and H.S. Baldwin, 'Αὐθεντέω and 1 Timothy 2:12: New Evidence concerning the Use of αὐθεντέω in 1 Timothy 2:12' (paper presented at the Annual ETS Conference, 20 November 1992).

3. Cf., e.g., G.W. Knight, *The Role Relationship of Men and Women* (Phillipsburg, NJ: Presbyterian and Reformed, rev. edn, 1985), p. 18 n. 1.

limited contribution of word studies, other creative approaches need to be explored. Is it possible that οὐδέ as a coordinating conjunction joins two words in a particular syntactical pattern which could shed light on the meaning of these words?

Syntactical Analyses

The need for syntactical background studies to understand 1 Tim. 2.12 has been recognized by Payne and Moo, who engaged in a detailed interchange on the syntactical significance of οὐδέ in 1 Tim. 2.12.[4] Payne argued that οὐδέ connects the two infinitives διδάσκειν and αὐθεντεῖν 'in order to convey a single coherent idea', that is as a hendiadys, so that the rendering of the passage should be: 'I do not permit a woman to teach *in a domineering manner*'.[5] Moo, however, has maintained that, while οὐδέ 'certainly usually joins "two *closely related* items", it does not usually join together words that restate the same thing or that are mutually interpreting'.[6] He has concluded that, while teaching and having authority are closely related, 'they are nonetheless distinct', referring also to 1 Tim. 3.2, 4-5 and 5.17 which distinguish those concepts.[7] Indeed, Payne's study is subject to improvement at several points.

1. Payne studies only Paul. A more comprehensive study of οὐδέ in the entire New Testament seems desirable to broaden the database available for comparison.

2. Payne studies all the occurrences of οὐδέ in Paul, even where it joins nouns, not verbs. However, one should sharpen the focus by studying the passages where οὐδέ joins verbs, since that is the construction found in 1 Tim. 2.12.[8]

3. Payne does not consider uses of μηδέ in Paul or elsewhere in the

4. Cf. P.B. Payne, 'οὐδέ in 1 Timothy 2:12' (paper presented at the Annual ETS Conference, 21 November 1986); D.J. Moo, '1 Timothy 2:11-15: Meaning and Significance', *TrinJ* NS 1 (1980), pp. 62-83; and *idem*, 'The Interpretation of 1 Timothy 2:11-15: A Rejoinder', *TrinJ* NS 2 (1981), pp. 198-222.

5. Cf. Payne, 'οὐδέ', p. 10.

6. Cf. D.J. Moo, 'What Does it Mean not to Teach or Have Authority over Men? 1 Timothy 2:11-15', in J. Piper and W. Grudem (eds.), *Recovering Biblical Manhood and Womanhood: A Response to Evangelical Feminism* (Wheaton, IL: Crossway, 1991), p. 187.

7. Cf. Moo, 'What Does it Mean', p. 187.

8. Studies of passages where οὐδέ links nouns yield similar results as studies of instances where οὐδέ connects verbs.

New Testament. Only seven instances remain where Paul uses οὐδέ to connect verbs (1 Cor. 15.50; 2 Cor. 7.12; Gal. 1.17; 4.14; Phil. 2.16; 2 Thess. 3.8; 1 Tim. 6.16). References including μηδέ in writings traditionally attributed to Paul provide eight further examples (Rom. 9.11, 16b; 14.21; 2 Cor. 4.2; Col. 2.21; 2 Thess. 2.2; 1 Tim. 1.3-4; 6.17). Two of these, 1 Tim. 1.3-4 and 6.17, occur in the same letter.

4. Payne starts with the assumption that αὐθεντεῖν means 'domineer'. However, the meaning of αὐθεντεῖν in 1 Tim. 2.12 should not be merely asserted, but be established by an inductive study of all the instances of οὐδέ joining verbs in the New Testament and extra-biblical Greek literature.

5. Since Payne presupposes that αὐθεντεῖν means 'domineer', he concludes that 'teach' and 'domineer' by themselves are conceptually too far apart to be joined by οὐδέ—which usually joins closely related terms—in a coordinating manner. Thus Payne views the second term joined by οὐδέ, in 1 Tim. 2.12, αὐθεντεῖν, as subordinate to the first, διδάσκειν. However, if αὐθεντεῖν were to mean 'to have authority' rather than 'to domineer', it would be quite closely related to διδάσκειν, 'to teach'. In that case, consistent with Payne's own observations on how οὐδέ generally functions, οὐδέ could well link the two closely related terms 'to teach' and 'to have authority' in a coordinating fashion. Payne's argument is circular, and his conclusion is unduly predetermined by his presupposition regarding the meaning of αὐθεντεῖν.

6. Payne's terminology is ambiguous when he calls two terms 'closely related'. He seems to use this terminology in the sense of 'essentially one' so that he can conclude that in 1 Tim. 2.12 'οὐδέ joins together two elements in order to convey a single coherent idea'. However, as will be shown below, two terms can be 'closely related' and yet be distinct. For example, Mt. 6.20 refers to heaven 'where thieves neither break in nor steal'. While 'breaking in' and 'stealing' are sequentially related and may be seen as components of essentially one event, that is burglary, the two activities are not so closely related as to lose their own distinctness. The burglar first breaks in, and then steals.

7. Payne's terminology categorizing the use of οὐδέ is inconsistent. At the beginning of his study, he terms words in his second category 'those which specify with greater clarity the meaning of one word or phrase by conjoining it with another word or phrase'.[9] Yet in his

9. Cf. Payne, 'οὐδέ', p. 1.

conclusion, he argues that 'οὐδέ joins together two elements in order to convey a single coherent idea'.[10] From beginning to end, Payne has subtly shifted from one category to another. While his initial definition allows for terms to be closely related and yet distinct, Payne's later categorization unduly narrows his earlier definition so that now closely related yet distinct terms seem excluded.

8. Payne only notes translations that support his own understanding of 1 Tim. 2.12, that is, those that render αὐθεντεῖν with 'domineer' or similarly negative connotations.[11] However, he fails to observe that NRSV, NIV, NASB and a host of other recognized translations do not render the term with a negative connotation. The NASB has 'exercise authority', the NIV and NRSV translate αὐθεντεῖν with 'to have authority'.[12]

Syntactical Parallels to 1 Timothy 2.12 in the New Testament[13]

The passage reads as follows: διδάσκειν δὲ γυναικὶ οὐκ ἐπιτρέπω οὐδὲ αὐθεντεῖν ἀνδρός, ἀλλ' εἶναι ἐν ἡσυχίᾳ. One can lay out the syntactical pattern found in 1 Tim. 2.12 this way: (1) negated finite

10. Payne, 'οὐδέ', p. 10.

11. Payne, 'οὐδέ', p. 10.

12. R.C. Kroeger and C.C. Kroeger, *I Suffer not a Woman: Rethinking 1 Tim. 2:11-15 in Light of Ancient Evidence* (Grand Rapids: Baker, 1991), pp. 83-84 and pp. 189-92, have recently argued for the presence of an 'infinitive of indirect discourse' in 1 Tim. 2.12. These authors translate the passage as 'I do not permit a woman to teach *that she is the author of man*', finding here an allusion to gnostic teaching. However, none of the instances of 'infinitives of indirect discourse' cited by the Kroegers includes οὐδέ. Moreover, a use of οὐδέ similar to ὅτι is unsubstantiated in the New Testament or elsewhere.

13. A few constraints should be noted. Although the title of this essay is '*Syntactical* Background Studies', the conclusions drawn from the syntax of 1 Tim. 2.12 will involve *semantic* judgments (especially in the two patterns of the usage of οὐδέ which will be identified). There are also other syntactical and semantic issues raised by 1 Tim. 2.12 that will not be dealt with in this study, such as the question whether ἀνδρός should be read with both διδάσκειν and αὐθεντεῖν or exactly how the ἀλλά-clause at the end of v. 12 relates to the preceding clause and which verb should be supplied there. Even the verbal aspect or verb tense of the verbs involved will not be dealt with at this stage of this investigation since, as will become evident, the major thesis of this essay is not materially affected by the aspect or tense of the verbs.

verb + (2) infinitive + (3) οὐδέ + infinitive, and, if available, + (4) ἀλλά + infinitive.[14]

Strictly speaking, there is only one close syntactical parallel to 1 Tim. 2.12 in the New Testament, Acts 16.21, where the same construction, a negated finite verb + infinitive + οὐδέ + infinitive, is found.[15] However, if one allows for verbal forms other than infinitives to be linked by οὐδέ, fifty-two further passages can be identified. These can be grouped into two patterns of the usage of οὐδέ.

> *Pattern 1*: two activities or concepts are viewed positively in and of themselves, but their exercise is prohibited or their existence denied owing to circumstances or conditions adduced in the context.
>
> *Pattern 2*: two activities or concepts are viewed negatively and consequently their exercise is prohibited or to be avoided or their existence is denied.

In both patterns, the conjunction οὐδέ coordinates activities of the same order, that is, activities that are both viewed either positively or negatively by the writer or speaker. The instances of *Pattern 1* in the New Testament can be listed as follows.

14. This syntactical pattern is not necessarily always found in this particular chronological order. For example, in 1 Tim. 2.12, the first infinitive precedes the negated finite verb so that the order there is (2), (1), (3) and (4). However, a study of preceding infinitives in Pauline literature indicates that it is hard to find any consistent significance in preceding rather than following infinitives. Cf. the nineteen instances of preceding infinitives in Pauline writings: Rom. 7.18; 8.8; 1 Cor. 7.36; 14.35; 15.50; 2 Cor. 8.10; 11.30; 12.1; Gal. 4.9, 17; Phil. 1.12; 2 Thess. 1.3; 1 Tim. 2.12; 3.5; 5.11, 25; 6.7, 16; 2 Tim. 2.13. At any rate, the central thesis of this essay is not affected by whether the first infinitive precedes or follows the negated finite verb. Likewise, the presence or absence of element (4) does not substantially affect the thesis of this paper.

15. This is one major reason why, after screening less close syntactical parallels, this study will proceed to search extrabiblical Greek literature for more exact parallels involving, as in 1 Tim. 2.12, two infinitives governed by a negated finite verb. However, the fact that, strictly speaking, there is only one close syntactical parallel to 1 Tim. 2.12 in the New Testament does not mean that New Testament passages where a negated finite verb governs two verb forms other than infinitives are without value for identifying general patterns of the usage of οὐδέ. Rather, the New Testament allows one to identify basic patterns of the usage of οὐδέ that can then be tested and refined by referring to extrabiblical Greek literature. This is the approach followed in the present study.

Pattern 1: Two activities or concepts are viewed positively in and of themselves, but their exercise is prohibited or their existence denied owing to circumstances or conditions adduced in the context.

Mt. 6.26	οὐ σπείρουσιν (sow)	οὐδὲ θερίζουσιν (harvest) οὐδὲ συνάγουσιν εἰς ἀποθήκας (gather into barns)
Mt. 6.28	οὐ κοπιῶσιν (labor)	οὐδὲ νήθουσιν (spin)
Mt. 7.6	μὴ δῶτε (give)	μηδὲ βάλητε (throw)
Mt. 7.18	οὐ δύναται ποιεῖν (can yield)	οὐδὲ ποιεῖν (yield)*
Mt. 10.14	μὴ δέξηται (receive)	μηδὲ ἀκούσῃ (listen)
Mt. 13.13	οὐκ ἀκούουσιν (hear)	οὐδὲ συνίουσιν (understand)
Mt. 22.46	οὐδεὶς ἐδύνατο ἀποκριθῆναι (could answer)	οὐδὲ ἐτόλμησέν ἐπερωτῆσαι (dared to ask)
Mt. 23.13	οὐκ εἰσέρχεσθε (enter)	οὐδὲ ἀφίετε εἰσελθεῖν (permit to enter)
Mk 6.11	μὴ δέξηται (receive)	μηδὲ ἀκούσωσιν (listen; cf. Mt. 10.14)**
Mk 8.17	οὔπω νοεῖτε (understand)	οὐδὲ συνίετε (understand)
Mk 13.15	μὴ καταβάτω (go down)	μηδὲ εἰσελθάτω (enter)
Lk. 6.44	οὐ συλλέγουσιν (pick)	οὐδὲ τρυγῶσιν (gather)
Lk. 12.24	οὐ σπείρουσιν (sow)	οὐδὲ θερίζουσιν (harvest; cf. Mt. 6.26)
Lk. 12.27	οὐ κοπιᾷ (labor)	οὐδὲ νήθει (spin; cf. Mt. 6.28)
Lk. 17.23	μὴ ἀπέλθητε (depart)	μηδὲ διώξητε (follow)
Lk. 18.4	οὐ φοβοῦμαι (fear [God])	οὐδὲ ἐντρέπομαι (care [about man])
Jn 14.17	οὐ θεωρεῖ (behold)	οὐδὲ γινώσκει (know)
Acts 4.18	μὴ φθέγγεσθαι (speak)	μηδὲ διδάσκειν (teach)
Acts 9.9	οὐκ ἔφαγεν (eat)	οὐδὲ ἔπιεν (drink)
Acts 16.21	οὐκ ἔξεστιν παραδέχεσθαι (accept)	οὐδὲ ποιεῖν (practice)
Acts 17.24-25	οὐκ κατοικεῖ (dwell)	οὐδὲ θεραπεύεται (be served)
Acts 21.21	μὴ περιτέμνειν (circumcise)	μηδὲ περιπατεῖν (walk [in customs])
Rom. 9.11	μήπω γεννηθέντων (born)	μηδὲ πραξάντων (done)
Rom. 9.16	οὐ τοῦ θέλοντος (wishing)	οὐδὲ τοῦ τρέχοντος (running)
Rom. 14.21	μὴ φαγεῖν (eat)	μηδὲ πιεῖν (drink)

1 Cor. 15.50	κληρονομῆσαι οὐ δύναται (can inherit)	οὐδὲ κληρονομεῖ (inherit)*
Gal. 1.16-17	οὐ προσανεθέμην (consult)	οὐδὲ ἀνῆλθον (go up)
Col. 2.21	μὴ ἅψῃ (touch)	μηδὲ γεύσῃ μηδὲ θίγῃς (taste, handle)
1 Tim. 2.12	διδάσκειν οὐκ ἐπιτρέπω (teach)	οὐδὲ αὐθεντεῖν ἀνδρός (have authority over a man)
1 Tim. 6.16	εἶδεν οὐδείς (see)	οὐδὲ ἰδεῖν δύναται (can see)
Heb. 10.8	οὐκ ἠθέλησας (desire)	οὐδὲ εὐδόκησας (be well-pleased)
1 Jn 3.6	οὐχ ἑώρακεν (see)	οὐδὲ ἔγνωκεν (know)
Rev. 12.8	οὐκ ἴσχυσεν (prevail)	οὐδὲ τόπος εὑρέθη (place be found)*

* = change of subject; ** = change from sg. to pl. verb form

A few explanations will flesh out this pattern. In Acts 16.21, the closest syntactical parallel to 1 Tim. 2.12 in the New Testament, the two terms in the infinitive, παραδέχεσθαι and ποιεῖν, are conceptual parallels. Neither 'accepting' nor 'practicing' carries negative connotations in and of itself. However, owing to circumstances indicated in the context, 'being Romans', the exercise of these otherwise legitimate activities is considered 'not lawful'. In Acts 21.21 Paul is told that there are reports that he forbids Jews living among Gentiles to carry out two activities viewed positively by the speakers, circumcising their children and walking according to Jewish customs. And in Gal. 1.16-17 Paul insists that, upon his conversion, he did not immediately consult with others nor go up to Jerusalem, two activities which are not intrinsically viewed negatively, to underscore that he had been divinely commissioned.

The New Testament occurrences of *Pattern 2* present themselves as follows.

Pattern 2: Two activities or concepts are viewed negatively and consequently their exercise is prohibited or their existence denied or to be avoided.

Mt. 6.20	οὐ διορύσσουσιν (break in)	οὐδὲ κλέπτουσιν (steal)
Mt. 12.19	οὐκ ἐρίσει (quarrel)	οὐδὲ κραυγάσει (cry out)
Lk. 3.14	μηδένα διασείσητε (extort money)	μηδὲ συκοφαντήσητε (accuse falsely)
Lk. 12.33	κλέπτης οὐκ ἐγγίζει (thief come near)	οὐδὲ διαφθείρει (destroy; cf. Mt. 6.20)*

Jn 4.15	μὴ διψῶ (thirst)	μηδὲ διέρχωμαι ἀντλεῖν (come to draw)
Jn 14.27	μὴ ταρασσέσθω (let be troubled)	μηδὲ δειλιάτω (be afraid)
Acts 2.27	οὐκ ἐγκαταλείψεις (abandon)	οὐδὲ δώσεις ἰδεῖν διαφθοράν (give to see decay)
2 Cor. 4.2	μὴ περιπατοῦντες ἐν πανουργίᾳ (walk in deceit)	μηδὲ δολοῦντες (distort)
2 Cor. 7.12	οὐκ ἕνεκεν τοῦ ἀδικήσαντος (the wrongdoer)	οὐδὲ ἕνεκεν τοῦ ἀδικηθέντος (the injured party)**
Gal. 4.14	οὐκ ἐξουθενήσατε (treat with contempt)	οὐδὲ ἐξεπτύσατε (scorn)
Phil. 2.16	οὐκ εἰς κενὸν ἔδραμον (run in vain)	οὐδὲ εἰς κενὸν ἐκοπίασα (labor in vain)
2 Thess. 2.2	μὴ σαλευθῆναι (become unsettled)	μηδὲ θροεῖσθαι (become alarmed)
2 Thess. 3.7-8	οὐκ ἠτακτήσαμεν (be idle)	οὐδὲ ἐφάγομεν (eat another's food)
1 Tim. 1.3-4	μὴ ἑτεροδιδασκαλεῖν (teach error)	μηδὲ προσέχειν μύθοις (pay attention to myths)
1 Tim. 6.17	μὴ ὑψηλοφρονεῖν (be arrogant)	μηδὲ ἠλπικέναι ἐπὶ πλούτου (put hope in wealth)
Heb. 12.5	μὴ ὀλιγώρει (despise)	μηδὲ ἐκλύου (consider lightly)
Heb. 13.5	οὐ μὴ ἀνῶ (leave)	οὐδ' οὐ μὴ ἐγκαταλίπω (forsake)
1 Pet. 2.22	ἁμαρτίαν οὐκ ἐποίησεν (commit sin)	οὐδὲ εὑρέθη δόλος (deceit be found)*
1 Pet. 3.14	μὴ φοβηθῆτε (be afraid)	μηδὲ ταραχθῆτε (be disturbed)
Rev. 7.16	οὐ πεινάσουσιν (hunger)	οὐδὲ διψήσουσιν (thirst)

* = change of subject; ** = used substantivally

The following comments further explain the second pattern, the prohibition or denial of two activities which are viewed negatively by the writer or speaker. In Jn 4.15 the Samaritan woman expresses her desire to avoid two things she views negatively, thirsting and having to come to the well to draw water. In 1 Thess. 3.7-8 Paul denies that at his previous visit he had engaged in two activities which he views negatively, being idle and eating another's food. A passage in the epistle under consideration, 1 Tim. 1.3-4, indicates the instruction to Timothy to command certain people to avoid two activities the author views negatively: teaching error, and holding to myths and endless genealogies. Later in the same epistle, in 1 Tim. 6.17, one finds the instruction to Timothy to command the rich in his congregation(s) to avoid two things viewed negatively by the writer, being arrogant and setting their hope on the uncertainty of riches.

These examples set forth the New Testament evidence that οὐδέ joins terms that denote activities that are either both viewed positively or negatively by the writer or speaker.[16] The implications of this observation for 1 Tim. 2.12 will be explored after the extrabiblical parallels preceding or contemporary with the New Testament have been considered as well.

Syntactical Parallels to 1 Timothy 2.12 in Extrabiblical Greek Literature

The IBYCUS system provides the modern scholar with unprecedented opportunities in the study of ancient literature. It has the capacity of producing more than simply word searches. Although the word entries are not tagged, that is, not morphologically defined, the IBYCUS system, properly managed, is capable of string searches (the search for two or more terms used in conjunction with one another in a given writing) which, properly sifted, yield syntactical units.

In the present case the search pattern presented itself as follows: οὐ, οὐκ or οὐχ, and οὐδέ. The system thus flags all instances where a negative and οὐδέ are used in the same context. Since the IBYCUS system operates with a context of about three lines, some of the references have the negative and οὐδέ too far apart or even in different clauses altogether, so that a manual weeding out of the references is necessary.

16. The following subcategories of this basic pattern may be identified: (1) Synonymous Concepts: Mt. 7.18; Mk 8.17; Jn 14.27; Acts 2.27; 1 Cor. 15.50; Gal. 4.14; Phil. 2.16; 2 Thess. 2.2; 1 Tim. 6.16; Heb. 10.8; 12.5; 13.5; 1 Pet. 3.14; (2) Conceptual Parallels: Mt. 6.28 = Lk. 12.27; Mt. 7.6; 10.14 = Mk 6.11; Mt. 12.19; Lk. 3.14; 6.44; 18.4; Jn 14.17; Acts 4.18; 17.24-25; Rom. 9.16; 2 Cor. 4.2; Col. 2.21; 2 Thess. 3.7-8; 1 Pet. 2.22; 1 Jn 3.6; Rev. 12.8; (3) Complementary Concepts: Acts 9.9; Rom. 14.21; 2 Cor. 7.12; Rev. 7.16; (4) Sequential Concepts: Mt. 6.20, 26 = Lk. 12.24; Mt. 13.13; Mk 13.15; Lk. 12.33; 17.23; Jn 4.15; Rom. 9.11; (5) Ascensive Concepts: Mt. 22.46; 23.13; Acts 16.21; (6) Specific to General or General to Specific: a. Specific to General: Acts 21.21; 1 Tim. 2.12; b. General to Specific: Gal. 1.16-17; 1 Tim. 1.3-4; 6.17. Note that there may be some overlap between these categories so that they should not be understood to be mutually exclusive but rather as indicating the most likely emphasis on the relationship between the two concepts linked by οὐδέ.

Furthermore, since it seemed wise to limit the search to negated *finite* verbs + infinitive + οὐδέ + infinitive, instances where the negative modifies, say, a participle, also need to be eliminated. Most importantly, however, only a small fraction of the passages printed out by the IBYCUS system are instances where the negated finite verb as well as οὐδέ are governing infinitives (as opposed to, for example, two finite verbs, or a finite verb and two or more nouns). Finally, the system also gives references of the relative pronoun οὗ, and instances where the subjects tied to οὐ and οὐδέ are different.

An extraordinary amount of work was required to extract from the initial printout the references relevant for the present study. In order to arrive at the 48 syntactical parallels to 1 Tim. 2.12, about 300 pages of data had to be sifted, with each page including about ten passages, for a total of about 3000 references. Thus only one out of 60 references, or about 1.5 per cent, was a true syntactical parallel to 1 Tim. 2.12. While this may appear to be an excessive amount of data and work for a relatively small collection of passages, the results are worth the effort, since this study provides for the first time exhaustive background data for the syntactical study of 1 Tim. 2.12. The IBYCUS system has enabled the researcher to study all the extant Greek literature directly relevant for the study of the syntax used in 1 Tim. 2.12 (i.e. literature from the third century BCE until the end of the first century CE)—the LXX, the papyri and inscriptions available on the IBYCUS, and all the extant works of Polybius, Dionysius Halicarnassensis, Diodorus Siculus, Josephus, Philo and Plutarch.

Following is the list of syntactical parallels to 1 Tim. 2.12.

LXX:

1. 1 Macc. 15.14: καὶ ἐκύκλωσεν τὴν πόλιν, καὶ τὰ πλοῖα ἀπὸ θαλάσσης συνῆψαν, καὶ ἔθλιβε τὴν πόλιν ἀπὸ τῆς γῆς καὶ τῆς θαλάσσης, καὶ (1) οὐκ εἴασεν οὐδένα (2) ἐκπορεύεσθαι (3) οὐδὲ εἰσπορεύεσθαι.[17]
2. Sir. 18.6: (1) οὐκ ἔστιν (2) ἐλαττῶσαι (3) οὐδὲ προσθεῖναι, καὶ οὐκ ἔστιν ἐξιχνιάσαι τὰ θαυμάσια τοῦ κυρίου.[18]

17. 'He surrounded the city, and the ships joined battle from the sea; he pressed the city hard from land and sea, and (1) permitted no one (2) to leave (3) or enter it.' This translation is taken from B.M. Metzger, *The Apocrypha of the Old Testament* (New York: Oxford University Press, 1977).

18. '[Who can measure his majestic power? And who can fully recount his mercies?] (1) It is not possible (2) to diminish (3) or increase them, nor is it possible

3. Isa. 42.24b: οὐχὶ ὁ θεός, ᾧ ἡμάρτοσαν αὐτῷ καὶ (1) οὐκ ἐβούλοντο ἐν ταῖς ὁδοῖς αὐτοῦ (2) πορεύεσθαι (3) οὐδὲ ἀκούειν τοῦ νόμου αὐτοῦ;[19]
4. Ezek. 44.13: καὶ (1) οὐκ ἐγγιοῦσι πρός με τοῦ (2) ἱερατεύειν μοι (3) οὐδὲ τοῦ προσάγειν πρὸς τὰ ἅγια υἱῶν τοῦ Ισραηλ οὐδὲ πρὸς τὰ ἅγια τῶν ἁγίων μου καὶ λήμψονται ἀτιμίαν αὐτῶν ἐν τῇ πλανήσει, ᾗ ἐπλανήθησαν.[20]
5. DanTh. 5.8: καὶ εἰσεπορεύοντο πάντες οἱ σοφοὶ τοῦ βασιλέως καὶ (1) οὐκ ἠδύναντο τὴν γραφὴν (2) ἀναγνῶναι (3) οὐδὲ τὴν σύγκρισιν γνωρίσαι τῷ βασιλεῖ.[21]

Epigraphy:

6. Attica.IG II(2).11589 (third century BCE):...(1) οὐκ ἄνσχετο (2) δῶρα δέχεσθαι (3) οὐδὲ κλύειν ἱκέτου Τισαμενοῖο πατρός.[22]
7. PZenPestm.21 (246 BCE): Νίκων δὲ ὁ κρινόμενος πρὸς Ἀντίπατρον (1) οὐκ ἔφατο (2) εἰληφέναι τὸ παιδάριον παρ' αὐτῶν (3) οὐδὲ ἔχειν αὐτὸ παρευρέσει οὐδεμιᾶι.[23]

Polybius (202–120 BCE):

8. *Hist.* 2.56.10: (1) δεῖ τοιγαροῦν οὐκ (2) ἐκπλήττειν τὸν συγγραφέα τερατευόμενον διὰ τῆς ἱστορίας τοὺς ἐντυγχάνοντας (3) οὐδὲ τοὺς ἐνδεχομένους λόγους ζητεῖν καὶ τὰ παρεπόμενα τοῖς ὑποκειμένοις ἐξαριθμεῖσθαι, καθάπερ οἱ τραγῳδιογράφοι, τῶν δὲ πραχθέντων καὶ ῥηθέντων κατ' ἀλήθειαν αὐτῶν μνημονεύειν πάμπαν, κἂν πάνυ μέτρια τυγχάνωσιν ὄντα.[24]

to trace the wonders of the Lord' (trans. Metzger, *Apocrypha*).

19. '[Who gave Jacob up for spoil, and Israel to plunderers?] Was it not God, against whom they have sinned, and in whose ways (1) they were not willing (2) to walk (3) nor to obey my law'? (my trans.).

20. 'And (1) they shall not come near to me (2) to serve as a priest to me, (3) nor to approach any of the holy things of the sons of Israel, nor to the holiest of my holy things; but they shall bear their dishonor in their shame by which they were deceived' (my trans.).

21. 'Then all the king's wise men came in, but (1) they could not (2) read the inscription (3) [n]or make known its interpretation to the king' (trans. Metzger, *Apocrypha*).

22. '...(1) he did not stand up (2) to receive gifts (3) nor to give ear to the suppliant, Tisamenoios the father [or: the father of Tisamenoios]' (my trans.).

23. 'Nikon the judge (1) did not say to Antipater (2) to take the boy from them (3) nor to hold him under any pretense' (my trans.).

24. 'A historical author (1) should not (2) try to thrill his readers by such exaggerated pictures, (3) nor should he, like a tragic poet, try to imagine the probable utterances of his characters or reckon up all the consequences probably incidental to the occurrences with which he deals, but simply record what really happened and

9. *Hist.* 5.10.5: (1) οὐ γὰρ ἐπ᾽ ἀπωλείᾳ δεῖ καὶ ἀφανισμῷ τοῖς ἀγνοήσασι (2) πολεμεῖν τοὺς ἀγαθοὺς ἄνδρας, ἀλλ᾽ ἐπὶ διορθώσει καὶ μεταθέσει τῶν ἡμαρτημένων, (3) οὐδὲ συναναιρεῖν τὰ μηδὲν ἀδικοῦντα τοῖς ἠδικηκόσιν, ἀλλὰ συσσῴζειν μᾶλλον καὶ συνεξαιρεῖσθαι τοῖς ἀναιτίοις τοὺς δοκοῦντας ἀδικεῖν.[25]
10. *Hist.* 6.15.8:...τούτους (1) οὐ δύνανται (2) χειρίζειν, ὡς πρέπει, ποτὲ δὲ τὸ παράπαν (3) οὐδὲ συντελεῖν...[26]
11. *Hist.* 30.5.8.4-6:... (1) οὐκ ἐβούλοντο (2) συνδυάζειν (3) οὐδὲ προκαταλαμβάνειν σφᾶς αὐτοὺς ὅρκοις καὶ συνθήκαις, (4) ἀλλ᾽ ἀκέραιοι διαμένοντες κερδαίνειν τὰς ἐξ ἑκάστων ἐλπίδας.[27]
12. *Hist.* 30.24.2.3-4:... (1) οὐ δοκοῦσι δὲ (2) γινώσκεσθαι παρὰ τοῖς ἀπαντῶσιν (3) οὐδὲ συνορᾶσθαι διότι λέλυνται σαφῶς, ἐὰν μή τι παράλογον ποιῶσι καὶ τῶν ἄλλων ἐξηλλαγμένον.[28]
13. *Hist.* 31.12.5-6:... τὴν δὲ σύγκλητον (1) οὐ τολμήσειν ἔτι (2) βοηθεῖν (3) οὐδὲ συνεπισχύειν τοῖς περὶ τὸν Λυσίαν τοιαῦτα διεργασαμένοις.[29]

Dionysius Halicarnassensis (first century BCE):

14. *De Thucydide* 7.13-15: Θουκυδίδῃ δὲ τῷ προελομένῳ μίαν ὑπόθεσιν, ᾗ παρεγίνετο αὐτός, (1) οὐκ ἥρμοττεν (2) ἐγκαταμίσγειν τῇ διηγήσει τὰς θεατρικὰς γοητείας (3) οὐδὲ πρὸς τὴν ἀπάτην

what really was said, however commonplace' (this and the following translations are taken from the Loeb Classical Library series).

25. 'For good men (1) should not (2) make war on wrong-doers with the object of destroying and exterminating them, but with that of correcting and reforming their errors, (3) nor should they involve the guiltless in the fate of the guilty, (4) but rather extend to those whom they think guilty the mercy and deliverance they offer to the innocent.'

26. '[For the processions they call triumphs, in which the generals bring the actual spectacle of their achievements before the eyes of their fellow-citizens,] (1) cannot (2) be properly organized and sometimes even cannot (3) be held at all, [unless the senate consents and provides the requisite funds].'

27. '[As they wished none of the kings and princes to despair of gaining their help and alliance,] (1) they did not desire (2) to run in harness with Rome (3) and engage themselves by oaths and treaties, (4) but preferred to remain unembarrassed and able to reap profit from any quarter.'

28. '[The inhabitants of Peraea were like slaves unexpectedly released from their fetters, who, unable to believe the truth, take longer steps than their natural ones] and (1) fancy that those they meet will (2) not know (3) and see for certain that they are free unless they behave in some strange way and differently from other men.'

29. '[For the Syrians would at once transfer the crown to him, even if he appeared accompanied only by a single slave,] while the senate (1) would not go so far as (2) to help (3) and support Lysias after his conduct.'

ἁρμόττεσθαι τῶν ἀναγνωσομένων, ἣν ἐκεῖναι πεφύκασι φέρειν αἱ συντάξεις, (4) ἀλλὰ πρὸς τὴν ὠφέλειαν...[30]

15. *Antiqu. Rom.* 10.12.3-5:...ἢ ὡς (1) οὐ δεῖ (2) κοινωνεῖν (3) οὐδὲ παρεῖναι τῇ ζητήσει τοὺς ἀνειληφότας τὴν τοῦ δήμου ἀρχήν.[31]

16. *De Comp. Verb.* 23.2-5: (1) οὐ ζητεῖ καθ' ἓν ἕκαστον ὄνομα ἐκ περιφανείας (2) ὁρᾶσθαι (3) οὐδὲ ἐν ἕδρᾳ πάντα βεβηκέναι πλατείᾳ τε καὶ ἀσφαλεῖ οὐδὲ μακροὺς τοὺς μεταξὺ αὐτῶν εἶναι χρόνους.[32]

Diodorus Siculus (c. 40 BCE):

17. *Bibl. Hist.* 3.30.2.8-9: (1) οὐ χρὴ δὲ (2) θαυμάζειν (3) οὐδὲ ἀπιστεῖν τοῖς λεγομένοις, πολλὰ τούτων παραδοξότερα κατὰ πᾶσαν τὴν οἰκουμένην γεγονότα διὰ τῆς ἀληθοῦς ἱστορίας παρειληφότας.[33]

18. *Bibl. Hist.* 3.37.9.1-4: διόπερ τηλικούτου μεγέθους ὄφεως εἰς ὄψιν κοινὴν κατηντηκότος (1) οὐκ ἄξιον (2) ἀπιστεῖν τοῖς Αἰθίοψιν (3) οὐδὲ μῦθον ὑπολαμβάνειν τὸ θρυλούμενον ὑπ' αὐτῶν.[34]

Josephus (37–100 CE):

19. *Apion* 2.6.1-3: (1) ἔστι μὲν οὖν οὐ ῥᾴδιον αὐτοῦ (2) διελθεῖν τὸν λόγον (3) οὐδὲ σαφῶς γνῶναι τί λέγειν βούλεται.[35]

20. *Apion* 2.212.1-2: (1) οὐ γὰρ ἐᾷ τὴν γῆν αὐτῶν (2) πυρπολεῖν (3) οὐδὲ τέμνειν ἥμερα δένδρα, ἀλλὰ καὶ σκυλεύειν ἀπείρηκεν τοὺς ἐν τῇ μάχῃ πεσόντας καὶ τῶν αἰχμαλώτων προυνόησεν.[36]

30. 'Thucydides, however, chose a single episode in which he personally participated: (1) it was therefore inappropriate for him (2) to adulterate his narrative with entertaining fantasies (3) or to arrange it in a way which would confuse his readers, as his predecessors' compositions would naturally do. (4) His purpose was to benefit his readers...'

31. '...or that the magistrates of the populace (1) ought not (2) to take part in or (3) be present at the inquiry.'

32. '[The polished style of composition, which I placed second in order, has the following character.] (1) It does not intend each word (2) to be viewed from all sides, (3) nor that every word shall stand on a broad, firm base, nor that the intervals of time between them shall be long...'

33. '(1) Nor is there any occasion (2) to be surprised at this statement (3) or to distrust it, since we have learned through trustworthy history of many things more astonishing than this which have taken place throughout all the inhabited world.'

34. 'Consequently, in view of the fact that a snake of so great a size has been exposed to the public gaze, (1) it is not fair (2) to doubt the word of the Ethiopians (3) or to assume that the report which they circulated far and wide was a mere fiction.'

35. 'His argument (1) is difficult (2) to summarize and his meaning (3) to grasp.'

36. '(1) He does not allow us (2) to burn up their country (3) or to cut down their fruit trees, and forbids even the spoiling of fallen combatants...'

21. *War* 5.199.3-5: κατὰ γὰρ τὰς ἄλλας (1) οὐκ ἐξῆν (2) παρελθεῖν γυναιξίν, ἀλλ' (3) οὐδὲ κατὰ τὴν σφετέραν ὑπερβῆναι τὸ διατείχισμα.[37]
22. *Ant*. 2.116.3-5: ὡς (1) οὐ προσῆκε μὲν αὐτὸν περὶ τἀδελφοῦ (2) δεδιέναι (3) οὐδὲ τὰ μὴ δεινὰ δι' ὑποψίας λαμβάνειν...[38]
23. *Ant*. 6.20.3-5:...(1) οὐκ (2) ἐπιθυμεῖν ἐλευθερίας (1) δεῖ μόνον, ἀλλὰ καὶ ποιεῖν δι' ὧν ἂν ἔλθοι πρὸς ὑμᾶς, (3) οὐδὲ βούλεσθαι μὲν ἀπηλλάχθαι δεσποτῶν ἐπιμένειν δὲ πράττοντας ἐξ ὧν οὗτοι διαμενοῦσιν.[39]
24. *Ant*. 6.344.5-6:...(1) οὐκ ἔγνω (2) φυγεῖν αὐτὸν (3) οὐδὲ φιλοψυχήσας προδοῦναι μὲν τοὺς οἰκείους τοῖς πολεμίοις καθυβρίσαι δὲ τὸ τῆς βασιλείας ἀξίωμα, ἀλλά...[40]
25. *Ant*. 7.127.1-3: τοῦτο τὸ πταῖσμα τοὺς 'Αμμανίτας (1) οὐκ ἔπεισεν (2) ἠρεμεῖν (3) οὐδὲ μαθόντας τοὺς κρείττονας ἡσυχίαν ἄγειν, (4) ἀλλὰ πέμψαντες πρὸς Χαλαμάν...[41]
26. *Ant*. 14.346.1-3: ὁ δὲ Ὑρκανὸν (2) ἀπολιπεῖν (1) οὐκ ἠξίου (3) οὐδὲ παρακινδυνεύειν τἀδελφῷ.[42]
27. *Ant*. 15.165.3-4: ὁ μὲν γὰρ Ὑρκανὸς ἐπιεικείᾳ τρόπου καὶ τότε καὶ τὸν ἄλλον χρόνον (1) οὐκ ἠξίου (2) πολυπραγμονεῖν (3) οὐδὲ νεωτέρων ἅπτεσθαι.[43]

37. 'For women (1) were not permitted (2) to enter by the others (3) nor yet to pass by way of their own gate beyond the partition wall.'

38. '[Judas, ever of a hardy nature, frankly told him] that (1) he ought not (2) to be alarmed for their brother (3) nor harbour suspicions of dangers that did not exist.'

39. '...(1) ye ought not to be content (2) to yearn for liberty, but should do also the deeds whereby ye may attain it, (3) nor merely long to be rid of your masters, while continuing so to act that they shall remain so.'

40. '[For he, although he knew of what was to come and his impending death, which the prophet had foretold,] yet (1) determined not (2) to flee from it (3) or, by clinging to life, to betray his people to the enemy and dishonour the dignity of kingship; instead...'

41. 'This defeat (1) did not persuade the Ammanites (2) to remain quiet (3) or to keep the peace in the knowledge that their enemy was superior. (4) Instead they sent to Chalamas...'

42. 'Phasael, however, (1) did not think it right (2) to desert Hyrcanus (3) or to endanger his brother.'

43. 'Now Hyrcanus because of his mild character (1) did not choose either then or at any other time (2) to take part in public affairs (2) or start a revolution...' (Note that 'to take part in public affairs' is not as neutral as this translation might suggest. Cf. LSJ, p. 1442: πολυπραγματέω: 'mostly in bad sense, to be a meddlesome, inquisitive busybody; esp. meddle in state affairs, intrigue'.)

Philo (c. 25 BCE–40 CE):

28. *Poster. C.* 84.5-7: (1) οὐ γὰρ (2) ἀναπτῆναι, θησίν, εἰς οὐρανὸν (3) οὐδὲ πέραν θαλάσσης ἀφικέσθαι (1) δεῖ κατὰ ζήτησιν τοῦ καλοῦ.[44]

Plutarch (40–120 CE):

29. *Rom.* 9.2.4-5: ὅτι γὰρ (1) οὐκ ἠξίουν οἱ τὴν Ἄλβην οἰκοῦντες (2) ἀναμιγνύναι τοὺς ἀποστάτας ἑαυτοῖς (3) οὐδὲ προσδέχεσθαι πολίτας...[45]
30. *Cor.* 27.4.1: τὰ γὰρ ἄλλα πάντα λυμαινόμενος καὶ διαφθείρων, τοὺς ἐκείνων ἀγροὺς ἰσχυρῶς ἐφύλαττε, καὶ (1) οὐκ εἴα (2) κακουργεῖν (3) οὐδὲ λαμβάνειν ἐξ ἐκείνων οὐδέν.[46]
31. *Tim.* 37.2.1: ὧν Λαφυστίου μὲν αὐτὸν πρός τινα δίκην κατεγγυῶντος (1) οὐκ εἴα (2) θορυβεῖν (3) οὐδὲ κωλύειν τοὺς πολίτας.[47]
32. *Comp. Arist. et Cat.* 4.2.1: (1) οὐ γὰρ ἔστι (2) πράττειν μεγάλα φροντίζοντα μικρῶν, (3) οὐδὲ πολλοῖς δεομένοις βοηθεῖν πολλῶν αὐτὸν δεόμενον.[48]
33. *Pyrrh.* 33.6.4: σπασάμενον γὰρ τὸ ξίφος ἢ κλίναντα λόγχην (1) οὐκ ἦν (2) ἀναλαβεῖν (3) οὐδὲ καταθέσθαι πάλιν, ἀλλ' ἐχώρει δι' ὧν ἔτυχε τὰ τοιαῦτα πάντα, καὶ περιπίπτοντες ἀλλήλοις ἔθνησκον.[49]
34. *Ages.* 32.3.3-4: ἐπεὶ δὲ φιλοτιμούμενος ὁ Ἐπαμεινώνδας ἐν τῇ πόλει μάχην συνάψαι καὶ στῆσαι τρόπαιον (1) οὐκ ἴσχυσεν (2) ἐξαγαγεῖν (3) οὐδὲ προκαλέσασθαι τὸν Ἀγησίλαον, ἐκεῖνος μὲν ἀναζεύξας πάλιν ἐπόρθει τὴν χώραν.[50]

44. '"For (1) it is not necessary", he says, (2) "to fly up into heaven, (3) nor to get beyond the sea in searching for what is good"'.

45. 'For that the residents of Alba (1) would not consent (2) to give the fugitives the privilege of intermarriage with them, (3) nor even receive them as fellow-citizens [is clear].'

46. 'For while he maltreated and destroyed everything else, he kept a vigorous watch over the lands of the patricians, and (1) would not suffer anyone (2) to hurt them (3) or take anything from them.'

47. 'Of these, Laphystius once tried to make him give surety that he would appear at a certain trial, and Timoleon (1) would not suffer the citizens (2) to stop the man (3) by their turbulent disapproval [lit.: nor to prevent him].'

48. '(1) It is impossible for a man (2) to do great things when his thoughts are busy with little things; (3) nor can he aid the many who are in need when he himself is in need of many things.'

49. 'For when a man had drawn his sword or poised his spear, (1) he could not (2) recover (3) or sheathe his weapon again, but it would pass through those who stood in its way, and so they died from one another's blows.'

50. 'Epaminondas was ambitious to join battle in the city and set up a trophy of victory there, but since (1) he could (2) neither force (3) nor tempt Agesilaus out of his positions, he withdrew and began to ravage the country.'

35. *Quom. Adul.* 64.E.7-8: ὁρᾷς τὸν πίθηκον; (1) οὐ δύναται τὴν οἰκίαν (2) φυλάττειν ὡς ὁ κύων, (3) οὐδὲ βαστάζειν ὡς ὁ ἵππος, οὐδ' ἀροῦν τὴν γῆν ὡς οἱ βόες.[51]
36. *Cons. ad Apoll.* 115.E.3: ἀνθρώποις δὲ πάμπαν (1) οὐκ ἔστι (2) γενέσθαι τὸ πάντων ἄριστον (3) οὐδὲ μετασχεῖν τῆς τοῦ βελτίστου φύσεως (ἄριστον γὰρ πᾶσι καὶ πάσαις τὸ μὴ γενέσθαι).[52]
37. *Reg. et Imp. Apopht.* 185.A.2: πρὸς δὲ τοὺς θαυμάζοντας τὴν μεταβολὴν ἔλεγεν ὡς '(1) οὐκ ἐᾷ με (2) καθεύδειν (3) οὐδὲ ῥᾳθυμεῖν τὸ Μιλτιάδου πρόπαιον'.[53]
38. *Act. Rom. et Graec.* 269.D.8-9: (1) οὐ δεῖ δὲ τῶν ἡμερῶν τὸν ἀκριβέστατον ἀριθμὸν (2) διώκειν (3) οὐδὲ τὸ παρ' ὀλίγον συκοφαντεῖν...[54]
39. *Act. Rom. et Graec.* 273.E.9-10: διὰ τί τοῖς μὴ στρατευομένοις μὲν ἐν στρατοπέδῳ δ' ἄλλως ἀναστρεφομένοις (1) οὐκ ἐξῆν ἄνδρα (2) βαλεῖν πολέμιον (3) οὐδὲ τρῶσαι;[55]
40. *Act. Rom. et Graec.* 291.B.3-4: διὰ τί τοῖς ἱερεῦσι τούτοις ἀρχὴν (1) οὐκ ἐφεῖτο (2) λαβεῖν (3) οὐδὲ μετελθεῖν;[56]
41. *De E Apud Delph.* 385.A.9:...(1) οὐκ ἦν εὐπρεπὲς (2) παράγειν (3) οὐδὲ παραιτεῖσθαι...[57]

51. 'You must have noticed the ape. (1) He cannot (2) guard the house like the dog, (3) nor carry a load like the horse, nor plough the land like oxen.'

52. 'But for men (1) it is utterly impossible (2) that they should obtain the best thing of all, (3) or even have any share in its nature (for the best thing for all men and women is not to be born).'

53. '[Themistocles while yet in his youth abandoned himself to wine and women. But after Miltiades, commanding the Athenian army, had overcome the barbarians at Marathon, never again was it possible to encounter Themistocles misconducting himself.] To those who expressed their amazement at the change in him, he said that "the trophy of Miltiades (1) does not allow me (2) to sleep (3) or to be indolent".'

54. 'But (1) we must not (2) follow out the most exact calculation of the number of days (3) nor cast aspersions on approximate reckoning [since even now, when astronomy has made so much progress, the irregularity of the moon's movements is still beyond the skill of mathematicians, and continues to elude their calculations].'

55. 'Why were men who were not regularly enlisted, but merely tarrying in the camp, (1) not allowed (2) to throw missiles at the enemy (3) or to wound them?'

56. 'Why were these priests (1) not allowed (2) to hold office (3) nor to solicit it?'

57. '[On many other occasions when the subject had been brought up in the school I had quietly turned aside from it and passed it over, but recently I was unexpectedly discovered by my sons in an animated discussion with some strangers, whom, since they purposed to leave Delphi immediately,] (1) it was not seemly (2) to try to divert from the subject, nor was it seemly for me (3) to ask to be excused from the discussion [for they were altogether eager to hear something about it].'

42. *De Def. Orac.* 426.B.1: (1) οὐ γὰρ ὡς σμήνους ἡγεμόνας δεῖ (2) ποιεῖν ἀνεξόδους (3) οὐδὲ φρουρεῖν συγκλείσαντας τῇ ὕλῃ μᾶλλον δὲ συμφράξαντας...[58]
43. *De Tranqu. Anim.* 474.A.12: (1) οὐ δεῖ τοῖς ἑτέροις (2) ἐξαθυμεῖν (3) οὐδ' ἀπαγορεύειν.[59]
44. *De Tranqu. Anim.* 475.D.3: ὅθεν (1) οὐ δεῖ παντάπασιν (2) ἐκταπεινοῦν (3) οὐδὲ καταβάλλειν τὴν φύσιν...[60]
45. *Quaest. Conviv.* 706.D.5: ἐρῶντι μὲν γὰρ πολυτελοῦς (1) οὐκ ἔστι τὴν Πηνελόπην (2) προσαγαγεῖν (3) οὐδὲ συνοικίσαι τὴν Πάνθειαν.[61]
46. *Quaest. Conviv.* 711.E.3: ὥσθ' ὁ οἶνος ἡμᾶς (2) ἀδικεῖν (1) οὐκ ἔοικεν (3) οὐδὲ κρατεῖν.[62]
47. *Aetia Phys.* 918.B.4:...ἡ δ' ἄγαν περίψυξις πηγνύουσα τὰς ὀσμὰς (1) οὐκ ἐᾷ (2) ῥεῖν (3) οὐδὲ κινεῖν τὴν αἴσθησιν;[63]
48. *Brut. Rat.* 990.A.11:...καὶ (1) οὐκ ἐᾷ (2) θιγεῖν (3) οὐδὲ λυπῆσαι τὴν γεῦσιν ἀλλὰ διαβάλλει καὶ κατηγορεῖ τὴν φαυλότητα πρὶν ἢ βλαβῆναι.[64]

58. '[Yet such an organization is altogether appropriate for the gods.] For (1) we must not (2) make them unable to go out, like the queens in a hive of bees, (3) nor keep them imprisoned by enclosing them with matter, or rather fencing them about with it.'

59. '(1) We should not (2) be disheartened (3) or despondent in adversity [but like musicians who achieve harmony by consistently deadening bad music with better and encompassing the bad with the good, we should make the blending of our life harmonious and conformable to our own nature].'

60. 'Therefore (1) we should not altogether (2) debase (3) and depreciate Nature [in the belief that she has nothing strong, stable, and beyond the reach of Fortune, but, on the contrary... we should face the future undaunted and confident...].'

61. 'If a man has a passion for a costly harlot, (1) we cannot (2) bring Penelope on stage, (3) nor marry Pantheia to him [but it is possible to take a man who is enjoying mimes and tunes and lyrics that are bad art and bad taste, and lead him back to Euripides and Pindar and Menander, "washing the brine from the ears with the clear fresh water of reason", in Plato's words].'

62. 'The wine (1) seems not (2) to be harming us (3) or getting the best of us.'

63. '[Why is ground that has become dewy unfavourable for hunting so long as the cold lasts?... A spoor does this when there is warmth to free and release it gently] whereas excessive chill freezes the scents and (1) does not allow them (2) to flow (3) and affect [i.e. move] our perception.'

64. '[It (our sense of smell) admits what is proper, rejects what is alien] and (1) will not let it (2) touch (3) or give pain to the taste, but informs on and denounces what is bad before any harm is done.'

These instances suggest that the construction 'negated finite verb + infinitive + οὐδέ + infinitive' is used to link two infinitives denoting concepts or activities which are either both viewed positively or negatively by the writer. The same two patterns of the usage of οὐδέ are found in *Pattern 1* where two activities or concepts are viewed positively in and of themselves, but where their exercise is prohibited or their existence denied due to circumstances or conditions adduced in the context, and in *Pattern 2* where two activities or concepts are viewed negatively and where consequently their exercise is prohibited or their existence is denied or to be avoided. The following chart documents the first pattern.

Pattern 1: Two activities or concepts are viewed positively in and of themselves, but their exercise is prohibited or their existence denied owing to circumstances or conditions adduced in the context.

1.	LXX: 1 Macc. 15.14	ἐκπορεύεσθαι (leave)	εἰσπορεύεσθαι (enter)
2.	LXX: Sir. 18.6	ἐλαττῶσαι (diminish)	προσθεῖναι (increase)
3.	LXX: Isa. 42.24b	πορεύεσθαι (walk)	ἀκούειν (obey)
4.	LXX: Ezek. 44.13	ἱερατεύειν (serve as priest)	προσάγειν (come near)
5.	LXX: DanTh. 5.8	ἀναγνῶναι (read)	γνωρίσαι (make known)
6.	Epig.: Attica	δέχεσθαι (receive gifts)	κλύειν (give ear to suppliant)
10.	Polybius, *Hist.* 6.15	χειρίζειν (be organized)	συντελεῖν (be held at all)
12.	Polybius, *Hist.* 30.24	γινώσκεσθαι (known)	συνορᾶσθαι (see)
13.	Polybius, *Hist.* 31.12	βοηθεῖν (help)	συνεπισχύειν (support)
15.	Dionysius Halicarnassensis, *Antiqu. Rom.* 10.12	κοινωνεῖν (take part in)	παρεῖναι (be present at)
19.	Josephus, *Apion* 2.6.1-3	διελθεῖν (discern)	γνῶναι (know)
21.	Josephus, *War* 5.199	παρελθεῖν (enter)	ὑπερβῆναι (pass by)
23.	Josephus, *Ant.* 6.20	ἐπιθυμεῖν (yearn for)	βούλεσθαι (want)*
25.	Josephus, *Ant.* 7.127	ἠρεμεῖν (remain quiet)	ἡσυχίαν ἄγειν (keep quiet)

28.	Philo, *Poster. C.* 84.5	ἀναπτῆναι (fly up)	ἀφικέσθαι (go beyond)*
29.	Plutarch, *Rom.* 9.2	ἀναμιγνύναι (intermarry)	προσδέχεσθαι (receive as citizen)
32.	Plutarch, *Comp.* 4.2	πράττειν (do great things)	βοηθεῖν (help)
33.	Plutarch, *Pyrrh.* 33.6	ἀναλαβεῖν (take again)	καταθέσθαι (sheathe again)
35.	Plutarch, *Adul.* 64.E	φυλάττειν (guard)	βαστάζειν (carry)
36.	Plutarch, *Apoll.* 115.E	γενέσθαι (obtain)	μετασχεῖν (have a share)
38.	Plutarch, *Act.* 269.D	διώκειν (follow)	συκοφαντεῖν (approximate)
40.	Plutarch, *Act.* 291.B	λαβεῖν (hold office)	μετελθεῖν (solicit office)
45.	Plutarch, *Conv.* 706.D	προσαγαγεῖν (bring on stage)	συνοικίσαι (marry)
47.	Plutarch, *Phys.* 918.B	ῥεῖν (flow)	κινεῖν (move)

* = preceding infinitive

Pattern 1 can be clarified by comment on the following instances. Polybius writes (10) that victory processions cannot be properly organized or sometimes be held at all unless the senate consents and provides the requisite funds. While 'organize' and 'hold' are both viewed positively in and of themselves by the writer, Polybius indicates that the holding of these processions is not possible unless certain conditions are met; the senate's consent and the requisition of appropriate funds. Again (13) Polybius writes that 'the senate would not go so far as to help or support Lysias after his conduct'. The writer views the two activities (here synonyms), 'helping' and 'supporting', positively in and of themselves, but the help is denied because of Lysias's unacceptable conduct. Josephus writes (23) that 'you ought not to be content to yearn for liberty...nor merely long to be rid of your masters'. While the writer views his readers' yearning for liberty and their longing to be rid of their masters positively in and of themselves, he indicates in the context why these longings by themselves are insufficient unless accompanied by action and change in behaviour.

The following chart lists the instances of the second pattern.

Pattern 2: Two activities or concepts are viewed negatively and consequently their exercise is prohibited or to be avoided or their existence is denied.

7.	Epig.: PZenPestm.	εἰληθέναι (take away)	ἔχειν (hold in pretense)
8.	Polybius, *Hist.* 2.56	ἐκπλήττειν (thrill)	ζητεῖν (seek to imagine)
9.	Polybius, *Hist.* 5.10.5	πολεμεῖν (make war)	συναναιρεῖν (involve guiltless)
11.	Polybius, *Hist.* 30.5	συνδυάζειν (run in harness)	προκαταλαμβάνειν (engage)
14.	Dionysius Halicarnassensis, *De Thucydide* 7.13	ἐγκαταμίσγειν (adulterate)	ἁρμόττεσθαι (confuse)
16.	Dionysius Halicarnassensis, *De Comp. Verb.* 23	ὁρᾶσθαι (be viewed)	βεβηκέναι (stand)
17.	Diodorus Siculus, *Bibl. Hist.* 3.30	θαυμάζειν (be surprised)	ἀπιστεῖν (distrust)
18.	Diodorus Siculus, *Bibl. Hist.* 3.37	ἀπιστεῖν (doubt)	ὑπολαμβάνειν (view as fictional)
20.	Josephus, *Apion* 2.212.1	πυρπολεῖν (burn)	τέμνειν (cut down)
22.	Josephus, *Ant.* 2.116	δεδίεναι (be alarmed)	λαμβάνειν (harbour suspicions)
24.	Josephus, *Ant.* 6.344	φυγεῖν (flee)	προδοῦναι (betray)
26.	Josephus, *Ant.* 14.346	ἀπολιπεῖν (desert)	παρακινδυνεύειν (endanger)*
27.	Josephus, *Ant.* 15.165	πολυπραγμονεῖν (intrigue)	ἅπτεσθαι (start a revolution)
30.	Plutarch, *Cor.* 27.4	κακουργεῖν (hurt)	λαμβάνειν (take from)
31	Plutarch, *Tim.* 37.2	θορυβεῖν (stop)	κωλύειν (hinder)
34.	Plutarch, *Ages.* 32.3	ἐξαγαγεῖν (force)	προκαλέσασθαι (tempt)
37.	Plutarch, *Reg. et Imp. Apopht.* 185.A	καθεύδειν (sleep)	ῥαθυμεῖν (be idle)
39.	Plutarch, *Act. Rom. et Graec.* 273.E	βαλεῖν (throw missiles)	τρῶσαι (wound)
41.	Plutarch, *De E Apud Delph.* 385.A	παράγειν (try to divert)	παραιτεῖσθαι (be excused)
42.	Plutarch, *De Def. Orac.* 426.B	ποιεῖν ἀνεξόδους (make unable)	φρουρεῖν (keep imprisoned)
43.	Plutarch, *De Tranqu. Anim.* 474.A	ἐξαθυμεῖν (be disheartened)	ἀπαγορεύειν (be despondent)

44.	Plutarch, *De Tranqu. Anim.* 475.D	ἐκταπεινοῦν (debase)	καταβάλλειν (depreciate)
46.	Plutarch, *Quaest. Conviv.* 711.E	ἀδικεῖν (harm)	κρατεῖν (get the best of)*
48.	Plutarch, *Brut. Rat.* 990.A	θιγεῖν (touch)	λυπῆσαι (give pain to)

* = preceding infinitive

A few examples from *Pattern 2* will highlight where two activities or concepts are both viewed negatively by the writer and where consequently their exercise is prohibited or their existence is denied or to be avoided. A papyrus (7) indicates that a judge ordered Antipater not 'to take the boy from them or to hold him under any pretense'. Clearly both activities, taking the boy away from them and holding him under any pretense, are viewed negatively by the judge who consequently denies the exercise of these activities. Josephus writes (27) that 'Hyrcanus because of his mild character did not choose...to meddle in state affairs or start a revolution'. 'Meddling in state affairs' and 'starting a revolution' are both viewed negatively by the writer who asserts that it was Hyrcanus's 'mild character' that kept him from engaging in these undesirable activities. In a writing by Plutarch (46) the existence of two negative effects of wine is denied: 'The wine seems not to be harming us or getting the best of us'.[65]

65. These passages may be categorized as follows: (1) Synonymous Concepts: Isa. 44.24b (LXX); Ezek. 44.13 (LXX); Polybius, *Hist.* 31.12; Dionysius Halicarnassensis, *Antiqu. Rom.* 10.12; Josephus, *Apion* 2.6.1-3; *Ant.* 2.116; 6.20; 7.127; Plutarch, *Tim.* 37.2; *Apoph.* 185.A; *Orac.* 426.B; *Tran.* 474.A; 475.D; *Conv.* 711.E; (2) Conceptual Parallels: Polybius, *Hist.* 2.56; 5.10.5; 30.5, 24; Dionysius Halicarnassensis, *Thuc.* 7.13; *De Comp.* 23; Diodorus Siculus, *Bibl. Hist.* 3.37; Josephus, *Apion* 2.212.1; *War* 5.199; *Ant.* 6.344; 14.346; Philo, *Poster. C.* 84.5; Plutarch, *Comp.* 4.2; *Ages.* 32.3; *Adul.* 64.E; *Act.* 269.D; *De E Apud Delph.* 385.A; *Conv.* 706.D; (3) Complementary Concepts: 1 Macc. 15.14 (LXX); Sir. 18.6 (LXX); (4) Sequential Concepts: DanTh 5.8 (LXX); PZenPestm. 21; Plutarch, *Pyrrh.* 33.6; *Phys.* 918.B; *Brut.* 990.A; (5) Ascensive Concepts: Attica.IG II (2).11589; Polybius, *Hist.* 6.15; Diodorus Siculus, *Bibl. Hist.* 3.30; Josephus, *Ant.* 15.165; Plutarch, *Rom.* 9.2; *Apoll.* 115.E; *Act.* 291.B; (6) Specific to General or General to Specific: a. Specific to General: Plutarch, *Act.* 273.B; b. General to Specific: Plutarch, *Cor.* 27.4.

Conclusion

The data from the New Testament and extrabiblical Greek literature equally display a clearly delineated use of οὐδέ. This conjunction always coordinates activities of the same order, that is, activities that are either both viewed positively or negatively by the writer or speaker. The following conclusions and implications for the interpretation of 1 Tim. 2.12 can be drawn.

1. Syntactically, there are only two acceptable ways of rendering 1 Tim. 2.12: (a) 'I do not permit a woman to teach or to have authority over a man', or (b) 'I do not permit a woman to teach error or to domineer over a man'. In the first instance both 'teaching' and 'exercising authority' would be viewed positively in and of themselves, yet for reasons to be gleaned from the context the writer does not permit these. In the latter case both 'teaching error' and 'domineering over a man' would be viewed negatively by the writer.

2. Since οὐδέ is a coordinating and not a subordinating conjunction, it is not permissible to make αὐθεντεῖν subordinate to διδάσκειν so that it in effect functions adverbially ('to teach in a domineering way'). Furthermore, while 'teaching' and 'exercising authority' may be perceived jointly in 1 Tim. 2.12, these concepts do not blend to the extent that they become one concept where the two constituent elements are no longer distinguishable.

3. A distinction should be made between the fact that two activities or concepts are viewed positively in and of themselves and that they may be prohibited owing to circumstances. In 1 Tim. 2.12, the phrase 'I do not permit' has by some been taken to mean that the writer views negatively the two activities, διδάσκειν and αὐθεντεῖν, in the sense of 'teaching in a domineering way'. However, judging by the evidence adduced, it is more likely that the writer prohibits for certain reasons the exercise of activities he otherwise views positively.

4. 1 Tim. 2.12 can thus legitimately be seen as an example of the first pattern, that is, the denial of two activities which are viewed positively in and of themselves, under contextually adduced circumstances. This is strongly suggested by the fact that the term διδάσκειν is consistently viewed positively in the New Testament when used absolutely, that is, unaccompanied by contextual qualifiers.[66] In passages such as

66. *Contra* Kroeger and Kroeger, *I Suffer not a Woman*, p. 81. See also Payne,

1 Tim. 4.11, 6.2 and 2 Tim. 2.2 διδάσκειν is viewed positively by the writer and linked with activities such as encouraging, exhorting and the passing on of apostolic tradition.[67]

5. Since the term διδάσκειν is used absolutely in the New Testament for an activity that is viewed positively in and of itself and since οὐδέ coordinates terms which are either both viewed positively or negatively, αὐθεντεῖν should be seen as denoting an activity that is viewed positively in and of itself as well. Thus 1 Tim. 2.12 is an instance of the first pattern where the exercise of two activities is prohibited or the existence of two concepts is denied by the writer owing to certain circumstances. Since the first part of 1 Tim. 2.12 reads 'But I do not permit a woman to teach', and the coordinating conjunction οὐδέ requires the second activity to be viewed correspondingly by the writer, αὐθεντεῖν should also be regarded positively and thus be rendered 'to have authority' and not 'to domineer'.

6. The immediate context of the passage supports the conclusion just stated. Framed by the *inclusio* of ἡσυχία at the beginning of 2.11 and at the end of 2.12, there are two corresponding pairs of terms: 'learning' in 2.11 corresponds to 'teaching' in 2.12, and 'full submission' in 2.11 relates to 'having authority' in 2.12. The author first expresses his desire for a woman to learn in full submission. He then registers his prohibition of the opposite, a woman's teaching or being in authority over a man. He closes by reiterating his desire for a woman to learn in submission. 'Learning' and 'teaching', 'full submission' and 'having authority' are contrasted, the former terms in the pair being viewed positively in the case of women, the latter ones negatively. Thus syntax and context join in suggesting that 1 Tim. 2.12 be rendered 'I do not permit a woman to teach or to have authority over a man'.

'οὐδέ', pp. 6-8, who argues that teaching is an activity viewed positively in and of itself in the New Testament and in Paul's writings.

67. Notably, in instances in the same letter where reference is made to *false* teaching, the term ἑτεροδιδασκαλεῖν is used (cf. 1 Tim. 1.3-4; 6.3), while in Titus 1.9-14 there is ample contextual indication that false teaching is in view, a feature that is absent from the context of 1 Tim. 2.12. *Contra* Kroeger and Kroeger, *I Suffer not a Woman*, p. 81.

THE MEANING OF Ἑλληνιστής IN ACTS IN LIGHT OF A DIACHRONIC ANALYSIS OF ἑλληνίζειν

H. Alan Brehm

The question of identifying the 'Hellenists' in Acts is one of the knottier problems facing the reconstruction of Christian origins. This question is a problematic one because Acts 6.1 reports the dissension in the Jerusalem congregation between two groups named 'Hellenists' and 'Hebrews', but the text itself does not explain the terms Ἑλληνιστής and Ἑβραῖος. Thus the question is complicated at the outset by the very wording of the text.

An answer to that question is not easy to find because of the fact that outside of Acts the term Ἑλληνιστής has been found only in certain Post-Nicene patristic writings. Although there has been no lack of attempts to answer the question of the identity of the Hellenists, any proposed answer must take into account the inherent uncertainty that remains. The reason for this uncertainty is twofold: (1) the fact that none of the answers solves every problem, and (2) the lack of a precise identification in the New Testament. Thus a basic uncertainty remains concerning the meaning of Ἑλληνιστής and the identity of the 'Hellenists' in Acts.

New Testament scholarship generally has endorsed a referential solution on the basis of the perceived lexical meaning of the terms, particularly in regard to the etymology of Ἑλληνιστής. While most agree that the term derives from the verb ἑλληνίζειν, there has been considerable debate as to whether this verb means 'to speak Greek (properly)' or 'to live like a Greek'.[1] Perhaps the oldest interpretation of the question

1. On the etymology of Ἑλληνιστής from the verb ἑλληνίζειν, see W.W. Goodwin, *A Greek Grammar* (Boston: Ginn, rev. edn, 1892), p. 191; F. Blass and A. Debrunner, *A Greek Grammar of the New Testament and Other Early Christian Literature* (trans. R.W. Funk; Chicago: University of Chicago Press, 1961), p. 59 (§109.8); T. Zahn, *Die Apostelgeschichte des Lukas* (Leipzig: Deichert,

understands the terms ‘Hebrew’ and ‘Hellenist’ with reference to a difference in language.[2] This viewpoint was expressed in the fourth century by John Chrysostom, who suggested that Luke called the ‘Hellenists’ by that name because they spoke Greek although they were ‘Hebrews’, or Jews, by ethnic descent.[3] Following Chrysostom, the consensus position has interpreted the term Ἑλληνιστής in Acts 6.1 as a reference to Jewish Christians who spoke Greek and has understood the term

3rd edn, 1922), I, p. 227 n. 6. Compare H.W. Smyth, *Greek Grammar* (rev. G.M. Messing; Cambridge: Harvard University Press, 1920), p. 246, where he says that verbs in -ιζω ‘express an adoption of *language*, *manners*, *opinions*, or *politics*’ and are derived from proper names. He suggests that ἑλληνίζειν is derived from Ἕλλην. For a similar opinion, see R. Kühner, *Ausführliche Grammatik der griechischen Sprache* (rev. F. Blass; Hannover: Hahn, 1892), II, p. 261. See also E. Schwyzer, *Griechische Grammatik* (Munich: Beck, 1959), I, pp. 730-37.

2. See, among others, Kühner, *Grammatik*, II, pp. 22-23; Schwyzer, *Grammatik*, I, pp. 118-19; Zahn, *Apostelgeschichte*, I, pp. 226-27; C.F.D. Moule, ‘Once More, who were the Hellenists?’, *ExpTim* 70 (1958–59), pp. 100-102; E. Haenchen, *The Acts of the Apostles: A Commentary* (trans. R.McL. Wilson *et al.*; Philadelphia: Westminster Press, 1971), pp. 260-61; M. Hengel, ‘Between Jesus and Paul: The “Hellenists”, the “Seven” and Stephen (Acts 6.1-15; 7.54–8.3)’, in *Between Jesus and Paul: Studies in the Earliest History of Christianity* (trans. J. Bowden; London: SCM Press, 1983; repr. Philadelphia: Fortress Press, 1983), p. 9; cf. also G.B. Winer, *A Grammar of the New Testament Diction* (trans. E. Masson; Edinburgh: T. & T. Clark, 2nd edn, 1860), p. 41.

3. John Chrysostom, *Homilies on Acts*, Homily 14 on Acts 6.1 (*PG* LX, p. 113): Ἑλληνιστὰς δὲ οἶμαι καλεῖν, τοὺς Ἑλληνιστὶ φθεγγομένους· οὗτοι γὰρ Ἑλληνιστὶ διελέγοντο Ἑβραῖοι ὄντες (‘Now the Hellenists I suppose he called those who spoke Greek; for although they were Hebrews they spoke Greek’). H.J. Cadbury (‘The Hellenists’, in K. Lake and H.J. Cadbury [eds.], *The Beginnings of Christianity* [London: Macmillan, 1933], V, pp. 72-73) argues from Chrysostom’s use of οἶμαι and ἴσως that he was just ‘guessing’ or at most ‘making inferences from the likeness of Ἑλληνισταί to the adverb Ἑλληνιστί’. H.-W. Neudorfer (*Der Stephanuskreis in der Forschungsgeschichte seit F.C. Baur* [Giessen: Brunnen, 1983], p. 20 n. 3) is more judicious in his evaluation that Chrysostom is clearly expressing an opinion, and ‘zugleich wird deutlich, daß der Terminus im späten vierten Jahrhundert bereits nicht mehr ohne weiteres verständlich war’. Compare also Chrysostom’s Homily 21 on Acts 9.29 (*PG* LX, p. 164), Ἑλληνιστὰς τοὺς Ἑλληνιστὶ φθεγγομένους λέγει; contrast Homily 25 on Acts 11.20 (*PG* LX, p. 191), ὅρα, Ἕλλησιν εὐαγγελίζονται. εἰκὸς γὰρ αὐτούς τε λοιπὸν εἰδέναι Ἑλληνιστί, καὶ ἐν Ἀντιοχείᾳ τοιούτους εἶναι πολλούς. In the last passage, Chrysostom quotes the text of Acts 11.20 as reading Ἑλληνιστάς, but he interprets it with reference to Ἕλληνες.

Ἑβραῖος as a reference to those who spoke Aramaic.[4]

The other major interpretation of the meaning of ἑλληνίζειν and Ἑλληνιστής has also found ample representation in twentieth-century New Testament scholarship. Many answer the question primarily with reference to culture. This approach includes three distinct interpretations. Some have argued that the terms 'Hellenist' and 'Hellenize' derive from ethnic distinctions and refer to non-Jews.[5] Others have argued that the terms derive from sectarian tensions among various groups in Judaism, and refer to an element in the Jerusalem congregation which was distinguished by its unique views on the ritual laws and the cultus.[6] A third group has taken the terms as deriving from the geographical distinction between Palestinian and Diaspora Jews.[7]

4. This interpretation was once so widespread that Henry Cadbury could call it the 'universal' one and Everett Ferguson labelled it the 'prevailing' one. See Cadbury, 'The Hellenists', pp. 60-61; E. Ferguson, 'The Hellenists in the Book of Acts', *ResQ* 12 (1969), p. 159. Both overstate the case to some extent. Thus, it is more accurate to say that a combination of the linguistic and cultural interpretations has represented a 'consensus' of sorts, to the extent that it is even possible to speak of a consensus. For an excellent survey of twentieth-century scholarship on the question, see Ferguson, 'Hellenists', pp. 159-80.

5. See, for example, G.P. Wetter, 'Das älteste hellenistische Christentum nach der Apostelgeschichte', *ARW* 21 (1922), pp. 410-12 (Gentiles); Cadbury, 'Hellenists', p. 65 (Gentiles); W. Grundmann, 'Das Problem der hellenistischen Christentums innerhalb der Jerusalemer Urgemeinde', *ZNW* 38 (1939), pp. 56-58 (Gentiles, explicitly following Wetter); E.C. Blackman, 'The Hellenists of Acts VI.1', *ExpTim* 48 (1936–37), pp. 524-25 (Proselytes).

6. See, for example, O. Cullmann, 'The Significance of the Qumran Texts for Research into the Beginnings of Christianity', in K. Stendahl (ed.), *The Scrolls and the New Testament* (New York: Harper & Brothers, 1957), pp. 19, 26-28; *idem*, *The Johannine Circle* (trans. J. Bowden; Philadelphia: Westminster Press, 1976), pp. 55-56; M. Simon, *St Stephen and the Hellenists in the Primitive Church* (London: Longmans, Green, 1958), pp. 89-94; E.E. Ellis, 'The Circumcision Party and the Early Christian Mission', in *Prophecy and Hermeneutic in Early Christianity: New Testament Essays* (WUNT, 18; Tübingen: Mohr [Paul Siebeck], 1978), pp. 118-19; cf. also J.B. Lightfoot, 'St Paul and the Three', in *St Paul's Epistle to the Galatians* (London: Macmillan, rev. edn, 1892), pp. 295-97; L. Goppelt, *Apostolic and Post-Apostolic Times* (trans. R.A. Guelich; New York: Harper & Row, 1970), pp. 53-54; and C. Spicq, 'L'Epître aux Hebreux, Apollos, Jean-Baptiste, les Hellénistes et Qumrân', *RevQ* 1 (1958–59), pp. 365-90.

7. See, for example, Ferguson, 'Hellenists', pp. 165-67; I.H. Marshall, 'Palestinian and Hellenistic Christianity: Some Critical Comments', *NTS* 19 (1972–73), p. 277; J.A.T. Robinson, 'The Destination and Purpose of St John's Gospel',

In addition to these two major views on the identity of the ‘Hellenists’ and ‘Hebrews’ in Acts, a significant element in critical scholarship has viewed the dissension as originating from a theological disagreement between the two groups. This viewpoint attributes to the ‘Hellenists’ a critical stance toward the Law and the Temple on the basis of a radical re-casting of Stephen’s speech in Acts 7.[8] It therefore reconstructs the ‘Circle of Stephen’ as representing a significant phase in the development of New Testament theology from Jesus to Paul.[9]

This study proposes to move beyond the impasse concerning the identity of the ‘Hellenists’ and the meaning of Ἑλληνιστής in Acts by utilizing modern methods of linguistic research. A diachronic survey of ἑλληνίζειν in the TLG database, analyzing the way the word was used over time, confirms that the two widely proposed views—language or culture as the basis for the name ‘Hellenist’—are supported by usage in the relevant period. The verb ‘Hellenize’ was used by Greek authors from the fifth century BCE to the second century CE to refer to speaking

NTS 6 (1960), p. 124; cf. also J.D.G. Dunn, *Unity and Diversity in the New Testament: An Inquiry into the Character of Earliest Christianity* (Philadelphia: Westminster Press, 1977), pp. 235-37.

8. See H.A. Brehm, ‘The Role of the “Hellenists” in Christian Origins: A Critique of Representative Models in Light of an Exegetical Study of Acts 6–8’ (PhD dissertation, Southwestern Baptist Theological Seminary, 1992), pp. 29-42, 175-82. See also C.C. Hill, *Hellenists and Hebrews: Reappraising Division within the Earliest Church* (Minneapolis: Fortress Press, 1992).

9. Compare, for example, F.C. Baur’s view of the dissension between the ‘Hellenists’ and ‘Hebrews’ in the Jerusalem congregation as foreshadowing the tension between Petrine and Pauline segments of early Christianity implied in the ‘parties’ at Corinth in F.C. Baur, *Paul, The Apostle of Jesus Christ: His Life and Work, his Epistles and his Doctrine* (trans. and ed. E. Zeller, rev. A. Menzies; London: Williams & Norgate, 2nd edn, 1876), I, pp. 38-41. See further the views of scholars in the Baur tradition, including W. Heitmüller, ‘Zum Problem Paulus und Jesus’, *ZNW* 13 (1912), pp. 329-30, reprinted in K.H. Rengstorf and U. Luck (eds.), *Das Paulusbild in der neueren deutschen Forschung* (Wege der Forschung, 24; Darmstadt: Wissenschaftliche Buchgesellschaft, 3rd edn, 1982), pp. 134-35 (cited hereafter in the reprinted edition); Grundmann, ‘Problem’, pp. 64, 65, 69-71, 73; R. Bultmann, *Theology of the New Testament* (trans. K. Grobel; New York: Scribners, 1951), I, pp. 55-57, 63; and *idem*, *The History of the Synoptic Tradition* (trans. J. Marsh; New York: Harper & Row; Oxford: Basil Blackwell, rev.edn, 1963), p. 303. See further, M. Goguel, *The Birth of Christianity* (trans. H.C. Snape; London: Allen & Unwin, 1953), p. 119; A.F. Loisy, *Les Actes des Apôtres* (Paris: E. Nourry, 1920), p. 297; Wetter, ‘Hellenistische Christentum’, pp. 414-17.

Greek correctly, especially in the case of a 'barbarian'. On the other hand, beginning with the first century BCE, authors could use the term to refer to the adoption of Greek thought or lifestyle. By the fifth century CE this was the predominant usage, especially in the case of a Ἑλληνιστής who embraced heretical or pagan beliefs and practices.

This diachronic survey suggests that the predominant usage of the term ἑλληνίζειν referred to the ability of a non-Greek to speak the language correctly. Since, however, diachronic analysis cannot demonstrate conclusively the meaning of any word in a specific context, it is necessary also to approach the problem from a synchronic perspective by examining the use of the term Ἑλληνιστής in Acts and in the New Testament as a whole.[10] This relates both to the syntagmatic relationships of Ἑλληνιστής to other words in the context of specific sentences and paragraphs and to the paradigmatic relationships of the word to other words which might serve as a substitute for it.

The syntagmatic relationships are rather limited since Ἑλληνιστής occurs only three times in the New Testament (Acts 6.1; 9.29; 11.20). Owing to this limitation, it is impossible to define conclusively Luke's use of the term. In fact, the syntagmatic analysis of Ἑλληνιστής in Acts raises questions regarding all of the proposed solutions to the problem. On the other hand, it does not rule out the view that the 'Hellenists' were so named for their use of the Greek language. The paradigmatic relationships of Ἑλληνιστής to other terms like Ἑβραῖος suggest that the term represents Luke's attempt to distinguish different groups within the Christian community with reference to their socio-religious or ethnic-cultural identity. Paradigmatic analysis also cannot arbitrate conclusively between the major views on the meaning of Ἑλληνιστής in Acts because the categories of religion, language, ethnic background, and culture are intertwined in Luke's identification of groups. Nevertheless, the view that language was the primary factor in the use of the term satisfies the overall diachronic and synchronic considerations better than the other views.

10. Cf. P. Cotterell and M. Turner, *Linguistics and Biblical Interpretation* (Downers Grove, IL: IVP, 1989), pp. 134-35.

ἑλληνίζειν *Referring to Language*[11]

The most prevalent use of the term ἑλληνίζειν in the canon of Greek authors in its simpler form is 'to speak Greek'.[12] The word is used by Greek authors as a substantival participle οἱ ἑλληνίζοντες ('those who Hellenize') to refer to those who adopted certain idioms of speech and those who used different pronunciations among the various dialects of Greek.[13] It denoted the correct use of grammar in Aristotle's use of the term to refer to the proper form of relative and demonstrative pronouns.[14] ἑλληνίζειν also denotes the pronunciation of names in Josephus's discussion of the difference between the name given to a certain island by the 'Εβραῖοι and the one used by those who 'Hellenized' it (ὑπὸ τῶν ἐξελληνισάντων αὐτήν), and his statement to the 'Ελλῆνες that the names in his account were Hellenized (ἡλλήνισται) for the sake of the document's euphony and with a view to his readers' pleasure.[15]

11. The survey of ἑλληνίζειν in Greek literature which follows represents a combination of diachronic and synchronic methods in that it traces the use of the term through the course of time within the context of outlining different idioms in both a syntagmatic and paradigmatic manner.

12. A search of the strings -λληνιζ-, -λληνισ-, and -ηλληνικ- in the Thesaurus Linguae Graecae (TLG) revealed 196 occurrences of ἑλληνίζειν and its cognate verb forms (ἀπελληνίζειν, ἐξελληνίζειν). Where the author has been able to check the reference, complete bibliographical information has been supplied. Where that is not the case, the texts cited below have been taken from TLG, and the citation system in the reference system in TLG has been used.

13. See, for an example of οἱ ἑλληνίζοντες with reference to idioms, Athenaeus (II–III CE), *Deipnosophistae* 6.231b: τι οἱ ἑλληνίζοντες οὐκ ἀργυρώματα καὶ χρυσώματά φασιν, ἀλλ' ἀργυροῦν κόσμον καὶ χρυσοῦν κόσμον. See C.B. Gulick, *Athenaeus: The Deipnosophists* (LCL; London: Heinemann, 1929), III, p. 40. Cf. also Galen (II CE), *De compositione medicamentorum secundum locos* 12.961.9 for an example of the terms applied to pronunciation. B.B. Warfield, 'The Readings Ἕλληνας and 'Ελληνιστάς, Acts XI.20', *JBL* 3 (1883), p. 112 suggests that οἱ ἑλληνίζοντες was the equivalent of 'Ελληνισταί in Greek literature.

14. Cf. Aristotle (IV BCE), *Soph. El.* 182a.14, 34; cf. also Alexander of Aphrodisias (II–III CE), *In Aristotelis sophisticos elenchos commentarium* 185.22, referring to the use of the feminine or masculine genders.

15. See Josephus (I CE), *Ant.* 1.128-29. See H. St J. Thackeray, *Josephus* (LCL; Cambridge, MA: Harvard University Press, 1978), IV, p. 62. Cf. also Dio Cassius (II–III CE), *Hist.* 53.14.6; 75.8.2. See E. Cary, *Dio's Roman History*

Along these lines, the phrase ἑλληνίζων τὴν φωνήν or ἑλληνίζων τῇ φωνῇ ('Hellenize the voice') commonly describes someone who spoke Greek but is not of Greek descent.[16] For example, Aeschines refers to a Scythian who was a barbarian 'from his mother' but who 'Hellenized' his speech.[17] A comparable idiom, ἑλληνίζειν τὴν γλῶσσαν ('Hellenize the tongue'), is used with the same connotation. This is represented by Thucydides, who speaks of certain Amphilochians who 'Hellenized' their speech in contrast with others who were βάρβαροι.[18] Furthermore, the phrase ἑλληνίζειν ἐπίστασθαι ('to

(LCL; Cambridge, MA: Harvard University Press, 1979), VI, p. 228; IX, p. 180. Cf. also Galen (II CE), *Inst. Log.* 4.6.9; Origen (II–III CE), *Commentarii in evangelium Joannis* 2.33.197; and Gregory of Nyssa (IV CE), *In inscriptiones Psalmorum* 5.90.19, where they contrast the way that the Ἑβραῖοι pronounced names with the way they were 'Hellenized' (ἐξελληνίζειν). Compare also Procopius (VI CE), *History of the Wars* 2 (= *Pers.*), 29.25; 3 (= *Vand.*), 21.2, 3, where he speaks of the Romans adopting Greek terminology. See H.B. Dewing, *Procopius* (LCL; London: Heinemann, 1914), I, p. 534; II, pp. 176, 178. Compare as well the phrase τὸ ὄνομα ἐξελληνίζειν in Plutarch (I–II CE), *Num.* 13.6.3; and Eusebius (IV CE), *Gospel Questions and Solutions addressed to Stephanus* (*PG* XXII, p. 925). See further Appian (I–II CE), *Sam.* 7.2, where the Tarentines jeered the Roman embassy when they did not 'Hellenize' well. See H. White, *Appian's Roman History* (LCL; Cambridge, MA: Harvard University Press, 1974), I, p. 78.

16. In addition to the examples cited in the text, see also Chariton (II CE?), *Chaereas and Callirhoe* 4.5.2. See W.E. Blake, *Charitonis Aphrodisiensis: De Chaerea et Callirhoe Amatoriarum Narrationum Libro octo* (Oxford: Clarendon Press, 1938), p. 63. See further Heliodorus (III CE?), *Aeth.* 9.25.3; cf. also Gregory of Nazianzus (IV CE), *In sanctum Pascha* (*PG* XXXVI, p. 636).

17. See Aeschines (IV BCE), *In Ctes.* 172.11, referring to a Scythian: τὰ δ' ἀπὸ τῆς μητρὸς Σκύθης Βάρβαρος ἑλληνίζων τῇ φωνῇ. See also Lucian of Samosota (II CE), *Dial. D.* 9.6, referring to a Mede who could not understand Greek. See A.M. Harmon, *Lucian* (LCL; London: Heinemann, 1936), V, p. 430. See further Eusebius (IV CE), *Life of Constantine* 2.44.1, where he refers to the delivery of a homily; Libanius, *Arg. D.* 3.9; Sopater (IV CE), Διαίρεσις ζητημάτων 5.50.6.

18. See Thucydides (V BCE), *Hist.* 2.68.5. See C.F. Smith, *Thucydides* (LCL; Cambridge, MA: Harvard University Press, 1980), I, p. 382. Cf. also Eusebius (IV CE), *Hist. Eccl.* 7.25.26, where he uses the phrase ἑλληνίζειν διάλεκτον καὶ γλῶσσαν. See J.E.L. Oulton and H.J. Lawlor, *Eusebius: The Ecclesiastical History* (LCL; Cambridge, MA: Harvard University Press, 1980), II, pp. 206, 208. See also Gregory of Nazianzus (IV CE), *Funebris oratio in laudem Basilii Magni Caesareae in Cappadocia episcopi* (orat. 43) 23.4.3, where he describes the orator or scholar as one who γλῶσσαν ἐξελληνίζει καὶ ἱστορίαν συνάγει καὶ μέτροις ἐπιστατεῖ

know how to Hellenize') refers to the ability to communicate in Greek, especially with reference to a barbarian,[19] or to speak Greek correctly, especially with reference to a Greek.[20]

Greek authors thus define the difference between ἀττικίζειν and ἑλληνίζειν in terms of the sound of the dialect.[21] Similarly, they use ἑλληνίζειν in conjunction with a variety of terms including σολοικίζειν ('commit a solecism'),[22] βαρβαρίζειν ('commit a barbarism'),[23] ῥωμαΐζειν ('speak Latin'),[24] αἰθιοπίζειν ('speak like

καὶ νομοθετεῖ ποιήμασιν, referring to the understanding of meter and formation of principles for poetry in connection with γλῶσσαν ἐξελληνίζειν. Compare also Procopius (VI CE), *Arc.* 20.17.10. See Dewing, *Procopius*, VI, p. 240.

19. See Xenophon (V–IV BCE), *Anab.* 7.3.25, where a cupbearer, in reply to the question regarding what another said in a different language, says that the foreigner ἑλληνίζειν...ἠπίστατο. Cf. also Philostratus (II–III CE), *VS* 1.489. See W.C. Wright, *Philostratus and Eunapius: The Lives of the Sophists* (LCL; London: Heinemann, 1922), p. 22. See also Heliodorus (III CE?), *Aeth.* 10.9.6, where he says that Sisimithres 'Hellenized' his report to the Gymnosophists so that the multitude of Ethiopians did not understand (ἑλληνίζων ὥστε μὴ τὸ πλῆθος ἐπαΐειν).

20. Cf. Plato (V–IV BCE), *Charm.* 159a; *Alc.* 111c. See W.R.M. Lamb, *Plato* (LCL; Cambridge, MA: Harvard University Press, 1960), VIII, pp. 26, 126. Cf. also Aristotle (IV BCE), *Rh.* 1413b, where ἑλληνίζειν ἐπίστασθαι is a requirement for the ability to express oneself properly in speech and writing. See J.H. Freese, *Aristotle* (LCL; London: Heinemann, 1925), XXII, p. 418. On the other hand, Olympiodorus (VI CE), *In Alc.* 95.18, comments on Socrates' statement in *Alcibiades* and further extends the definition of what it means to teach ἑλληνίζειν with reference to language, contrasting those who teach 'Hellenizing', or τὸ ἁπλῶς Ἑλλήδι φωνῇ μόνῃ κεχρῆσθαι, with the scholars who teach τὸ ἀπταίστως διαλέγεσθαι. This suggests that teaching ἑλληνίζειν is contrasted with truly teaching the Greek language. Cf. also *In Alc.* 91.8; 96.5, 18.

21. See Posidippus (III BCE), *Fragmenta* 28.3, σὺ μὲν ἀττικίζεις, ἡνίκ' ἂν φωνὴν λέγῃς αὐτοῦ τινές, οἱ δ' Ἕλληνες ἑλληνίζομεν.

22. Cf. Galen (II CE), *De methodo medendi* 10.71.6; Eusebius (IV CE), *Hist. Eccl.* 7.25.26 (quoting Dionysius); cf. Oulton and Lawlor, *Eusebius*, II, pp. 206, 208.

23. Cf. Lucian of Samosota (II CE), *Philops.* 16.13; Aelius Herodianus (II CE), Περὶ σολοικισμοῦ καὶ βαρβαρισμοῦ 311.12; cf. also 308-309. Cf. also Rufus (I–II CE), *De corporis humani appellationibus* 19.19.3; cf. also Eusebius (IV CE), *Hist. Eccl.* 7.25.26 (quoting Dionysius); cf. Oulton and Lawlor, *Eusebius*, II, pp. 206, 208. See also Thucydides (V BCE), *Hist.* 2.68.5, where he speaks of certain Amphilochians who 'Hellenized' their speech in contrast with others who were βάρβαροι. See Smith, *Thucydides*, I, p. 382.

24. Philostratus (II–III CE), *VA* 5.36.50, where Apollonius advises Vespasian to

an Ethiopian'),[25] or ἑβραΐζειν ('speak Aramaic')[26] to contrast various modes of speaking.[27] For example, Strabo describes those who 'commit barbarism' as οἱ κακῶς ἑλληνιζόντες ('those who Hellenize poorly'), and defines this with reference to not being able to ἀρτιστομεῖν, or 'to speak in good idiom or accurately'.[28]

In this regard, Greek authors define the matter of learning to ἑλληνίζειν in terms of acquiring a proficiency with the language. As a prime example, Aristotle says ἔστι δ' ἀρχὴ τῆς λέξεως τὸ ἑλληνίζειν ('to Hellenize is the beginning of speech'), referring to the correct use of the Greek language.[29] He lists a number of specific examples of what constitutes τὸ ἑλληνίζειν, including the proper use of connecting particles like μέν and δέ, the use of specific rather than

appoint governors over the Greeks who speak Greek. See F.C. Conybeare, *Philostratus: The Life of Apollonius of Tyana* (LCL; London: Heinemann, 1912), I, p. 556.

25. Heliodorus (III CE?), *Aeth.* 10.39.1.5, where he says that a certain Sisimithres did not 'Hellenize' his report to the king so that those who 'Ethiopize' understood (οὐχ ἑλληνίζων ἀλλ' ὥστε καὶ πάντας ἐπαΐειν αἰθιοπίζων), in contrast to a previous statement that the aforementioned Sisimithres 'Hellenized' a report so that those who 'Ethiopize' did not understand.

26. See Josephus (I CE), *War* 6.96, where he uses ἑβραΐζων to describe how he delivered Titus's offer to spare Jerusalem to John of Gischala and the multitude in Aramaic (τά τε τοῦ Καίσαρος διήγγελλεν ἑβραΐζων). See Thackeray, *Josephus*, III, p. 402.

27. Compare also Procopius (VI CE), *History of the Wars* 7 (= *Goth.*) 26.24, where he describes a certain John of Gilacius who neither spoke Greek (ἑλληνίζειν ἠπίστατο) nor Latin, Gothic, nor any other language except Armenian (οὗτος ὁ Γιλάκιος οὔτε ἑλληνίζειν ἠπίστατο οὔτε Λατίνην ἢ Γοτθικὴν ἢ ἄλλην τινὰ ἢ Ἀρμενίαν μόνην ἀφεῖναι φωνήν). See Dewing, *Procopius*, IV, p. 384.

28. See also Strabo (I BCE–I CE), *Geog.* 14.2.28, where he contrasts ἑλληνισμός with βαρβαροθωνεῖν, βαρβαρίζειν, καρίζειν and σολοικίζειν. H.L. Jones, *The Geography of Strabo* (LCL; Cambridge, MA: Harvard University Press, 1970), VI, pp. 306-307, who translates this as 'the art of speaking Greek'. While it is true that he says that they cannot 'speak accurately' because they have not entered into ἑλληνισμός, which may bring in a broader cultural reference, the focus of ἑλληνίζειν in this context is clearly the ability to speak Greek correctly. On the definition of ἀρτιστομεῖν, see LSJ, I, p. 249, where they refer to this passage in Strabo's *Geography* as an example.

29. Aristotle (IV BCE), *Rh.* 1407a. See Freese, *Aristotle*, XXII, pp. 370-75. Cf. also Strabo (I BCE–I CE), *Geog.* 2.3.4, where he narrates the account of Ptolemy Euergetes handing over an Indian to be taught to speak Greek (ἑλληνίζειν) in order to recount his voyage from India. See Jones, *Geography of Strabo*, I, p. 376.

generic terms, the avoidance of ambiguous terms, the strict maintenance of the distinction between genders, and the observance of number.[30] In another context Aristotle says that the style of written compositions is 'most precise' (ἀκριβεστάτη) and requires that one 'know how to Hellenize' (ἑλληνίζειν ἐπίστασθαι), again relating ἑλληνίζειν to a high level of proficiency with the language.[31] Similarly, Dionysius of Halicarnassus contrasts the quality of 'speaking finely' (καλλιειπεῖν) with the more distasteful practice of others who 'Hellenize badly' (κάκιον ἑλληνίζουσα).[32] Moreover, Sextus Empiricus demonstrates that there was a debate in his day about whether it was better to learn to ἑλληνίζειν by imitation, that is, by observing how the majority of Greeks spoke, or by acquiring philological understanding and studying the etymology of the language.[33] Finally, Greek authors demonstrate their understanding of the meaning of ἑλληνίζειν to signify the correct

30. In addition, see Aelius Herodianus (II CE), Περὶ σολοικισμοῦ καὶ βαρβαρισμοῦ 308-309 (cf. also 311), where he lists ἑλληνισμός as one of the virtues of speech (ἀρεταὶ λόγου), along with clarity (σαφήνεια), conciseness (συντομία), the use of literal expressions (κυριολογία), good arrangement of words (εὐσυνθεσία), and speciousness (εὐπρέπεια), and defines ἑλληνισμός as speech that is sound and accurate or contains proper arrangements of the parts of speech (ἑλληνισμὸς μὲν οὖν ἐστὶ λέξις ὑγιὴς καὶ ἀδιάστροφος ἢ λόγου μερῶν πλοκὴ κατάλληλος). See also Diogenes Laertius (III CE), *Vit.* 7.59.1-2, where he also lists ἑλληνισμός as one of the virtues of speech (ἀρεταὶ λόγου), along with clarity (σαφήνεια), conciseness (συντομία), propriety (πρέπον), and correct style (κατασκευή). He defines ἑλληνισμός somewhat differently as speech that is 'faultless with reference to artistic and not casual usage' (ἑλληνισμὸς μὲν οὖν ἐστι φράσις ἀδιάπτωτος ἐν τῇ τεχνικῇ καὶ μὴ εἰκαία συνηθεία), and contrasts this with βαρβαρισμός, or the violation of Greek usage, and with σολοικισμός, or incongruous usage. See R.D. Hicks, *Diogenes Laertius: Lives of Eminent Philosophers* (LCL; London: Heinemann, 1925), II, pp. 166, 168.

31. Aristotle (IV BCE), *Rh.* 1413b. Compare also Freese, *Aristotle*, XXII, p. 419, where he translates this phrase as 'a knowledge of good Greek'.

32. Dionysius of Halicarnassus (I BCE), *Dem.* 5.21; cf. *Pomp.* 2.5.4. Cf. also Rufus (I–II CE), *De corporis humani appelationibus* 133.3, where he laments the names created by certain Egyptian healers who φαύλως ἑλληνίζειν; and Gregory of Nazianzus (IV CE), *Contra Julianem imperatorem 1* (*PG* XXXV, p. 636), where he contrasts those who practice ἑλληνίζειν with ἀλογία and ἀγροικία (the first of which clearly refers to language, while the second may refer to the practice of Greek customs).

33. Sextus Empiricus (II–III CE), *Math.* 1.176-247 (esp. 176-94, 235, 247). He also defines ἑλληνισμός in terms of proper usage of the Greek language. See H. Mutschmann, *Sexti Emperici opera* (Leipzig: Teubner, 1961), III, pp. 46-61.

use of the Greek language by qualifying the term with adverbs such as ἀκριβῶς, ὀρθῶς, καθαρῶς, ἀμέμπτως, σαφῶς and βεβαίως.[34]

ἑλληνίζειν *Referring to Thought or Way of Life*

On the other hand, Greek authors also use ἑλληνίζειν in a context which implies a meaning beyond the use of language. In this regard they employ the idiom ἑλληνίζειν τὴν γνώμην ('Hellenize the understanding'), which carries the implication of adopting a Greek way of thinking. For example, Aristides describes a barbarian as one who ἑλληνίζειν οἶδεν οὐ μόνον τοῖς ῥήμασιν, ἀλλὰ καὶ τῇ γνώμῃ.[35] Yet in these references Greek authors are primarily concerned with the relationship between thought and language. In fact, Sextus Empiricus may indicate this kind of relationship between an understanding of the Greek language and the Greek way of life when he says that ἑλληνίζειν means to learn from the language what is 'Hellenistic'.[36]

34. ἀκριβῶς: Rufus (I–II CE), *De corporis humani appelationibus* 65.15.7, where he associates ἑλληνίζειν ἀκριβῶς with γράμματα ἐπίστασθαι; cf. also Galen (II CE), *In Hippocratis librum iii epidemiarum commentaria iii* 17a.625.53; Eusebius (IV CE), *Hist. Eccl.* 7.25.26, where he quotes a letter of Dionysius, remarking on the style of Revelation in contrast to that of the Fourth Gospel and 1 John that διάλεκτον μέντοι καὶ γλῶσσαν οὐκ ἀκριβῶς ἑλληνίζουσαν αὐτου. See Oulton and Lawlor, *Eusebius*, II, pp. 206, 208. ὀρθῶς: Aelius Herodianus (II CE), Περὶ σολοικισμοῦ καὶ βαρβαρισμοῦ 311.12, where he defines ἑλληνισμός as τὸ πάσαις ταῖς διαλέκτοις ὀρθῶς χρῆσθαι. καθαρῶς: Lucian of Samosota (II CE), *Philops.* 34.9. ἀμέμπτως: Sextus Empiricus (II–III CE), *Math.* 1.235. Compare also Clement of Alexandria (II–III CE), *Strom.* 2.1.3 (*PG* VIII, p. 934). σαφῶς: Rufus (I–II CE), *De corporis humani appelationibus* 19.9.8, where he speaks of those who no longer 'Hellenize precisely' because they dwell among barbarians. βεβαίως: Heliodorus (III CE?) *Aeth.* 2.30.1.

35. Aristides (II CE), Ὑπὲρ τῆς πρὸς Ἀθηναίους εἰρήνης 403.11. See W. Dindorf, *Aristides* (Hildesheim: Georg Olms, 1964), I, p. 605. Compare also Ῥόδιοι περὶ ὁμονοίας 571, where he speaks of those σφόδρα ἑλληνίζοντες. See Dindorf, *Aristides*, I, p. 843. While Hengel recognizes that the former reference contains an 'extended meaning', he claims that the latter is 'purely linguistic'. See Hengel, *Between Jesus and Paul*, p. 141 n. 55. Cf. also Synesius (IV–V CE), *Aegyptii sive de providentia* 2.7.35, which speaks of ἑλληνίζειν in contrast to αἰγυπτιάζειν in a context that goes beyond language and refers to mode of thought. In addition, Agatharchides (II BCE) describes a Persian as ὃν καὶ ἑλληνίσαι γλῶσσαν καὶ γνώμην (cited by Photius [IX CE], in *Bibl.* 250.442a.23).

36. Sextus Empiricus (II–III CE), *Math.* 1.184; cf. also 1.176, 186, 189, 190,

In other cases, however, the term ἑλληνίζειν clearly refers to the adoption of Greek thought or a Greek way of life.[37] The word is used in this manner by Philo to praise Augustus as the one who 'Hellenized' (ἀφελληνίσας) the most important parts of the barbarian world.[38] ἑλληνίζειν contains this idea in the context of Porphyry's accusation that Origen had adopted a Greek way of thought that included 'Hellenizing' his opinions regarding 'material things and the Deity'.[39] It has a similar connotation in a text where Heliodorus describes a Persian woman who 'Hellenized' the understanding and who had an extreme love for Greek customs and association.[40] The term also implies the adoption of a Greek way of life when Sozomen describes those who 'conducted themselves in a pious and manly fashion in philosophy and in the household virtues' in connection with the practice of ἑλληνίζειν.[41]

In the context of this development of the term, the church fathers use it with a negative connotation. Eusebius employs ἑλληνίζειν with

192, where he enters the debate over how one acquires language. See Mutschmann, *Sexti Emperici opera*, III, pp. 46, 48-49.

37. Compare also Josephus, who quotes an account from Clearchus of Soli of how Aristotle met a certain Jew who was 'Greek not in language alone, but also in soul' (ἑλληνικὸς ἦν οὐ τῇ διαλέκτῳ μόνον, ἀλλὰ καὶ τῇ ψυχῇ). See Josephus (I CE), *Ap.* 1.180. See Thackeray, *Josephus*, I, p. 234.

38. Philo Judaeus (I BCE–I CE), *Leg.* 147.5. See F.H. Colson, *Philo* (LCL; Cambridge, MA: Harvard University Press, 1962), X, p. 74. See also E.M. Smallwood, *Philonis Alexandrini: Legatio ad Gaium* (Leiden: Brill, 2nd edn, 1970), p. 229, where she suggests that this statement refers to 'the general diffusion of Greek culture under the *pax Romana*'.

39. Porphyry (III CE), *Contra Christianos* 39.30: κατὰ δὲ τὰς περὶ τῶν πραγμάτων καὶ τοῦ θείου δόξας Ἑλληνίζων. Contrast Eusebius (IV CE), *Hist. Eccl.* 6.19.7, where he cites Porphyry and disputes his claim that Origen had in effect become thoroughly Hellenized. See Oulton and Lawlor, *Eusebius*, II, p. 58. See also Epiphanius (IV CE), *Anc.* 12.8.2; *Adv. Haeres.* 25.157.3, 6; 159.21, 25; and *passim*; *Anac.* 25.163.1; 164.9, 14, where he lists the various 'sects' that originated with ἑλληνισμός, including Platonists, Aristotelians, Pythagoreans, Stoics, Epicureans, etc., which suggests that the term refers to Greek thought.

40. Heliodorus (III CE?), *Aeth.* 7.14.2: καὶ Περσὶς οὖσα τὸ γένος σφόδρα ἑλληνίζει τὴν γνώμην χαίρουσα καὶ προστρέχουσα τοῖς ἐντεῦθεν, ἦθός τε καὶ ὁμιλίαν τὴν Ἑλληνικὴν εἰς ὑπερβολὴν ἠγάπηκε. Cf. 2.21.4, where he also speaks of an Egyptian who 'Hellenized' his dress (στολή).

41. Sozomen (V CE), *Hist. Eccl.* 3.14.28: εὐσεβῶς καὶ ἀνδρείως ἐν φιλοσοφίᾳ ἐπολιτεύσαντο καὶ ταῖς οἰκείαις ἀρεταῖς.

reference to Antiochus IV Epiphanes' program of forced Hellenization in Jerusalem, which served as the occasion for the Maccabean revolt.[42] In this connection the fourth- and fifth-century Church Fathers generally refer to someone who adopted heretical beliefs or Greek practices that are contrary to Christianity by means of the term ἑλληνίζειν.[43] They particularly use the term Ἑλληνιστής with this in mind. For example, Sozomen says that those who defend the term 'consubstantial' for Christ's relationship with God the Father consider their opponents in the Arian controversy as Ἑλληνισταί.[44] Furthermore he reports the account of soldiers who had offered incense in pagan sacrifice, where they lamented that they had done it in ignorance 'entirely as if it is to say that they Hellenized the hand only while the mind did not cooperate' (εἴ γε ὅλως εἰπεῖν ἔστι, μόνην ἑλληνίσαι τὴν χεῖρα μὴ συμπραξάσης τῆς διανοίας).[45] In addition Sozomen repeatedly refers to non-Christian Greeks as Ἑλληνισταί, especially in a context of antagonism or a contrast between pagan beliefs and Christianity.[46]

42. Eusebius (IV CE), *Dem. Evang.* 8.2.71: καθ' ὃν 'Αντίοχος τοὺς 'Ιουδαίους πολιορκήσας ἑλληνίζειν κατηνάγκαζεν; cf. also *Dem. Evang.* 10.1.10; *Commentaria in Psalmos* (*PG* XXIII, p. 833), where he adds that Antiochus 'compelled the Jews to hellenize and abandon their ancestral customs' (ἑλληνίζειν καὶ παραβαίνειν τὰ πάτρια ἀνάγκαζεν 'Ιουδαίους), making clear that ἑλληνίζειν included the adoption of Greek customs. Sozomen (V CE) uses ἑλληνίζειν in a manner similar to Eusebius when he refers to the expectation by the non-Christian Greeks that Attalus would 'Hellenize' and restore their temples, festivals, and sacrifices (*Hist. Eccl.* 9.9.1). Compare also Gregory of Nazianzus (IV CE), *Contra Juianem imperatorem 1* (*PG* XXXV, p. 636), where he contrasts those who practice ἑλληνίζειν with ἀγροικία, or crudeness, which may imply a reference to the practice of Greek customs.

43. See, for example, Gregory of Nyssa (IV CE), *Oratio catechetica magna* 19.1; cf. also Gregory of Nazianzus (IV CE), *In theophania* (*PG* XXXVI, p. 320); *In sanctum Pascha* (*PG* XXXVI, p. 628); Athanasius, *Contra Sabellianos* (*PG* XXVIII, p. 97), *Quaestiones ad Antiochum ducem* (*PG* XXVIII, p. 597), *Oratio quarta contra Arianos* 10.6, comparing those who practiced 'Judaizing' (ἰουδαΐζειν) with those who practiced 'Hellenizing' (ἑλληνίζειν). See also *Apocalypse of John* 21.4, where ἑλληνισμός is listed along with idolatry, solar and astral religion, and various heresies. See C. Tischendorf, *Apocalypses Apocryphae Mosis Esdrae Pauli Iohannis, item Mariae Dormitio* (Leipzig: Mendelssohn, 1866), p. 88.

44. Sozomen (V CE), *Hist. Eccl.* 2.18.3.

45. Sozomen, *Hist. Eccl.* 5.17.12.

46. Sozomen, *Hist. Eccl.* 2.32.3; 3.17.1; 4.26.4; 5.3.9; 5.5.7; 5.7.4, 6, 7; 5.10.8, 13, 14; 5.11.4, 11; 5.15.4; 5.16.4, 12; 5.19.9; 5.21.3; 6.35.1, 4; 6.37.14; 7.15.8, 10, 11, 14; 7.20.5; 7.28.5. Cf. also *passim*, for Sozomen's use of

Some Synchronic Observations

A synchronic analysis of usage of 'Ἑλληνιστής in Acts calls attention to the basic uncertainty concerning the meaning of the term.[47] One of the reasons for this uncertainty is because the term 'Ἑλληνιστής has three different connotations in three different contexts. In Acts 6.1 it clearly refers to a group in the Jerusalem congregation. In Acts 9.29, however, it clearly refers to non-believing opponents of Paul, and in comparison with Acts 6.9 probably refers to Jews. In Acts 11.20 yet a third connotation surfaces, for there it contrasts with the 'Ιουδαίοις of 11.19. Therefore it must refer to a segment of the non-Jewish population of Antioch. In short, the fact that 'Ἑλληνιστής has three different connotations in the New Testament frustrates the best attempts to explain it.[48] The problem is compounded by the fact that variant readings raise questions about the originality of the term in Acts 9.29 and 11.20. It is clear that 'Ἑλληνιστάς is the more original reading in Acts 9.29. That 'Ἑλληνιστάς is also the more original reading in Acts 11.20 may be argued on the basis of external evidence and transcriptional probabilities.[49]

An analysis of the syntagmatic relations of 'Ἑλληνιστής in Acts raises questions about standard solutions to the identity of the

ἑλληνισμός for Greek culture and practices, especially in connection with the practice of idolatry.

47. See Cadbury, 'Hellenists', pp. 60, 64 n. 5, 73. He says in light of Chrysostom's uncertainty, 'it is worth while to remind ourselves how little we really know of the word Hellenist'.

48. Cadbury records the comments of A.D. Nock ('The Hellenists', p. 70 n. 1): 'The curious thing is the matter-of-fact way in which the word is used in vi. 1. Any Greek reader outside the Christian circles would have been puzzled, I think. Now the two certain examples are vi. 1 and ix. 29, both relating to Jerusalem. Have we here a *Schlagwort*, whose meaning was familiar at the time but which disappeared from use?... 'Ἑλληνιστής does seem to me to mean something quite definite.' The problem is that the references in Acts 9.29 and 11.20 have to do with groups *outside* Christian circles.

49. See Brehm, 'Hellenists', pp. 139-44. See further Warfield, '"Ἕλληνας and 'Ἑλληνιστάς', pp. 125-26; Ferguson, 'The Hellenists', pp. 176-77. Contrast Wetter, 'Hellenistische Christentum', pp. 418-19; Hengel, 'Between Jesus and Paul', p. 8; Cadbury, 'Hellenists', p. 71. The latter only judge one or two of the occurrences to be original, but in each case their textual judgment seems influenced by their theory about the meaning of 'Ἑλληνιστής.

'Hellenists'. In the first place, the fact that Luke speaks of other Greek-speaking Jews elsewhere in Acts without calling them 'Hellenists' remains an obstacle to an exclusively linguistic solution to the problem.[50] In the second place, the usage of Ἑλληνιστής in Acts also brings to light a problem with the interpretation of the 'Hellenists' as Jews opposed to the Temple or as ritually lax Jews. This interpretation fails to make sense of the fact that Luke also calls the Jewish opponents of Paul in Acts 9.29 'Hellenists' and not 'Hebrews'. If it is correct to associate these Jewish 'Hellenists' in Acts 9.29 with the opponents of Stephen in Acts 6.9, then one must ask why they would have persecuted Stephen and the rest of the Christian 'Hellenists' for opposing the Temple or for having a lax attitude toward the cultus and the ritual law.[51] If Ἑλληνιστής signifies Jews who opposed the Temple or had a lax attitude toward the Law, then Jewish 'Hellenists' would have shared that perspective with the Christian 'Hellenists'.[52] This objection applies generally to the attempts to identify the 'Hellenists' primarily on the basis of culture, since Luke does not call the opponents of Stephen 'Hebrews'.

An analysis of the paradigmatic relations of Ἑλληνιστής in Acts shows that it occurs in the context of Luke's attempt to distinguish different groups within the Christian community from one another and from those outside the community with reference to their socio-religious or ethnic-cultural identity. Luke specifically contrasts the Ἑλληνισταί in Acts with two other groups, the Ἑβραῖοι (Acts 6.1) and the Ἰουδαῖοι (Acts 11.19). Other groups in Acts include ἔθνη, Ἕλληνες,

50. Acts 18.2, 24; 21.27; 24.19; cf. Wetter, 'Hellenistische Christentum', p. 410; Marshall, 'Palestinian and Hellenistic Christianity', pp. 271-78.

51. For the identification of Stephen's opponents in Acts 6.9 with those of Paul in Acts 9.29, see G. Schneider, 'Stephanus, die Hellenisten und Samaria', in J. Kremer (ed.), *Les Actes des Apôtres: Traditions, rédaction, théologie* (Leuven: Leuven University Press, 1979), p. 220. *Pace* Cadbury's objections against pressing 'the loose connexions of an obscure passage' too hard ('Hellenists', p. 60).

52. See also Haenchen, *The Acts of the Apostles*, pp. 260-61 n. 3, where he points out a similar inconsistency, saying, 'But the real difficulty lies in the implicit contradiction at the heart of Cullmann's picture—on the one hand the Hellenists must be "syncretistic" to the extent of beginning the mission to the Gentiles, on the other they must be closely connected with Qumran, which is more legalistic than the legalists'. See also Ferguson, 'Hellenists', pp. 174-75; and R. Scroggs, 'The Earliest Hellenistic Christianity', in *Religions in Antiquity: Essays in Memory of E.R. Goodenough* (Leiden: Brill, 1968), p. 180.

ἀλλόφυλοι, προσήλυτοι and the ἀκροβυστία, all of which have either a socio-religious or ethnic-cultural connotation.[53] The phrase τινες τῶν ἀπὸ τῆς αἱρέσεως τῶν Φαρισαίων πεπιστευκότες (Acts 15.5) represents a group of believers distinguished by their former membership in the sect of the Pharisees and perhaps by implication also their continued adherence to pharisaic teachings. On the other hand, οἱ ἐκ περιτομῆς (Acts 10.45; 11.1-2, 18) designates a group in the Jerusalem congregation, but the precise referent of the expression is unclear.[54] Other group names like ζηλωταὶ τοῦ νόμου (Acts 21.20), οἱ φοβούμενοι/σεβόμενοι τὸν θεόν (Acts 10.2, 22, 35; 13.16, 26; 16.14; 17.4; 18.7; 18.13; cf. also 13.43, 50; 17.17), τινες ἀπὸ τῆς Ἰουδαίας (Acts 15.1), κύπριοι and κυρηναῖοι (Acts 11.20), do not fall into socio-religious or ethnic-cultural semantic domains, but upon closer examination have such a connotation in Acts.[55]

Within the context of the paradigmatic relations of Ἑλληνιστής in Acts, Luke's contrast between this group and the Ἑβραῖοι and Ἰουδαῖοι is of primary importance. Luke uses Ἑβραῖος only in Acts 6.1, but does not clearly define it. The context of Acts suggests that Luke distinguishes the Ἑβραῖοι as believing Jews from the Ἰουδαῖοι as non-believing Jews. The term occurs elsewhere in the New Testament only in Paul's writings. An examination of the syntagmatic relations of Ἑβραῖος in Paul also raises questions about several of the proposed solutions to the question of the identity of the 'Hebrews', and thus also the 'Hellenists', in Acts. Paul implies that his opponents called themselves Ἑβραῖοι, but he makes a point of saying that he could claim for

53. See J.P. Louw, E.A. Nida, *et al.* (eds.), *Greek–English Lexicon of the New Testament Based on Semantic Domains* (2 vols.; New York: United Bible Societies, 1988): ἔθνη (11.37; 11.55), Ἕλληνες (11.40; 11.90), ἀλλόφυλοι (11.43), προσήλυτοι (11.54), and the ἀκροβυστία (11.52, 53).

54. Louw and Nida, *Greek–English Lexicon*: περιτομῆς (11.51). Contrast Ellis, 'Circumcision Party', pp. 116-17. For a critique of Ellis's views, see Brehm, 'Hellenists', pp. 54-60. The term does not appear in Acts until after the conversion of Cornelius and the group of Gentile συγγενεῖς and φίλοι gathered at his house (Acts 10.24). Perhaps in that context the need arose for Luke to distinguish between the Jewish Christians and the Gentile believers.

55. Louw and Nida, *Greek–English Lexicon*: ζηλωταὶ τοῦ νόμου (25.77: Attitude), οἱ φοβούμενοι/σεβόμενοι τὸν θεόν (53.53, 58: Religious activities), τινες ἀπὸ τῆς Ἰουδαίας (93.170: Names of places), κύπριοι (93.509: Names of persons), κυρηναῖοι (93.511: Names of persons). This highlights a limitation with Louw and Nida's work.

himself exactly the same privileges as his opponents (2 Cor. 11.22). In Phil. 3.5 Paul also identifies himself as a Ἑβραῖος ἐξ Ἑβραίων. This makes the problem particularly acute, because Paul does not just claim that he once was a Ἑβραῖος, he claims that he *is* one.

This creates a problem for all of the proposed solutions to the identity of the 'Hebrews' in Acts. While it would appear to be true that Paul continued to observe Jewish customs after his conversion and call to evangelize the Gentiles, this cannot be construed to mean that he was 'ritually strict'.[56] It also constitutes an obstacle to the interpretation that attributes a difference of cultural orientation to the Ἑβραῖοι and Ἑλληνισταί in Acts 6.1, because Paul, a Jew from the Diaspora who seemingly crossed all cultural boundaries, could claim to be a 'Hebrew'.[57] Paul's claim raises an objection against the view that proposes to solve the problem by attributing a theological difference to the 'Hellenists' and 'Hebrews', making the Hebrews out to be the forerunners of Paul's 'Judaizing' opponents, because in spite of Paul's polemics against his opponents' false gospel (2 Cor. 11.2-4), he claims to share with them the distinction of being a Ἑβραῖος.[58] Furthermore, the

56. Contrast Cullmann, 'Significance', p. 19; Ellis, 'Circumcision Party', pp. 118-19, 121-22. Contrast also G.F. Hawthorne, *Philippians* (WBC; Waco, TX: Word Books, 1983), p. 133, where he suggests that while Paul could have been labeled a Hellenist because he was born outside of Palestine, he rejected that label on the basis of his rabbinic training in Jerusalem, his adoption of Aramaic as his language, and his observance of Jewish customs. Cf. similarly J.B. Lightfoot, *St Paul's Epistle to the Philippians* (London: Macmillan, 1913), p. 147. At the same time, however, Paul maintained that he could become 'all things to all men', including Jews, those under the law, the 'lawless', and the weak (1 Cor. 9.19-23).

57. Contrast Ferguson, 'Hellenists', pp. 165-67; Marshall, 'Palestinian and Hellenistic Christianity', p. 277. While many acknowledge that Judaism participated in the interaction of cultures characteristic of the Hellenistic age, the assumption that Diaspora Jews were somehow more open culturally speaking persists. On the other hand, both Philo and Josephus depict Diaspora Jews as adopting Greek language and customs on the one hand while at the same time continuing to observe circumcision, the Sabbath, purity codes and food laws, and continuing to revere the Temple. See Philo, *Migr. Abr.* 89-94; *Spec. Leg.* 1.66-70, 257; Josephus, *War* 2.591; *Ant.* 12.120; 13.74-79; 14.213-16, 225-27; 16.160-78; 18.312-13, 322-23, 340, 348, 350; 20.38-48 (regarding the circumcision of a *proselyte*, not a Jew); *Life* 74. See also E.R. Goodenough, *Jewish Symbols in the Greco-Roman Period*. I. *The Archaeological Evidence from Palestine* (New York: Pantheon, 1953), pp. 33-41, 54-58. See further, Brehm, 'Hellenists', pp. 127-38.

58. Contrast Grundmann, 'Problem', p. 54; Bultmann, *Theology*, I, pp. 54-56.

fact that Paul, although he calls himself a 'Hebrew', most certainly could speak Greek as well as Aramaic suggests that any linguistic distinctions could not have been absolute and mutually exclusive.[59] Thus the solution to the meaning of Ἑβραῖος in Paul must conform to the fact that the apostle, writing at the earliest toward the end of his third missionary journey and perhaps as late as his imprisonment in Rome, could still claim to be a 'Hebrew'.

On the other hand, the question of identifying the 'Hellenists' and 'Hebrews' might be answered in a manner which seems to have been overlooked. That is, it is possible that Paul uses Ἑβραῖος differently than Luke does. The contexts of 2 Cor. 11.22 and Phil. 3.5 suggest that Paul uses the term Ἑβραῖος with reference to pure Jewish descent and a strict adherence to the Law.[60] In that case, Paul calls himself a Ἑβραῖος in 2 Cor. 11.22 in reply to his opponents' boasting of pure Jewish descent as Ἑβραῖοι, Ἰσραηλῖται and σπέρμα Ἀβραάμ.[61] Paul calls himself Ἑβραῖος ἐξ Ἑβραίων in Phil. 3.5 again to emphasize, along with the demonstrations of his former zeal in observing the Law, the purity of his Jewish identity.

This meaning, however, does not fit the context of Acts because Luke calls Paul's Jewish opponents, who may also include Stephen's accusers in Acts 6.9 and who seem to have no deficiency in their zeal for the Law, Ἑλληνισταί (Acts 9.29) rather than Ἑβραῖοι. Luke's use of the terms Ἑλληνιστής and Ἑβραῖος occurs in the context of his attempt to distinguish different groups of people in the Christian community with reference to their socio-religious or ethnic-cultural identity. Thus the comparison of Ἑβραῖος in Paul and Luke suggests that they are using the term in two different ways and that it is inappropriate

59. See Beza, *Annotationes*, on Acts 6.1, quoted in Neudorfer, *Stephanuskreis*, p. 21 n. 18. See also Zahn, *Apostelgeschichte*, I, p. 228. While he adopts the linguistic interpretation of the terms, he recognizes that the two groups cannot be conceived as mutally exclusive. Cf. also Marshall, 'Palestinian and Hellenistic Christianity', pp. 277-78. Contrast Hengel, 'Between Jesus and Paul', pp. 6-11. To insist that the primary reference of the term is to one who speaks Aramaic as his mother tongue does not avoid this objection.

60. H. Lietzmann, *An Die Korinther I–II* (HNT; Tübingen: Mohr [Paul Siebeck], 5th edn, 1969), p. 150; C.K. Barrett, *The Second Epistle to the Corinthians* (New York: Harper & Row, 1973), p. 293; R.P. Martin, *2 Corinthians* (WBC; Waco, TX: Word Books, 1986), pp. 374-75, 387.

61. Cf. also Rom. 11.1, where Paul calls himself Ἰσραηλίτης and σπέρμα Ἀβραάμ.

to try to read connotations of ritual purity, not to mention a specific theological orientation, into Luke's use of the term.

Conclusion

The meaning of Ἑλληνιστής in Acts is difficult to define because of the lack of evidence in the New Testament. Thus an inherent uncertainty regarding the identity of the 'Hellenists' must qualify every proposed solution to the problem. Beyond that, the lack of evidence makes it impossible to justify elaborate reconstructions about their role in Christian origins. In the context of this impasse, modern methods of linguistic research produce insights that at least shed some clearer light on the question.

In the first place, a diachronic analysis of ἑλληνίζειν in Greek literature confirms the two widely proposed views on language and culture as the basis for the name 'Hellenist'. While diachronic analysis cannot determine any particular author's usage, this survey suggests that the predominant meaning of ἑλληνίζειν concerns language, while an extended meaning with reference to the adoption of a Greek way of life appears with regularity only in the works of Eusebius and other fourth-century and later Church Fathers. Furthermore, it is fair to say that the negative connotation of the term ἑλληνίζειν, or indeed of Ἑλληνιστής, in patristic sources cannot serve to explain the meaning of Ἑλληνιστής in Acts 6.1, for it is scarcely possible that Luke regarded that group as heretical or pagan.[62] Moreover, the patristic references concerning the adoption of Greek culture and thought must be balanced with others that explicitly pertain to language, particularly in cases where the language of the Ἑβραῖοι is said to have been 'Hellenized'.[63]

In the second place, an analysis of the syntagmatic relations of Ἑλληνιστής in Acts underscores the impossibility of conclusively

62. See J.L. Lindhammer, *Der von dem heiligen Evangelisten beschriebenen Apostel-Geschichte ausführliche Erklärung und Anwendung* (Halle, 2nd edn, 1734), p. 241; quoted in Neudorfer, *Stephanuskreis*, p. 22 n. 23. On the other hand, it is important to recognize the question of whether classical Greek literature would have influenced Luke more than Hellenistic literature.

63. See Brehm, 'Hellenists', pp. 118-19. Compare also the Syriac translation of Ἑλληνιστάς in Acts 9.29 as 'those who knew Greek', which demonstrates that the Syrian fathers of the fifth century who were responsible for this version understood it in this fashion. See Cadbury, 'Hellenists', p. 72.

defining the meaning of the term, since it occurs in three different contexts with three different connotations. The fact that Luke can use ʽΕλληνιστής in Acts to refer to Jewish Christians, Jewish opponents of Paul, and Syrian converts raises questions regarding all of the proposed solutions. Although the factor of language does not answer all the questions, it could plausibly define these three groups.

In the third place, an analysis of the paradigmatic relations of ʽΕλληνιστής in Acts highlights Luke's efforts to distinguish different groups in the Christian community from one another and from other groups in the broader social context on the basis of their socio-religious or ethnic-cultural identity. This confirms that the basis for Luke's use of these terms is cultural, but cannot distinguish between the various options because criteria of religion, ethnic background, culture and language are interrelated. The paradigmatic analysis of ʽΕλληνιστής focuses primarily upon the contrast with ʽΕβραῖος in Acts 6.1, and thus on Paul's use of the latter. Once again a syntagmatic analysis raises questions about the standard solutions because Paul not only claims that he once was a 'Hebrew', but also that he still is one. In the context of this claim it appears that he is affirming the purity of his Jewish identity. This meaning, however, does not fit Acts because Luke uses the term ʽΕλληνιστής to describe those Jews who opposed Paul, and by implication also those who accused Stephen out of their zeal for the Law and the Temple. Therefore in Acts the term ʽΕβραῖος may simply distinguish believing Jews from the ʼΙουδαῖοι who did not believe and in some cases persecuted the Way. It does not have a linguistic reference.

ʽΕλληνιστής in Acts identifies Jewish Christians, Jewish opponents of Paul, and Syrian converts on the basis of the fact that they had adopted Greek language and/or culture.[64] The diachronic analysis of the use of ἑλληνίζειν suggests that the term primarily distinguishes the 'Hellenists' from the 'Hebrews' on the basis of the fact that they spoke Greek. While this does not answer every question raised by the syntagmatic and paradigmatic analysis of the word in Acts, it does satisfy the overall evidence better than the other proposed solutions to the identity of the 'Hellenists'.

64. See Brehm, 'Hellenists', p. 143 n. 112.

τί οὖν; THE INFERENTIAL QUESTION IN PAUL'S LETTER TO THE ROMANS WITH A PROPOSED READING OF ROMANS 4.1

Micheal W. Palmer

In the analysis which follows I have been heavily influenced by a number of studies, only some of which address discourse analysis in any direct way. My theoretical perspective is influenced by the work of Geoffrey Leech in his *Principles of Pragmatics*, for example, a work which mentions discourse analysis only in passing.[1] My approach to Paul's use of inferential questions might be more aptly titled 'text rhetoric' than 'discourse analysis', though I would argue that an analysis of text rhetoric *is* one form of discourse analysis.

By 'discourse marker' I mean a linguistic unit (often, but not always a word) which signals a relationship between discourse units larger than individual sentences or utterances. The inferential question marks local discontinuities (changes in direction) and heightens cohesion (the way the larger argument hangs together), yet it may serve these functions in multiple ways in any persuasive text.[2]

Paul did not, perhaps, consciously employ inferential questions as an intentional literary device using the techniques of formal rhetoric or even the more loosely defined diatribe,[3] but that he did, nonetheless, use

1. G. Leech, *Principles of Pragmatics* (LLL; London: Longman, 1983). J.G. du Plessis has applied Leech's principles of pragmatics to a number of New Testament texts. See especially, 'Why did Peter Ask his Question and how did Jesus Answer him? or: Implicature in Luke 12.35-48', *Neot* 22 (1988), pp. 311-24, and 'Pragmatic meaning in Matthew 13:1-23', *Neot* 21 (1987), pp. 33-56.

While in this paper I do not explain Leech's work, I do acknowledge its impact on the way I see the problems I address.

2. For a recent discussion of local discontinuities, see S.H. Levinsohn, *Discourse Features of New Testament Greek: A Coursebook* (Dallas: Summer Institute of Linguistics, 1992), pp. 13-16.

3. See S.K. Stowers, *The Diatribe and Paul's Letter to the Romans* (Chico, CA: Scholars Press, 1981).

inferential questions in ways similar to those found in these genres is evident. The dialogical form of argumentation, with its use of censure, was in wide use, and it is *not* necessary therefore to insist that Paul consciously used its devices—fully understanding their function—in order to acknowledge their presence in his letters.

I argue simply that Paul presents a consistent pattern in his usage of inferential questions which effectively strengthens his argument, though he does in fact use such questions in a variety of ways: to present and censure false conclusions, to focus his argument—providing occasions for summary statements and theses—and, less frequently, simply to maintain interest. What follows τί οὖν (or other introductory formulae for such questions) is basically consistent, with an inference demanded, a response given, then a defense of that response.

The examples in the appendix at the end of this essay demonstrate the two major functions of the questions and the patterns they follow.[4] These two uses of inferential questions—which account for almost all such questions in Romans (though many are not listed in the appendix)—serve decidedly different functions. Questions which imply a false inference attempt to eliminate from the argument potentially distracting possibilities of interpretation and thereby maintain the direction and force of the argument, while questions which lack such an implied false inference serve to create pauses in thought (focus) in which a crucial principle may be deduced from the argument with optimum clarity.

S.K. Stowers describes the diatribe, which has obvious parallels in Romans, as 'discourses and discussions in the school where the teacher employed the "Socratic" method of censure and protreptic'.[5] These two aspects of instruction are paralleled in the two main functions of the inferential question, or perhaps more clearly, the inferential question is used to create moments of high focus in which censure and protreptic might successfully take place.

This tactic of creating focus is sometimes more forced than others. In 3.5, for example, the false inference which Paul wishes to censure (that God is unjust to inflict wrath) is tangential to the context, and he is forced to make the inferential question conditional, introducing in the protasis a condition on which the false inference may be predicated: 'if

4. I am indebted for some insights in the analysis of these examples to Stowers, *Diatribe*, pp. 119-22.

5. Stowers, *Diatribe*, p. 76.

our unrighteousness shows the righteousness of God...' The same false inference, however (that God is unjust—that our sin serves to show his justice, so he is *un*just to punish us), is reintroduced in 6.1 in a more natural context where it fits easily into the argument without the conditional clause.

I. 3.5
Set up: conditional clause in 3.5

εἰ δὲ ἡ ἀδικία ἡμῶν θεοῦ δικαιοσύνην συνίστησιν, [But if our unrighteousness shows the righteousness of God,]

Inferential Question

τί ἐροῦμεν; μὴ ἄδικος ὁ θεὸς ὁ ἐπιφέρων τὴν ὀργήν; [What shall we say? That God is unjust to inflict wrath?]

II. 6.1
Context: 5.20

νόμος δὲ παρεισῆλθεν, ἵνα πλεονάσῃ τὸ παράπτωμα· οὗ δὲ ἐπλεόνασεν ἡ ἁμαρτία, ὑπερεπερίσσευσεν ἡ χάρις [Law entered, causing the trespass to increase; but where sin increased, grace abounded even more]

Inferential Question: 6.1

τί οὖν ἐροῦμεν; ἐπιμένωμεν τῇ ἁμαρτίᾳ ἵνα ἡ χάρις πλεονάσῃ; [What then shall we say? Shall we continue in sin so that grace may increase?]

The way the question relates to its context has a great bearing on its effectiveness, and for this reason the question in 3.5 seems almost incidental while in 6.1 it captures a logical objection to a statement presented in 5.20 ('where sin increased, grace abounded even more'), thereby engaging the reader in meaningful dialogue.

Paul is quite effective in his use of inferential questions as occasions to censure possible false conclusions in 3.1-9. There he affirms both ends of a paradox—the Jews have an advantage, yet they are no better off than the Gentiles—and leads the reader through two other inferential questions and two more objections to his argument. This cluster of inferential questions marks the shift from the responsibility of the Jew living among Gentiles to be a faithful witness (ch. 2) to the value of being a Jew.

τί οὖν (in 3.1) calls for an inference from the argument of 2.17-29. The call for an inference is focused on a possible objection to Paul's argument by two parallel questions: 'Do the Jews have any advantage?' (τί οὖν τὸ περισσὸν τοῦ 'Ιουδαίου...;) and 'Is there any value in circumcision?' (τίς ἡ ὠφέλεια τῆς περιτομῆς;). Both questions are answered immediately with the phrase πολὺ κατὰ πάντα τρόπον ('much in every way') which is then defended.

The appositional/parallel relationship of the two questions—even at the level of syntactic structure[6]—generates a surplus of meaning from the combination of περισσόν ('advancement') and ὠφέλεια ('advantage, worth'). That meaning is the idea of worth or value. There is worth in being a Jew, and Paul affirms this.

In v. 3 the conditional clause εἰ ἠπίστησάν τινες sets the context for a new yet related false inference—one whose refutation will become crucial to Paul's entire argument.[7] Does God's faithfulness depend on human faithfulness? His answer is μὴ γένοιτο, which he immediately defends.

Again, in v. 5, a conditional clause (εἰ δὲ ἡ ἀδικία ἡμῶν θεοῦ δικαιοσύνην συνίστησιν... 'but if our unrighteousness demonstrates the righteousness of God...') is used to set the context for a third false inference whose refutation will also become a significant strand in the overall argument (see 6.1-14): 'Is God unjust?' (τί ἐροῦμεν; μὴ ἄδικος ὁ θεὸς...;). Again the answer is μὴ γένοιτο (v. 6).[8]

In v. 9 Paul returns to the original question from 3.1 to add a corrective. He does so by posing the inferential question in a slightly different way (one which has consistently puzzled commentators). προεχόμεθα replaces τὸ περισσόν, and no qualifying appositional statement is used. Paul's defense of the response οὐ πάντως would seem to rule out προεχόμεθα being taken as passive (in which case it could be translated 'are we any *worse* off?') and, instead, argues for its being taken as *middle* voice (in which case it should be translated, 'are we any *better* off?'). This reading makes the question more directly related to that in 3.1 ('Do the Jews have any advantage?'), but without the limitation of

6. Notice that the parallel units (τὸ περισσόν/ἡ ὠφέλεια and τοῦ 'Ιουδαίου/τῆς περιτομῆς) have the same phrase-level status and bear the same head or modifier relationship to the rest of their own phrase in the two questions.

τί οὖν [$_{NP}$τὸ περισσὸν [$_{NP}$τοῦ 'Ιουδαίου]]...;
τίς [$_{NP}$ἡ ὠφέλεια [$_{NP}$τῆς περιτομῆς]];

7. Stowers, *Diatribe*, p. 133, suggests that Paul's use of τί γάρ here may be unique.

8. Rom. 3.7-8 uses a slightly different question to elaborate the same point.

ὠφέλεια. Hence, the relation of 3.9 to 3.1 must be one of corrective—there *is* an advantage in being a Jew, but not an *inherent* one. As John A.T. Robinson has written, 'The Jews have many advantages, yet ultimately they are in no better case'.[9] Paul attempts to maintain the claim that there is value in being a Jew, yet he attempts to skirt the implication that God has played favorites.

Through the use of inferential questions in this passage, then, Paul has addressed four possible unsanctioned interpretations of his argument. Notice the way in which the individual questions and their responses are *linked* in a structure which we may call *chaining*.

3.1-2

Question: What then is the advantage of the Jew, or what is the value of circumcision?

Response: Much in every way.

Defense: First, that *they* were entrusted with the oracles of God.

3.3-4

Question: So what? If some were unfaithful, will *their* unfaithfulness nullify the faithfulness of God?

Response: By no means.

Defense: Let God be true though *every human* be false...

3.5-6(8)

Question: And if *our* unfaithfulness establishes the justice of God, what shall we say? Is God unjust to inflict wrath [on us]? (I speak in human terms.)

Response: By no means.

Defense: For then how would God judge the world?

Each unit is linked to the following one by a semantic overlap between the *defense* of one argument and the *inferential question* introducing the next. In 3.2 (i.e. the defense of Paul's rejection of the false inference

9. J.A.T. Robinson, *Wrestling with Romans* (Philadelphia: Westminster Press, 1979), p. 35. See P.S. Minear who argues that Paul was dealing with Jewish Christians who were convinced of the value of their circumcision (3.1), but who also thought of it as something which made them better off (3.9) than their Gentile brothers (*The Obedience of Faith: The Purposes of Paul in the Epistle to the Romans* [London: SCM Press, 1971], p. 47).

from 3.1) '*they* [the Jews] were entrusted with the oracles of God'. In 3.3 *their* unfaithfulness (failure to live up to the trust placed in them?) is the focus of the question implying a false conclusion. This overlap of meaning links the two arguments.

In 3.4 (i.e. the defense of Paul's rejection of the false inference from 3.3) *they* has been broadened to *every human/person*. In the following question implying a false conclusion (3.5) *our* unfaithfulness serves as the point of departure for the false inference that God is unjust. Again, the overlap with the previous defense (*every person* includes *us*) links the new argument to its context.

By chaining the arguments in this way, Paul effectively marks each local discontinuity (change in direction) and increases cohesion (the way that the larger argument hangs together). In this way he has maximized what we may call the *processibility* of the discourse.[10]

We may postulate a *processibility maxim* which recommends that for effective discourse, arguments should be presented in such a manner as to make it easy for the reader to decode their message with as little rereading as possible.[11] In fact, Paul quite consistently follows such a maxim, constructing his arguments using either chaining or chiastic structures (whether or not those arguments involve inferential questions, and whether or not his strategy in fact proves successful). Deviations from these patterns can cause a reduction in processibility, and a consequent loss of clarity and cohesion.

The inferential question *without* an implied false inference also presents a consistent pattern in the letter to the Romans. The element of censure is absent and the reader is not asked to pass judgment on the inference. The sense of polemic characteristic of the questions implying a false conclusion, is greatly reduced. Paul uses this form particularly well.

Rom. 8.31 offers an excellent example. After a discussion of Christian hope and the sovereignty of God, Paul asks, τί οὖν ἐροῦμεν πρὸς ταῦτα; and then responds with the rhetorical question, εἰ ὁ θεὸς ὑπὲρ ἡμῶν, τίς καθ' ἡμῶν; The question functions as a statement of the thesis toward which Paul's local argument has been building: God's sovereign faithfulness can overcome any obstacle. Focus is achieved by

10. See Leech's processibility maxim for phonological, syntactic and semantic processes in Leech, *Principles of Pragmatics*, pp. 64-66.

11. I have adapted Leech's processibility maxim to the needs of discourse analysis. See Leech, *Principles of Pragmatics*, pp. 64-66 for his processibility maxim as applied to phonology, syntax and semantics.

the simple (inferential) question: τί οὖν ἐροῦμεν πρὸς ταῦτα; The response to that question implies, not a false conclusion which needs refutation, but the logical conclusion to the preceding argument. The same effect is achieved (though the point is less crucial) in 9.30 and again in 11.7.

One other aspect of Paul's usage of inferential questions is worthy of a brief notice. The formula λέγω οὖν ('I ask, then') in 11.1 and 11.11 replaces the formula τί οὖν ἐροῦμεν. Its usage serves the same function as the inferential question implying a false conclusion. The characteristic response μὴ γένοιτο is used in both cases. The difference between the two formulae (λέγω οὖν versus τί οὖν ἐροῦμεν) is mainly structural, though there is a sense in which the relationship between the author and the reader is altered. By posing the question in the first person singular (λέγω οὖν), Paul places himself over against the reader; a dynamic which may impact the reader's response.

Now let us consider the problematic case of 4.1. In 3.27–4.12, as in 3.1-9, Paul has clustered several inferential questions into a larger argument—again marking a significant development in the overall discourse, the shift from focus on the failure of life under the Law to the assertion of a righteousness which is 'apart from law'. The problem of context becomes particularly acute here.

R.B. Hays has argued that on grammatical and syntactic grounds a question mark should follow τί οὖν ἐροῦμεν.[12] The subject of εὑρηκέναι, he argues, is to be carried over from ἐροῦμεν in the preceding phrase, rendering the verse, 'What then shall we say? Have we found Abraham (to be) our forefather according to the flesh?'[13] This rendering, Hays says, fits Paul's argument rather well, in fact, better than the traditional rendering, if we take into consideration the entire context rather than simply 4.2-8.

UBSGNT Text
τί οὖν ἐροῦμεν εὑρηκέναι Ἀβραὰμ τὸν προπάτορα ἡμῶν κατὰ σάρκα;

Hays's Proposed Punctuation
τί οὖν ἐροῦμεν; εὑρηκέναι Ἀβραὰμ τὸν προπάτορα ἡμῶν κατὰ σάρκα;

12. R.B. Hays, 'Have we Found Abraham to be our Forefather according to the Flesh? A Reconsideration of Romans 4:1', *NovT* 27 (1985), pp. 76-98.

13. Hays, 'Have we Found Abraham', p. 81.

As punctuated in the *UBSGNT* text, the verse assumes the structure of an inferential question *not* implying a false conclusion. Hays's punctuation assumes the opposite category.

Quite apart from the textual difficulties, the sentence as traditionally punctuated poses several problems. On the analogy of the LXX text of Gen. 18.3 (εὑρίσκειν χάριν),[14] the text can be taken to mean:

> A. What then shall we say that Abraham, our forefather according to the flesh, found/achieved?

This interpretation raises immediate problems because it presupposes that Abraham is the forefather of the addressees κατὰ σάρκα,[15] a position which is complicated by 11.13 (ὑμῖν δὲ λέγω τοῖς ἔθνεσιν).[16] Even if we assume that Paul is speaking here only to the Jewish addressees in a mixed group, he argues in 4.11-12 that Abraham is the father of us *all*, both the circumcised and the uncircumcised. If Paul did mean for the question to be taken in this way, then his following discussion not only leaves the question unanswered, it undermines its basic assumption—that Abraham is our forefather κατὰ σάρκα.

The syntax of the question punctuated in this way is ambiguous, however, and it may be read as:

> B. What then shall we say that Abraham, our forefather, found/achieved according to the flesh?

If we accept this second proposal, Paul's ensuing discussion fails to address the question, which asks *what* Abraham found, and discusses only *how* he found what he did.[17] Even if we ignore this problem, however, the question of what he found κατὰ σάρκα still goes completely unanswered.

14. See also Lk. 1.30, Acts 7.46 and Heb. 4.16. εὑρεῖν ἔλεος occurs in 2 Tim. 1.18.

15. I find it highly unlikely that Paul's first readers would have interpreted ἡμῶν as an *exclusive* first person plural pronoun indicating only Paul and those with him. There is nothing in the context to indicate such an understanding. It is much more likely that ἡμῶν should be taken as *inclusive*, including the addressees.

16. Though clearly at least some of the intended readers were Jewish. See, for example, 2.17.

17. U. Luz, *Das Geschichtverständnis des Paulus* (Munich: Chr. Kaiser Verlag, 1968), p. 174 n. 148. See also W. Sanday and A.C. Headlam, *A Critical and Exegetical Commentary on the Epistle to the Romans* (New York: Scribners, 1895), pp. 98-99.

The RSV followed Codex Vaticanus in omitting the infinitive (εὑρηκέναι), producing the reading:

C. What then shall we say about Abraham our forefather according to the flesh.

Aside from the fact that the manuscript evidence weighs heavily against this reading, it suffers from one of the same difficulties as reading A above ('What then shall we say that Abraham, our forefather according to the flesh, found?'). It assumes that the addressees (though not necessarily the readers) are all Jewish.

The NRSV translators have abandoned this reading in favor of reading A—a decision which has better manuscript support, but does not resolve the problem.

I find Hays's syntactic analysis, on the other hand, quite convincing. My intent here, however, is not to ask whether Hays's proposed punctuation is *correct* on syntactic grounds, but simply whether it is *plausible* on discourse grounds, given Paul's normal discourse structures with the inferential question.

I must differ from Hays regarding the *immediate* context. His rendering does fit the overall argument better than the traditional one, but we must wonder why no one recognized this before Hays.

The reason is quite understandable from an analysis of the immediate discourse. Rather than following a single argument through to its conclusion, Paul has fused two related arguments:

A. God is just in that he treats Jews and Gentiles on the same basis (both are saved by faith); and
B. Because we are saved by faith we have no grounds for boasting.

Paul handles this strategy of fusing multiple lines of argument quite well in other parts of the letter, yet here the fusion is not clearly delineated, creating contextual ambiguity. The semantic noise which results becomes most intense precisely at 4.1, making its relevance all but unintelligible or at least difficult to discern for the average reader.

The inferential questions in 3.27 (ποῦ οὖν ἡ καύχησις; and διὰ ποίου νόμου;) begin the confusion by making explicit what was, until that point, only an implication (that there is no room for boasting), and elevating it to the apparent status of a fundamental step in the argument. The reader, then, must readjust his or her projection of where the argument is going. In v. 29 Paul returns to his major point (God treats both and Gentiles on the same basis; he is God of both), but the static created by vv. 27-28 intensifies as the reader realizes that the readjustment in those verses (27-28) was to some degree mistaken. Again the reader must refocus, attempting to resolve the ambiguity. By v. 30, the semantic noise is intense enough to render a proper reading somewhat unlikely.

Hays proposes a full stop at the end of v. 29 and a comma after πίστεως in v. 30, rendering the verse as an elliptical conditional sentence.[18] Hays's punctuation of vv. 29-30 contrasts with the usual punctuation as follows:

> *UBSGNT* Punctuation:
> ἢ Ἰουδαίων ὁ θεὸς μόνον; οὐχὶ καὶ ἐθνῶν; ναὶ καὶ ἐθνῶν, εἴπερ εἷς ὁ θεὸς ὃς δικαιώσει περιτομὴν ἐκ πίστεως καὶ ἀκροβυστίαν διὰ τῆς πίστεως.
> [Or is God the God of Jews only? Is he not the God of Gentiles also? Yes, of Gentiles also, since God is one; and he will justify the circumcised on the basis of faith and the uncircumcised through faith.]
>
> Hays's Proposed Punctuation:
> ἢ Ἰουδαίων ὁ θεὸς μόνον; οὐχὶ καὶ ἐθνῶν; ναὶ καὶ ἐθνῶν. εἴπερ εἷς ὁ θεὸς ὃς δικαιώσει περιτομὴν ἐκ πίστεως, καὶ ἀκροβυστίαν διὰ τῆς πίστεως.
> [Or is God the God of Jews only? Is he not the God of Gentiles also? Yes, of Gentiles also. If indeed God, who will justify the circumcised on the basis of faith, is one, he will also justify the uncircumcised through faith.]

Due to the confusion created in the previous few verses, however, such a reading, though it may well be what Paul intended, is all but obvious. A misreading at this point adds to the confusion and the reader is caught off guard by the inferential question in v. 31 (νόμον οὖν καταργοῦμεν διὰ τῆς πίστεως; 'Do we, therefore, overturn the Law by faith?'). This question, which is crucial for Paul's argument, is robbed of much of the force it should receive. The question and its response function in the same way that all of the others dealing with false conclusions function. It demands an inference, provides one (which is false), rejects it, then moves to a defense of that rejection. Had a great deal of semantic noise not been created by the preceding verses, this pattern would be quite clear to the reader and he or she would confront 4.1 with confidence, expecting a defense of νόμον ἱστάνομεν ('we uphold the law', 3.31), and of how it is true in relation to vv. 29-30. Given the present contextual ambiguity, however, one arrives at 4.1 with uncertainty.

Rom. 4.1 introduces Abraham to the argument with no forewarning. In addition, the inferential question raised here does *not* fit the pattern

18. Hays, 'Have we Found Abraham', p. 84. Hays proposes that the unexpressed verb of the elliptical clause should be δικαιώσει.

completely. It demands an inference not from Paul's immediate argument, but from who knows where? (I would say from the experience of the first readers.) Hays, attempting to defend his reading, asserts that the inference is demanded from the position *against* which Paul is arguing,[19] but this is little help and quite unlikely given the consistency of Paul's usage at this point. He generally calls for an inference from his *own* argument. (See for example 1 Cor. 3.5; 6.15; 9.18; 14.15; Gal. 3.19 and 21, in addition to the examples examined here.) A more plausible suggestion is that Paul is simply inconsistent in this one case. He begins with the inferential question τί οὖν ἐροῦμεν; but then offers a question that does not represent an inference at all, but a matter of common knowledge to his readers, who were well aware that Abraham was *not* the physical forefather of them all (that is, *not* their forefather κατὰ σάρκα). For this reason, the customary μὴ γένοιτο is not necessary, and the question in 4.1 is given no immediate response.

But even if one did recognize 4.1 as the beginning of a defense of the way in which Paul 'upholds the Law' (νόμον ἱστάνομεν, 3.31), and a defense of his claim that Jews and Gentiles are saved in the same way (3.29-30), as it certainly is, the reader would have this assessment challenged once again when he or she reaches 4.2, which relates the example of Abraham back to the inferential question in 3.27 (ποῦ οὖν ἡ καύχησις) rather than to the ones in 3.29 and 3.31 ('Ιουδαίων ὁ θεὸς μόνον; and νόμον οὖν καταργοῦμεν διὰ τῆς πίστεως;).

What can we say, then, about the relationship of the inferential question in 4.1 to its immediate context? In order for it to function as an integral part of Paul's overall argument that God is righteous, saving Jews and Gentiles in the same way (by faith)—and an analysis of its function in relation to the overall structure of the letter is the goal of discourse analysis—it must be understood to relate back to the rhetorical question in 3.29, 'Is God the God of the Jews only?' ('Ιουδαίων ὁ θεὸς μόνον;) and forward to 4.9-12, 'Abraham is the father of all who have faith like his faith'.

This relationship is obscured, however, in both directions. The rhetorical questions in 3.29 and their response in 3.29-30 are bracketed on either side by secondary (supporting) inferential questions: the question about boasting in 3.27 and the question about overthrowing the Law in v. 31. On the other side, 4.1 is separated from its response by applications of the example of Abraham to these secondary questions in

19. Hays, 'Have we Found Abraham', p. 87.

3.27 and 3.31. The order of these applications of the example of Abraham is not the same as the order of the related inferential questions. Neither do the applications bear a chiastic relationship to the questions which they address. As a result of the unusual ordering, the processibility of the text is much lower than was the case in 3.1-9.

3.27-28	Boasting excluded
3.29-30	God is the God of both Jews and Gentiles and saves both in the same way.
3.31	Paul upholds the Law.
4.1	What then shall we say? Have we found Abraham to be our father according to the flesh?
4.2-8	Application of Abraham to the boasting question
4.3-11	Application of Abraham to the Law question. Paul cites the Law (Gen. 15.6) as supporting evidence for his argument and gives an exposition of its meaning.
4.9-12	Application of Abraham to the One God question

These interrelationships make it extremely difficult to argue convincingly for or against a particular reading in 4.1 on the basis of the immediate context, since the example of Abraham is applied to all three of the inferential questions preceding 4.1 (3.27; 3.29; 3.31). The issue of the correct reading must, therefore, be decided using a combination of methods from analysis of syntax, usage of similar questions elsewhere, and analysis of the whole discourse of which this section is but one unit.

The problems of interpretation in 4.1 stem not from its syntactic structure, which is easily accounted for since Hays's article—though the syntax is recognizably ambiguous—but from the fact that Paul has used the inferential question here in a more complex set of interrelationships than is usually the case.

My own examination of inferential questions elsewhere is consistent with Hays's syntactic analysis in that the structure of 4.1 and the example which follows it are significantly similar to the structure of units incorporating an inferential question that suggests a false conclusion, but here the false conclusion (that Abraham is our forefather κατὰ σάρκα) is *clearly* false to some readers on the basis of their own experience (11.13), so that no immediate refutation is necessary. For other readers the question would imply no false conclusion (since Abraham *was* their father κατὰ σάρκα). In either case, Paul *could not* include the usual emphatic negation μὴ γένοιτο, so we should not be surprised by its absence. Because of this same split in his addressees, Paul could not effectively give an immediate response to the question. He must first set the context in which the answer would make sense—he must make the discourse processible.

The example of Abraham, while addressing all three of the inferential questions from 3.27, 29 and 31, addresses them in overlapping sections, providing strong cohesion to the unit 4.2-12. Paul's use of the Law (4.3-11) provides the defense of—and overlaps with—his argument that Abraham has nothing to boast about before God (4.2-8). This same treatment of the example from Scripture (4.3-11) supports and overlaps with his argument that both the circumcised and the uncircumcised are children of Abraham (4.9-12).

The entire unit (4.2-12), then, may serve as an extended defence of the argument (which becomes clear only after looking back from 4.12) that Abraham is the father of us all, *not* κατὰ σάρκα, but κατὰ πίστιν.

The overall discourse also argues for taking Hays's proposal seriously. If Paul's question is one about the sense in which Abraham is our father (κατὰ σάρκα [4.1] or κατα πίστιν [4.11-12]) rather than a question about what we find to be the case about Abraham who is assumed to *be* our father according to the flesh (the traditional reading), then the example of Abraham fits much more naturally into a letter which is addressed at least in part to Gentile readers (see, for example, 11.13) for whom Abraham was clearly *not* their father *according to the flesh* (κατὰ σάρκα) and to Jewish readers to whom Paul wished to express the conviction that not all Jews were 'children of Abraham' (9.6-8).

If we understand the overall coherence of the discourse to be based on the argument that God is just, accepting both Jews and Gentiles on the same basis, and take the questions in 3.27 and 3.31, along with their development in the example of Abraham, to be secondary to this main unifying thread, then the local discourse—even if somewhat complex—also supports Hays's reading.[20]

The central issue in the *local* discourse becomes the question of whether God is one—both God of Jews and God of Gentiles. The question about Abraham, then, becomes a question about the sense in which

20. For a brief discussion of main-line versus supportive material in (narrative) discourse, see R.E. Longacre, *The Grammar of Discourse* (New York: Plenum, 1983), pp. 14-17.

he is the father of all those who are worshipers of this one God. The question about boasting supports the one-God question by working out one of its implications, that no group is inherently better than any other. The question of overthrowing the Law also supports this same central question by eliminating the possible objection that accepting God as God of both Jews and Gentiles would require a disregard for the Law.

The inferential question in Paul's letter to the Romans, then, is used primarily to mark local discontinuities and heighten cohesion. Its effectiveness in performing these functions varies between the difficult entanglement of 3.27–4.12, the skillful orientation of 3.1-9, and the climactic beauty of 8.31.

> τί οὖν ἐροῦμεν; εὑρηκέναι Ἀβραὰμ τὸν προπάτορα ἡμῶν κατὰ σάρκα; (Rom. 4.1).
> μὴ γένοιτο,
> ἀλλὰ κατὰ πίστιν.

Appendix: Examples of Inferential Questions in Paul's Letter to the Romans[21]

I. Questions with suggested false conclusions.[22]

A. 3.1-2

1. τί οὖν introduces an objection in the form of a double question implying a false conclusion [There is no advantage in being a Jew]. τί οὖν τὸ περισσὸν τοῦ Ἰουδαίου ἢ τίς ἡ ὠφέλεια τῆς περιτομῆς; (3.1)
2. *Response (Censure)*: πολὺ κατὰ πάντα τρόπον (3.2a)
3. *Defense*: Introduced by γάρ,[23] alludes to Scripture (Deut. 4.7-8; Pss. 103.7; 147.19-20) to refute the implied false conclusion. πρῶτον μὲν γὰρ ὅτι ἐπιστεύθησαν τὰ λόγια τοῦ θεοῦ. (3.2b)

B. 3.3-4

1. τί γάρ; introduces an objection in the form of a question implying a false conclusion to the argument in 2.17-29 [God is unfaithful]. τί γάρ; εἰ ἠπίστησάν τινες, μὴ ἡ ἀπιστία αὐτῶν τὴν πίστιν τοῦ θεοῦ καταργήσει; (3.3)

21. The basic structure of much of what is presented in this list of examples was suggested by Stowers, *Diatribe*. See esp. pp. 119-22, for an outline of his view of the major features of objections and false conclusions in Romans. While Stowers's main concern is not the role of inferential questions, he does outline all of the passages I have cited in section I below.

22. Although 3.27b-28 and 3.29-30 do not use τί οὖν, they do fit the pattern presented here.

23. But note that γάρ is missing in B D* G Y 81 365 1506 2464* pc latt sy[p] bo[mss].

2. *Response (Censure)*: μὴ γένοιτο (3.4a)
3. *Defense*: Introduced by δέ, uses Scripture (Pss. 116.11; 51.4). γινέσθω δὲ ὁ θεὸς ἀληθής, πᾶς δὲ ἄνθρωπος ψεύστης, καθὼς γέγραπται,

   ὅπως ἂν δικαιωθῇς ἐν τοῖς λόγοις σου
   καὶ νικήσεις ἐν τῷ κρίνεσθαί σε (3.4b).

C. 3.5-6[24]

1. εἰ δέ introduces a conditional clause ending in τί ἐροῦμεν; which in turn introduces an objection in the form of a question implying a false conclusion [God is unjust]. εἰ δὲ ἡ ἀδικία ἡμῶν θεοῦ δικαιοσύνην συνίστησιν, τί ἐροῦμεν; μὴ ἄδικος ὁ θεὸς ὁ ἐπιφέρων τὴν ὀργήν; (3.5)
   Clarification: κατὰ ἄνθρωπον λέγω (3.5).
2. *Response (Censure)*: μὴ γένοιτο (3.6a)
3. *Defense*: A rhetorical question introduced by ἐπεί. ἐπεὶ πῶς κρινεῖ ὁ θεὸς τὸν κόσμον; (3.6b)

D. 3.9-20

1. τί οὖν; reintroduces the question from 3.1, but with a slightly different implication due to the intervening discussion. A false conclusion is implied [Jews are better off, as regards salvation, than Gentiles]. τί οὖν; προεχόμεθα;
2. *Response (Censure)*: οὐ πάντως· (3.9b)
3. *Defense*: is introduced by γάρ and utilizes Scripture (Pss. 14.1-3; 53.1-3; Eccl. 7.20; Pss. 5.9; 140.3; 10.7; Isa. 59.7-8; Prov. 1.16; Ps. 36.1). προῃτιασάμεθα γὰρ Ἰουδαίους τε καὶ Ἕλληνας πάντας ὑφ' ἁμαρτίαν εἶναι,

   καθὼς γέγραπται ὅτι
   οὐκ ἔστιν δίκαιος οὐδὲ εἷς...

   οἴδαμεν δὲ ὅτι ὅσα ὁ νόμος λέγει τοῖς ἐν τῷ νόμῳ λαλεῖ, ἵνα πᾶν στόμα φραγῇ καὶ ὑπόδικος γένηται πᾶς ὁ κόσμος τῷ θεῷ· διότι ἐξ ἔργων νόμου οὐ δικαιωθήσεται πᾶσα σὰρξ ἐνώπιον αὐτοῦ, διὰ γὰρ νόμου ἐπίγνωσις ἁμαρτίας (3.9c-20).

E. 3.31 (and ch. 4)

1. οὖν is used in a question implying a false conclusion [Paul is overthrowing the Law]. νόμον οὖν καταργοῦμεν διὰ τῆς πίστεως; (3.31)
2. *Response (Censure)*: μὴ γένοιτο·

24. While 3.7-8 does not fully fit the pattern I am discussing, it does begin with two questions implying a false understanding of Paul's argument then provides a response in the form of a retort.

3. *Defense*: consists of a counterstatement introduced by ἀλλά and the example of Abraham which follows in ch. 4. ἀλλὰ νόμον ἱστάνομεν (3.31). [See also the example of Abraham in ch. 4.]

F. 4.1 [This problematic case is discussed in the essay.]

G. 6.1-11

1. τί οὖν ἐροῦμεν; introduces an objection in the form of a question (resuming the objections of 3.3-8) which implies a false conclusion [Sin increases God's grace and is therefore desirable]. τί οὖν ἐροῦμεν; ἐπιμένωμεν τῇ ἁμαρτίᾳ, ἵνα ἡ χάρις πλεονάσῃ; (6.1)
2. *Response (Censure)*: μὴ γένοιτο (6.2a)
3. *Defense*: is introduced by two rhetorical questions. οἵτινες ἀπεθάνομεν τῇ ἁμαρτίᾳ, πῶς ἔτι ζήσομεν ἐν αὐτῇ; ἢ ἀγνοεῖτε ὅτι, ὅσοι ἐβαπτίσθημεν εἰς Χριστὸν Ἰησοῦν, εἰς τὸν θάνατον αὐτοῦ ἐβαπτίσθημεν;...οὕτως καὶ ὑμεῖς λογίζεσθε ἑαυτοὺς εἶναι νεκροὺς μὲν τῇ ἁμαρτίᾳ ζῶντας δὲ τῷ θεῷ ἐν Χριστῷ Ἰησοῦ (6.2-11).

H. 6.15-18

1. τί οὖν; introduces a question implying a false conclusion [We are free to sin because we live under grace rather than Law]. τί οὖν; ἁμαρτήσωμεν, ὅτι οὐκ ἐσμὲν ὑπὸ νόμον ἀλλὰ ὑπὸ χάριν; (6.15)
2. *Response (Censure)*: μὴ γένοιτο (6.15b).
3. *Defense*: is introduced by a rhetorical question and involves a discussion of baptism (6.16-18). οὐκ οἴδατε ὅτι ᾧ παριστάνετε ἑαυτοὺς δούλους εἰς ὑπακοήν, δοῦλοί ἐστε ᾧ ὑπακούετε, ἤτοι ἁμαρτίας εἰς θάνατον ἢ ὑπακοῆς εἰς δικαιοσύνην;... ἐδουλώθητε τῇ δικαιοσύνῃ (6.16-18).

I. 7.7-12

1. τί οὖν ἐροῦμεν; introduces a question implying a false conclusion [The Law is sinful]. τί οὖν ἐροῦμεν; ὁ νόμος ἁμαρτία; (7.7)
2. *Response* (*Censure*): μὴ γένοιτο (7.7b)
3. *Defense*: consists of a counterstatement introduced by ἀλλά and a defense of the counterstatement introduced by γάρ. The defense utilizes Scripture (Exod. 20.17; Deut. 5.21). ἀλλὰ τὴν ἁμαρτίαν οὐκ ἔγνων εἰ μὴ διὰ νόμου· τήν τε γὰρ ἐπιθυμίαν οὐκ ᾔδειν εἰ μὴ ὁ νόμος ἔλεγεν, οὐκ ἐπιθυμήσεις...ὥστε ὁ μὲν νόμος ἅγιος καὶ ἡ ἐντολὴ ἁγία καὶ δικαία καὶ ἀγαθή. (7.7c-12)

J. 7.13-25

1. οὖν introduces a question implying a false conclusion [Good is the cause of evil]. τὸ οὖν ἀγαθὸν ἐμοὶ ἐγένετο θάνατος; (7.13)
2. *Response* (*Censure*): μὴ γένοιτο (7.13b).

3. *Defense*: involves a counterstatement introduced by ἀλλά and a defense of the counterstatement introduced by γάρ, and alludes to Scripture. ἀλλὰ ἡ ἁμαρτία, ἵνα φανῇ ἁμαρτία, διὰ τοῦ ἀγαθοῦ μοι κατεργαζομένη θάνατον, ἵνα γένηται καθ' ὑπερβολὴν ἁμαρτωλὸς ἡ ἁμαρτία διὰ τῆς ἐντολῆς. οἴδαμεν γὰρ ὅτι ὁ νόμος πνευματικός ἐστιν, ἐγὼ δὲ σάρκινός εἰμι πεπραμένος ὑπὸ τὴν ἁμαρτίαν...ἄρα οὖν αὐτὸς ἐγὼ τῷ μὲν νοῒ δουλεύω νόμῳ θεοῦ τῇ δὲ σαρκὶ νόμῳ ἁμαρτίας (7.13c-25).

K. 9.14-18

1. τί οὖν ἐροῦμεν; introduces a question implying a false conclusion [God is unjust]. τί οὖν ἐροῦμεν; μὴ ἀδικία παρὰ τῷ θεῷ; (9.14)
2. *Response* (*Censure*): μὴ γένοιτο (9.14b)
3. *Defense*: introduced by γάρ; utilizes Scripture. τῷ Μωϋσεῖ γὰρ λέγει,

   ἐλεήσω ὃν ἂν ἐλεῶ
   καὶ οἰκτιρήσω ὃν ἂν οἰκτίρω.

   ἄρα οὖν οὐ τοῦ θέλοντος οὐδὲ τοῦ τρέχοντος ἀλλὰ τοῦ ἐλεῶντος θεοῦ...ἄρα οὖν ὃν θέλει ἐλεεῖ, ὃν δὲ θέλει σκληρύνει (9.15-18)

L. 11.1-6

1. λέγω οὖν introduces a question implying a false conclusion [God has rejected his people]. λέγω οὖν, μὴ ἀπώσατο ὁ θεὸς τὸν λαὸν αὐτοῦ; (11.1)
2. *Response (Censure)*: μὴ γένοιτο (11.1)
3. *Defense*: is introduced by γάρ and utilizes Scripture. καὶ γὰρ ἐγὼ Ἰσραηλίτης εἰμί, ἐκ σπέρματος Ἀβραάμ, φυλῆς Βενιαμίν... λεῖμμα κατ' ἐκλογὴν χάριτος γέγονεν... (11.1b-6)

M. 11.11-16

1. λέγω οὖν introduces a question implying a false conclusion [The Jews fell permanently from God's favor]. λέγω οὖν, μὴ ἔπταισαν ἵνα πέσωσιν; (11.11)
2. *Response (Censure)*: μὴ γένοιτο (11.11b)
3. *Defense*: opens with a counterstatement introduced by ἀλλά. ἀλλὰ τῷ αὐτῶν παραπτώματι ἡ σωτηρία τοῖς ἔθνεσιν εἰς τὸ παραζηλῶσαι αὐτούς...εἰ γὰρ ἡ ἀποβολὴ αὐτῶν καταλλαγὴ κόσμου, τίς ἡ πρόσλημψις εἰ μὴ ζωὴ ἐκ νεκρῶν; εἰ δὲ ἡ ἀπαρχὴ ἁγία, καὶ τὸ φύραμα, καὶ εἰ ἡ ῥίζα ἁγία, καὶ οἱ κλάδοι (11.11c-16)

II. Inferential questions as occasions for conclusions and summary statements:

A 3.27-28

1. ποῦ οὖν introduces a question demanding a deduction from what precedes v. 27. ποῦ οὖν ἡ καύχησις; (3.27a)
2. *Deduction*: ἐξεκλείσθη...διὰ νόμου πίστεως (3.27; a logical conclusion to the argument of 3.21-26).[25]
3. *Defense*: introduced by γάρ. λογιζόμεθα γὰρ δικαιοῦσθαι πίστει ἄνθρωπον χωρὶς ἔργων νόμου (3.28).

B 8.31-39

1. τί οὖν ἐροῦμεν introduces a question demanding a deduction from what precedes. τί οὖν ἐροῦμεν πρὸς ταῦτα; (8.31)
2. *Deduction*: εἰ...ἡμῶν; constitutes a rhetorical question expressing the conclusion of the foregoing argument. εἰ ὁ θεὸς ὑπὲρ ἡμῶν, τίς καθ' ἡμῶν; (8.31b)
3. *Defense*: the deduction is clarified and defended (1) by a series of rhetorical questions whose answers Paul assumes to be self-evident, and (2) by positive assertions. The defense utilizes Scripture (Ps. 44.22). ὅς γε τοῦ ἰδίου υἱοῦ οὐκ ἐφείσατο ἀλλὰ ὑπὲρ ἡμῶν πάντων παρέδωκεν αὐτόν, πῶς οὐχὶ καὶ σὺν αὐτῷ τὰ πάντα ἡμῖν χαρίσεται;...πέπεισμαι γὰρ ὅτι οὔτε θάνατος οὔτε ζωὴ...οὔτε τις κτίσις ἑτέρα δυνήσεται ἡμᾶς χωρίσαι ἀπὸ τῆς ἀγάπης τοῦ θεοῦ τῆς ἐν Χριστῷ Ἰησοῦ τῷ κυρίῳ ἡμῶν (8.32-39).

C. 9.30-33

1. τί οὖν ἐροῦμεν; demands a deduction from what precedes.
2. *Deduction*: ὅτι (v. 30)...ἔφθασεν (v. 31) provides the logical conclusion. ὅτι ἔθνη τὰ μὴ διώκοντα δικαιοσύνην κατέλαβεν δικαιοσύνην, δικαιοσύνην δὲ τὴν ἐκ πίστεως, Ἰσραὴλ δὲ διώκων νόμον δικαιοσύνης εἰς νόμον οὐκ ἔφθασεν.
3. *Defense*: introduced by the rhetorical question διὰ τί and utilizes Scripture (Isa. 28.16). διὰ τί; ὅτι οὐκ ἐκ πίστεως ἀλλ' ὡς ἐξ ἔργων· προσέκοψαν τῷ λίθῳ τοῦ προσκόμματος, καθὼς γέγραπται... (9.32-33).

25. The part omitted (...) represents yet another inferential question fitting the pattern discussed above. διὰ ποίου νόμου; is an inferential question which introduces a second question [τῶν ἔργων;] which implies a false conclusion [that boasting is excluded on the basis of works]. This false conclusion is then rejected out of hand [οὐχί] and the rejection is supported by a counterstatement introduced by ἀλλά: ἀλλὰ διὰ νόμου πίστεως.

D. 11.7-10

1. τί οὖν; demands a deduction from the foregoing argument.
2. *Deduction*: ὃ ἐπιζητεῖ...ἐπωρώθησαν provides a summary of the preceding argument. ὃ ἐπιζητεῖ Ἰσραήλ, τοῦτο οὐκ ἐπέτυχεν, ἡ δὲ ἐκλογὴ ἐπέτυχεν· οἱ δὲ λοιποὶ ἐπωρώθησαν (11.7b)
3. *Defense*: consists of an argument from Scripture. καθὼς γέγραπται,

ἔδωκεν αὐτοῖς ὁ θεὸς πνεῦμα κατανύξεως,
ὀφθαλμοὺς τοῦ μὴ βλέπειν
καὶ ὦτα τοῦ μὴ ἀκούειν,
ἕως τῆς σήμερον ἡμέρας.

καὶ Δαυὶδ λέγει,

γενηθήτω ἡ τράπεζα αὐτῶν εἰς παγίδα...
καὶ τὸν νῶτον αὐτῶν διὰ παντὸς σύγκαμψον

INDEXES

INDEX OF BIBLICAL REFERENCES

OLD TESTAMENT

NEW TESTAMENT

Index of Authors

JOURNAL FOR THE STUDY OF THE NEW TESTAMENT

Supplement Series

38 MATTHEW'S MISSIONARY DISCOURSE:
A LITERARY CRITICAL ANALYSIS
Dorothy Jean Weaver

39 FAITH AND OBEDIENCE IN ROMANS:
A STUDY IN ROMANS 1–4
Glenn N. Davies

40 IDENTIFYING PAUL'S OPPONENTS:
THE QUESTION OF METHOD IN 2 CORINTHIANS
Jerry L. Sumney

41 HUMAN AGENTS OF COSMIC POWER:
IN HELLENISTIC JUDAISM AND THE SYNOPTIC TRADITION
Mary E. Mills

42 MATTHEW'S INCLUSIVE STORY:
A STUDY IN THE NARRATIVE RHETORIC OF THE FIRST GOSPEL
David B. Howell

43 JESUS, PAUL AND TORAH:
COLLECTED ESSAYS
Heikki Räisänen

44 THE NEW COVENANT IN HEBREWS
Susanne Lehne

45 THE RHETORIC OF ROMANS:
ARGUMENTATIVE CONSTRAINT AND STRATEGY AND PAUL'S
DIALOGUE WITH JUDAISM
Neil Elliott

46 THE LAST SHALL BE FIRST:
THE RHETORIC OF REVERSAL IN LUKE
John O. York

47 JAMES AND THE Q SAYINGS OF JESUS
Patrick J. Hartin

48 TEMPLUM AMICITIAE:
ESSAYS ON THE SECOND TEMPLE PRESENTED TO ERNST BAMMEL
Edited by William Horbury

49 PROLEPTIC PRIESTS
PRIESTHOOD IN THE EPISTLE TO THE HEBREWS
John M. Scholer

50 PERSUASIVE ARTISTRY:
STUDIES IN NEW TESTAMENT RHETORIC IN HONOR OF
GEORGE A. KENNEDY
Edited by Duane F. Watson

51 THE AGENCY OF THE APOSTLE:
A DRAMATISTIC ANALYSIS OF PAUL'S RESPONSES TO CONFLICT IN 2 CORINTHIANS
Jeffrey A. Crafton

52 REFLECTIONS OF GLORY:
PAUL'S POLEMICAL USE OF THE MOSES–DOXA TRADITION IN 2 CORINTHIANS 3.12-18
Linda L. Belleville

53 REVELATION AND REDEMPTION AT COLOSSAE
Thomas J. Sappington

54 THE DEVELOPMENT OF EARLY CHRISTIAN PNEUMATOLOGY WITH SPECIAL REFERENCE TO LUKE–ACTS
Robert P. Menzies

55 THE PURPOSE OF ROMANS:
A COMPARATIVE LETTER STRUCTURE INVESTIGATION
L. Ann Jervis

56 THE SON OF THE MAN IN THE GOSPEL OF JOHN
Delbert Burkett

57 ESCHATOLOGY AND THE COVENANT:
A COMPARISON OF 4 EZRA AND ROMANS 1–11
Bruce W. Longenecker

58 NONE BUT THE SINNERS:
RELIGIOUS CATEGORIES IN THE GOSPEL OF LUKE
David A. Neale

59 CLOTHED WITH CHRIST:
THE EXAMPLE AND TEACHING OF JESUS IN ROMANS 12.1–15.13
Michael Thompson

60 THE LANGUAGE OF THE NEW TESTAMENT:
CLASSIC ESSAYS
Edited by Stanley E. Porter

61 FOOTWASHING IN JOHN 13 AND THE JOHANNINE COMMUNITY
John Christopher Thomas

62 JOHN THE BAPTIZER AND PROPHET:
A SOCIO-HISTORICAL STUDY
Robert L. Webb

63 POWER AND POLITICS IN PALESTINE:
THE JEWS AND THE GOVERNING OF THEIR LAND 100 BC–AD 70
James S. McLaren

64 JESUS AND THE ORAL GOSPEL TRADITION
Edited by Henry Wansbrough

65 THE RHETORIC OF RIGHTEOUSNESS IN ROMANS 3.21-26
Douglas A. Campbell

66 PAUL, ANTIOCH AND JERUSALEM:
A STUDY IN RELATIONSHIPS AND AUTHORITY IN EARLIEST CHRISTIANITY
Nicholas Taylor

67 THE PORTRAIT OF PHILIP IN ACTS:
A STUDY OF ROLES AND RELATIONS
F. Scott Spencer

68 JEREMIAH IN MATTHEW'S GOSPEL:
THE REJECTED-PROPHET MOTIF IN MATTHAEAN REDACTION
Michael P. Knowles

69 RHETORIC AND REFERENCE IN THE FOURTH GOSPEL
Margaret Davies

70 AFTER THE THOUSAND YEARS:
RESURRECTION AND JUDGMENT IN REVELATION 20
J. Webb Mealy

71 SOPHIA AND THE JOHANNINE JESUS
Martin Scott

72 NARRATIVE ASIDES IN LUKE–ACTS
Steven M. Sheeley

73 SACRED SPACE:
AN APPROACH TO THE THEOLOGY OF THE EPISTLE TO THE HEBREWS
Marie E. Isaacs

74 TEACHING WITH AUTHORITY:
MIRACLES AND CHRISTOLOGY IN THE GOSPEL OF MARK
Edwin K. Broadhead

75 PATRONAGE AND POWER:
A STUDY OF SOCIAL NETWORKS IN CORINTH
John Kin-Man Chow

76 THE NEW TESTAMENT AS CANON:
A READER IN CANONICAL CRITICISM
Robert Wall and Eugene Lemcio

77 REDEMPTIVE ALMSGIVING IN EARLY CHRISTIANITY
Roman Garrison

78 THE FUNCTION OF SUFFERING IN PHILIPPIANS
L. Gregory Bloomquist

79 THE THEME OF RECOMPENSE IN MATTHEW'S GOSPEL
Blaine Charette

80 BIBLICAL GREEK LANGUAGE AND LINGUISTICS:
OPEN QUESTIONS IN CURRENT RESEARCH
Edited by Stanley E. Porter and D.A. Carson

81 THE LAW IN GALATIANS
In-Gyu Hong

82 ORAL TRADITION AND THE GOSPELS:
THE PROBLEM OF MARK 4
Barry W. Henaut

83 PAUL AND THE SCRIPTURES OF ISRAEL
Edited by Craig A. Evans and James A. Sanders

84 FROM JESUS TO JOHN:
ESSAYS ON JESUS AND NEW TESTAMENT CHRISTOLOGY IN HONOUR OF MARINUS DE JONGE
Edited by Martinus C. De Boer

85 RETURNING HOME:
NEW COVENANT AND SECOND EXODUS AS THE CONTEXT FOR 2 CORINTHIANS 6.14–7.1
William J. Webb

86 ORIGINS OF METHOD:
TOWARDS A NEW UNDERSTANDING OF JUDAISM AND CHRISTIANITY—ESSAYS IN HONOUR OF JOHN C. HURD
Edited by Bradley H. McLean

87 WORSHIP, THEOLOGY AND MINISTRY IN THE EARLY CHURCH:
ESSAYS IN HONOUR OF RALPH P. MARTIN
Edited by Michael Wilkins and Terence Paige

88 THE BIRTH OF THE LUKAN NARRATIVE
Mark Coleridge

89 WORD AND GLORY:
ON THE EXEGETICAL AND THEOLOGICAL BACKGROUND OF JOHN'S PROLOGUE
Craig A. Evans

90 RHETORIC IN THE NEW TESTAMENT:
ESSAYS FROM THE 1992 HEIDELBERG CONFERENCE
Edited by Stanley E. Porter and Thomas H. Olbricht

91 MATTHEW'S NARRATIVE WEB:
OVER, AND OVER, AND OVER AGAIN
Janice Capel Anderson

92 LUKE:
INTERPRETER OF PAUL, CRITIC OF MATTHEW
Eric Franklin

93 ISAIAH AND PROPHETIC TRADITIONS IN THE BOOK OF REVELATION:
VISIONARY ANTECEDENTS AND THEIR DEVELOPMENT
Jan Fekkes

94 JESUS' EXPOSITION OF THE OLD TESTAMENT IN LUKE'S GOSPEL
Charles A. Kimball

95 THE SYMBOLIC NARRATIVES OF THE FOURTH GOSPEL:
THE INTERPLAY OF FORM AND MEANING
Dorothy A. Lee

96 THE COLOSSIAN CONTROVERSY:
WISDOM IN DISPUTE AT COLOSSAE
Richard E. DeMaris

97 PROPHET, SON, MESSIAH:
NARRATIVE FORM AND FUNCTION IN MARK 14–16
Edwin K. Broadhead

98 FILLING UP THE MEASURE:
POLEMICAL HYPERBOLE IN 1 THESSALONIANS 2.14-16
Carol J. Schlueter

99 PAUL'S LANGUAGE ABOUT GOD
Neil Richardson

100 TO TELL THE MYSTERY:
ESSAYS ON NEW TESTAMENT ESCHATOLOGY IN HONOR OF ROBERT H. GUNDRY
Edited by Thomas E. Schmidt and Moisés Silva

101 NEGLECTED ENDINGS:
THE SIGNIFICANCE OF THE PAULINE LETTER CLOSINGS
Jeffrey A.D. Weima

102 OTHER FOLLOWERS OF JESUS:
MINOR CHARACTERS AS MAJOR FIGURES IN MARK'S GOSPEL
Joel F. Williams

103 HOUSEHOLDS AND DISCIPLESHIP:
A STUDY OF MATTHEW 19–20
Warren Carter

104 THE GOSPELS AND THE SCRIPTURES OF ISRAEL
Edited by Craig A. Evans and W. Richard Stegner

105 THE BIBLE, THE REFORMATION AND THE CHURCH:
ESSAYS IN HONOUR OF JAMES ATKINSON
Edited by W.P. Stephens

106 JEWISH RESPONSIBILITY FOR THE DEATH OF JESUS IN LUKE–ACTS
Jon A. Weatherly

107 PROLOGUE AND GOSPEL:
THE THEOLOGY OF THE FOURTH EVANGELIST
Elizabeth Harris

108 GOSPEL IN PAUL:
STUDIES ON CORINTHIANS, GALATIANS AND ROMANS FOR RICHARD N. LONGENECKER
Edited by L. Ann Jervis and Peter Richardson

109 THE NEW LITERARY CRITICISM AND THE NEW TESTAMENT
Edited by Elizabeth Struthers Malbon and Edgar V. McKnight

110 THE DAVIDIC MESSIAH IN LUKE–ACTS:
THE PROMISE AND ITS FULFILLMENT IN LUKAN CHRISTOLOGY
Mark L. Strauss

112 THE TEMPTATIONS OF JESUS IN EARLY CHRISTIANITY
J.B. Gibson

113 DISCOURSE ANALYSIS AND OTHER TOPICS IN BIBLICAL GREEK:
Edited by Stanley E. Porter and D.A. Carson